BIG
DEAL!

RICHARD SYDENHAM
& JOHN WRAGG

BIG
DEAL!

100
MANAGERS
THEIR GREATEST SIGNING
AND THE ONE WHO GOT AWAY!

First published by Pitch Publishing, 2022
Reprinted 2025
2

Pitch Publishing
9 Donnington Park,
85 Birdham Road,
Chichester, West Sussex,
PO20 7AJ
www.pitchpublishing.co.uk
info@pitchpublishing.co.uk

A CIP catalogue record is available for this book
from the British Library.

ISBN 978 1 80150 793 6

Printed and bound on FSC® certified paper in line with
our continuing commitment to ethical business practices,
sustainability and the environment.

Typesetting and origination by Pitch Publishing
Printed and bound in India by Replika Press Pvt. Ltd.

Contents

Nothing More Exciting in Football than the Swoop 11
Me, Managers and the Transfer Market 15
'I never enjoyed transfer deadline day as a manager' 18

1. Micky Adams by John Wragg 23
2. Graham Alexander by Richard Sydenham. . . .26
3. Sam Allardyce by John Wragg 29
4. Jimmy Armfield by Richard Sydenham 32
5. Len Ashurst by Richard Sydenham 34
6. Ron Atkinson by Richard Sydenham 37
7. John Barnwell by Richard Sydenham 40
8. Dave Bassett by Richard Sydenham 44
9. Billy Bingham by Richard Sydenham 47
10. Tony Book by Richard Sydenham 49
11. Ken Brown by Richard Sydenham 51
12. Steve Bruce by John Wragg 54
13. Alan Buckley by Richard Sydenham. 57
14. Keith Burkinshaw by Richard Sydenham 61
15. George Burley by Richard Sydenham 65
16. Terry Butcher by Richard Sydenham. 68
17. Frank Clark by Richard Sydenham 71
18. Allan Clarke by Richard Sydenham 74
19. Nigel Clough by John Wragg 77
20. John Coleman by Richard Sydenham 81
21. Steve Coppell by Richard Sydenham 84
22. Alan Curbishley by John Wragg 88
23. Keith Curle by Richard Sydenham. 92
24. Tommy Docherty by Richard Sydenham 95
25. Alan Durban by Richard Sydenham 98
26. Sean Dyche by Richard Sydenham. 101
27. Sven-Göran Eriksson by John Wragg 104

28. Roy Evans by Richard Sydenham 108
29. Brian Flynn by Richard Sydenham 110
30. Gerry Francis by Richard Sydenham. 114
31. Trevor Francis by Richard Sydenham 117
32. Barry Fry by Richard Sydenham 120
33. Johnny Giles by Richard Sydenham 123
34. Bobby Gould by Richard Sydenham 126
35. Harry Gregg by Richard Sydenham 129
36. Bryan Hamilton by Richard Sydenham 132
37. David Hay by Richard Sydenham 135
38. Kenny Hibbitt by Richard Sydenham 137
39. Glenn Hoddle by Richard Sydenham 140
40. Brian Horton by John Wragg 144
41. Gérard Houllier by John Wragg 147
42. Mark Hughes by John Wragg 151
43. Kenny Jackett by Richard Sydenham 155
44. Dave Jones by John Wragg. 158
45. Joe Jordan by Richard Sydenham 162
46. Kevin Keegan by Richard Sydenham 165
47. Jürgen Klopp by John Wragg. 169
48. Paul Lambert by Richard Sydenham. 175
49. Lennie Lawrence by John Wragg 179
50. Gordon Lee by Richard Sydenham 183
51. Neil Lennon by John Wragg. 186
52. Brian Little by Richard Sydenham. 190
53. Lou Macari by Richard Sydenham. 194
54. Don Mackay by Richard Sydenham 198
55. Malcolm Macdonald by Richard Sydenham . . 202
56. Mick McCarthy by John Wragg 205
57. Steve McClaren by Richard Sydenham 209
58. Roy McFarland by Richard Sydenham. . . . 212
59. Mark McGhee by John Wragg. 215

60. John McGovern by Richard Sydenham 219
61. Sammy McIlroy by Richard Sydenham 222
62. Alex McLeish by Richard Sydenham 225
63. Lawrie McMenemy by Richard Sydenham . . 230
64. Gary Megson by John Wragg 236
65. Gordon Milne by Richard Sydenham 240
66. David Moyes by John Wragg 243
67. Alan Mullery by Richard Sydenham. 247
68. Phil Neal by Richard Sydenham 250
69. John Newman by Richard Sydenham 253
70. Terry Neill by Richard Sydenham 255
71. Chris Nicholl by Richard Sydenham. 260
72. David O'Leary by John Wragg. 263
73. Martin O'Neill by John Wragg 267
74. David Pleat by Richard Sydenham. 271
75. Tony Pulis by John Wragg 274
76. Claudio Ranieri by John Wragg 277
77. Kevin Ratcliffe by John Wragg 280
78. Harry Redknapp by Richard Sydenham 283
79. Peter Reid by John Wragg 287
80. Bryan Robson by Richard Sydenham 290
81. Brendan Rodgers by John Wragg 293
82. Joe Royle by Richard Sydenham 297
83. John Rudge by John Wragg 300
84. Bobby Saxton by Richard Sydenham 303
85. John Sillett by Richard Sydenham 305
86. Dean Smith by John Wragg 308
87. Denis Smith by Richard Sydenham 310
88. Graeme Souness by Richard Sydenham 313
89. Gordon Strachan by John Wragg 316
90. Dave Stringer by Richard Sydenham 319
91. Gerry Summers by Richard Sydenham 322

92. Brian Talbot by Richard Sydenham 324
93. Stan Ternent by Richard Sydenham 327
94. Colin Todd by Richard Sydenham 330
95. John Toshack by John Wragg 332
96. Graham Turner by Richard Sydenham 337
97. Mark Warburton by Richard Sydenham . . . 341
98. Neil Warnock by John Wragg 345
99. Howard Wilkinson by Richard Sydenham . . 348
100. Terry Yorath by Richard Sydenham 352
Appendix 1 354
Appendix 2 359

'There are so many interesting things about making signings, why you scout that long, why you watch players for so long. And you HAVE to talk to them as well.

'I always say, you can have two players, a world-class player and a top player. But if the world-class player is an arsehole and the top player is a great guy … then, I take the top player because an arsehole in the group can cause you more problems than you can solve.

'The top player, he can easily become a world-class player.'

Jürgen Klopp

Nothing More Exciting in Football than the Swoop

Introduction by Richard Sydenham

'VILLA SWOOP for star striker' or whoever was the in-demand player of the day. Those type of headlines on the back page of the *Birmingham Evening Mail* would be enough to excite me as a youngster for many a day.

Not that my beloved Villa made too many blockbuster signings, but any newcomer was exciting and energising to a young supporter. I well recall the day in March 1986 when we signed two former players, Steve Hunt and Andy Blair. We were fighting against relegation and severely lacking in the midfield area with Steve Hodge and Paul Birch woefully under-supported in that part of the field after Steve McMahon and Dennis Mortimer had left.

Neither Hunt nor Blair were household names, but both made a crucial difference to stave off the drop, albeit for a season anyway. I would have certainly nagged my dad to take me to see their home debuts at Villa Park. Why? Because transfers create a buzz at a football club, and not much has changed in that regard.

In those days it felt like newspaper rumours had enough truth to them to believe. That might be because journalists were able to form closer working relationships with managers then, if not full-on friendships, so managers would look after their trusted journo mates with the latest transfer scoop. Now, in a world of press officers and stage-managed media activity that has created distance between clubs and the media, the transfer stories feel more like an educated stab in the dark. Therefore, we get the clickbait website headlines and loose gossip in the media that is less likely to mean a transfer story will actually happen.

Those frequent speculation headlines are so prevalent because editors know these kinds of stories grab fans' attention and subsequently sell newspapers, or generate click-throughs in the modern age we're now in.

When I wrote my previous football book, *Ticket to the Moon, Aston Villa: The Rise and Fall of a European Champion*, I was able to obtain boardroom minutes. In doing so I gleaned amazing inside knowledge of what the football club were discussing and there was nothing more interesting than the conversations surrounding their transfer targets and players of their own who they were planning to sell. Transfers are always big news and, ultimately, they change teams and the course of history – sometimes for the better, sometimes not.

Why did I choose to create this book? This following sentence taken from a recent headmaster's newsletter at my son's school, prior to Remembrance Sunday, kind of explains it: 'We are now at that time of the year when it is customary to remember the fallen of all wars, to reflect on our own families' stories, and to tell and retell those stories that belong to the communities in which we live.' So, while my motivation wasn't about victims of war, it was about telling and the subsequent retelling of how some of the most iconic transfers came about in football history. If we don't find these things out, too many great, untold stories eventually die, untold.

My first interviewee for the book was Alan Durban, in the lounge of a tennis club near Wolverhampton. Many more were on the phone. My chat with Lawrie McMenemy was at the Potter's Heron in Romsey over a four-hour lunch and what a fascinating man he was, which you will understand for yourself when reading his memories – just a natural storyteller.

I wanted to produce this book as a mark of respect to the role of the football manager through the years and the impact of how transfers set the level of a club's ambitions. Look how quickly Blackburn Rovers transformed their aspirations through the wealth of Sir Jack Walker. They followed 26 years outside of the top flight with league finishes of fourth, second and eventually the championship in the next three years. The powerhouse signings of players like Alan Shearer, Chris Sutton and David Batty allowed them to win a Premier League.

Leicester City's shocking Premier League title win in 2015/16 may not have been the result of the kind of investment of some of their wealthier rivals, but the fact they were still able to win the league was a nod to shrewd transfer business. The capturing of players like Jamie Vardy, Riyad Mahrez, N'Golo Kanté and Robert Huth showed how there will always be a place for clever scouting and that club greats do not always have to arrive via record sums of money.

The contents of this book demonstrate how some of the most celebrated managers down the years view their best signing or signings as a player who they secured for next to nothing, measuring their eventual success against scant investment. Keith Burkinshaw's choice is such an example. Other managers will have listed a player they had to spend serious money on due to their market value but who still proved to be a great servant to the club. Ron Atkinson's selection would typify the latter example.

I also felt it was important to include managers in the book who have been loyal or successful at those clubs who do not always command the headlines. The former England and Derby County legendary defender Roy McFarland, for example, mostly spent his managerial career in the lower leagues as did several others in the book. Hopefully supporters of some of these clubs – and others – will enjoy hearing the stories behind the transfers at their club.

Me, Managers and the Transfer Market

By co-author John Wragg

SVEN-GÖRAN ERIKSSON summed it up perfectly when I was talking to him about this book.

'What a good idea,' he said. 'That is different. I like it.'

I certainly thought it was a good idea when Richard Sydenham asked me to get involved with him on the book, and I'm glad he did. The managers I spoke to were all very cooperative and seemed to enjoy the concept.

For the best signing of Sven's career and the one that got away, you'll have to delve further into the book, but like other managers it's fair to say he didn't find it easy.

Sven took a weekend to think about it and then, promptly, at the time when we had arranged for me to call him at his Swedish home, he gave me his contribution.

He has a public perception as a Casanova, something he would not deny by the way and why should he? But Sven is also one of the most helpful managers you could meet. I've interviewed him when he was managing in Japan, at home in Sweden, when he was England manager and Leicester City manager.

The Leicester interview was on an ice-cold, snowy day in the depths of an English winter. It was dark by

15

4pm. The training ground was frozen, so much so there was no hot water, and the players – and Sven – had got in their cars to train at the Walkers Stadium and get a hot shower.

As we talked I asked Sven why he was still in football management. He had been in charge of big clubs, had big players work for him, had been England boss, had all the money he needed. Wouldn't he rather be retired and on a cruise to the Caribbean or somewhere?

'Well,' said Sven, looking out of his office window into the darkness and the cold, 'today, yes.'

It is in untold, personal little cameos like that when you get to know someone, create, if not a friendship, then certainly a respect that allows a sports journalist to do his or her job better.

In 40 years on national newspapers, from the *Daily Mail* to the launch of the *Daily Star* to over 30 years with the *Daily Express* you collect experiences, tears, laughs, knocks and some exceptional times.

The managers I have interviewed for this book are in general the ones I got to know well. There are some I kept secrets for. David O'Leary's revelation of the player who got away is something I knew at the time and never reported and has never been told in 15 years – until now.

There's only one manager who I disliked and that was the late Ronnie Allen, when manager of West Bromwich Albion. He told a bare-faced lie to myself and another national journalist and said that Bryan Robson was not being sold to Manchester United.

I wrote that for the *Daily Express* and was made to look foolish when it was confirmed that Robson was a United player. I got my own back by writing exclusively a few weeks later that Allen was about to get the sack. And he was sacked. Trust, you see, is a two-way thing.

When David Platt's transfer from Aston Villa to Bari entered unexpectedly long talks, Platt's agent, the excellent Tony Stephens, brought some crates of beer in for parched reporters waiting at Villa Park. A smile and a bit of thought goes a long way.

Ron Atkinson, though, didn't know whether to laugh or cry when he revealed that Aston Villa chairman Doug Ellis had negotiated the fee for Platt DOWN by agreeing a friendly with Bari, which was never played.

Someone I would have liked to have interviewed for the book is Graham Taylor. Graham is someone who became a real friend and I miss him to this day. We got to know each other through a row caused when he unwittingly gave *The Sun* a story that I was chasing and for which he apologised to me, my *Daily Express* sports editor and the editor.

He was such a genuine, principled, funny, engaging man who I was close to and saw suffer all through his England reign, a disappointment he never forgave himself for until his last day on this earth.

Brian Clough would have been another. I used to play him at squash at Nottinghamshire County Cricket Club, which is just a short stroll over the road from Forest's ground. I could never beat him. One day, as we walked back to the City Ground, Cloughie said, 'Eh, John, you do know I cheat, don't you?'

I said, 'Yes Brian, I do know that.' But I could never have brought it up, could I, and risk losing all those great stories he came up with.

Malcolm Allison; John Bond; Bobby Robson; Dave Sexton; Ron Saunders; Jim Smith. All these legends of yesteryear would have graced this book, but I think there's enough to be going on with.

Enjoy the book and, as Cloughie would say, 'Well done, hope you like it. Ta-ra.'

'I never enjoyed transfer deadline day as a manager'

Foreword by Harry Redknapp

CONTRARY TO my reputation, I wouldn't say I loved transfer deadline day or being on telly or anything like that. I'm well known for being interviewed through my car window by a Sky Sports reporter, but that's the way I live my life – if I can help someone I will. Those reporters get sent by Sky to stand outside the football ground all day. So, when you turn up at 8am on a cold, wet January morning, they're out there freezing cold. They have got a job to do so if I can help them in any way, I will.

It's not that I want to stop but their boss is looking at them and if they can get an interview with me and ask, 'What's happening Harry?' I will always tell them what's going on and that to me is what life is about. Why shouldn't I help someone? When they were off screen, I'd bring them in for a cup of tea and a few biscuits or I'd give them some lunch. They're freezing cold stood out there all day. That's just the way I am.

I never particularly enjoyed transfer deadline day as a manager. My summer as Birmingham City manager in more recent times was a good example. I was excited about building a new team – like I did at Portsmouth – but eight weeks in when you can't get all your original targets in, it can be frustrating. Getting deals over the line is not easy.

We're now in times when directors of football have a role to play but, me personally, I always wanted to be the one who picks the players. Once anyone else at the club starts choosing the players for me I'd rather pack up. That's what management is about. I'd always say to them, 'If the players I bring in are no good, then sack me.' If I bring a load of rubbish players in and six months down the line the team is struggling, it's down to me. I have to be the one who picks the players because it's me who the crowd starts shouting at when the team isn't winning, it won't be anyone else.

The transfer market can produce some great stories. That Bournemouth team of mine that beat Ron Atkinson's Manchester United in the FA Cup in 1984 was basically a team of players we had put together on free transfers mostly – and we beat Man United who were all internationals! That's the magic of both the FA Cup and the transfer market. And when I was assistant manager to Dave Webb before that, we took Nigel Spackman to Bournemouth when he was just a sub for Andover in a pre-season friendly when we played against them. He came on as sub and we ended up buying him for about a grand – for a kid who couldn't even get into Andover's team! Once again, that's the magic of the transfer market. Webby probably saw more in Nigel than me and when we paid a grand for him people thought we were mad. But the lad went on to play for Chelsea, Liverpool and Rangers!

People talk about me as a manager who loves to spend money but that hasn't always been the case. I bought the big Yugoslav Ivan Golac from Southampton on a free for Bournemouth when there was probably no better right-back in the country. What a player he was. Quite often actually I have walked into teams that are struggling and when you're struggling what do you need to do? There is no magic wand, you have to change things around. When I went to Portsmouth after West Ham, I had to do something drastic because they had been struggling in the Championship [the First Division at the time] for several seasons. I knew I couldn't get them promotion with those same players if that's the best they had been doing for so long; I had to get some new players in. I took Paul Merson on a free, I took Arjan de Zeeuw from Wigan, Matty Taylor from Luton for 50 grand and he went for four or five million in the end, I took Steve Stone from Villa on a free, and many others. When I am dealing in the transfer market it is because the clubs I am at need changes to bring better results.

People ask me whether I ever worried about spending other people's money – and especially such large sums as we see now, but the answer is simple. You do want value for money as a manager but, ultimately, it is the chairman who decides whether to pay the money; I just pick the players. You'd say, 'Is there any chance of getting this boy in?' And they'd come back with their answer and usually take it chairman to chairman. Transfers a few years ago used to be more between manager to manager. You'd ring someone up and ask an opinion: 'What's he like?' 'Is he a good trainer?' If you lie to someone you'll fall out so most people were pretty honest. We'd always have a glass of wine or a lager after a match so we were all pretty friendly anyway. But that doesn't happen now since the influx of so many foreign managers. I'd ring someone like Jim Smith and he'd tell me straight about a player. Maybe he'd say, 'Harry, that lad is a bit of a nuisance, but maybe you could handle him.' That's how it went.

I used to help out managers at other clubs if I could. When I was West Ham manager, because I'd had such a great time at Bournemouth I loaned them Rio Ferdinand and I loaned them Jermain Defoe. Mel Machin was there as director of football when it looked like they were getting relegated and he rang me up and said, 'Harry, have you got any strikers? We're desperate, we can't score goals.' I said, 'Yeah I've got a kid here for you.' Mel said, 'Who's that?' I told them I had this five-foot-six, 18-year-old kid by the name of Defoe. Mel said, 'You must be joking, we need a proper bloke in this league.' I said, 'Mel, he's going to be a star. I tell you what, take him for a week and after that if you want to loan him we'll let you and if not just tell him he's there for a bit of experience.'

I had a call back from Mel after his first practice match on Monday afternoon: 'Harry, we want to loan him for the season. We had a practice match and he scored five goals!' He went on to score 19 goals for them that season and they finished seventh! Those are the great stories of the transfer market, how moves can just change things for clubs. That has always been the case.

There is so much money involved with transfers now that we see so many big transfer fees being spent. I wouldn't like to say what's the best transfer that has ever been made because there have been too many for me to think about. But if you ask me for the most iconic transfer business ever, then I would have to say when Keith Burkinshaw signed Ossie Ardiles and Ricky Villa. That was at a time when there were very few foreign players in England. Bobby Robson signed two fantastic players from Holland – Arnold Muhren and Frans Thijssen – when he was Ipswich manager. They were top-drawer. But the way Tottenham went and signed two players who had just won the World Cup that summer [in 1978], it was just an amazing deal – the whole country was excited. It was a very exciting time for British football in general, to see these guys arrive. I went to see them play a few times and all the ticker tape was on the pitch. It was like the World Cup all over again. One match was against Altrincham in the FA Cup and this lad by the name of [John] King kicked Ossie all over the pitch, he never knew what had hit him!

Harry Redknapp

MICKY ADAMS

Managed: Fulham (1996–1997, player-manager);
Swansea City (1997, player-manager); Brentford
(1997–1998, player-manager); Nottingham
Forest (1999, caretaker); Brighton & Hove Albion
(1999–2001 & 2008–2009); Leicester City
(2002–2004); Coventry City (2005–2007);
Port Vale (2009–2010 & 2011–2014); Sheffield
United (2010–2011); Tranmere Rovers (2014–
2015); Sligo Rovers (2015)

MY BIG DEAL

Bobby Zamora: Bristol Rovers to Brighton & Hove
Albion for £100,000 in 2000

We initially got him on loan from Bristol Rovers. We were
in the Second Division when it seemed everybody was
playing with a big centre-forward. We were looking around
for one. I'd rung around a few clubs and I spoke to Ian
Holloway, who was down at Rovers, to see what he'd got, if
he'd got anybody that fitted the bill. He said he'd got a lad
who had just been on loan at Bath playing in the Southern
League and had scored a few goals there, I think it was 11
in eight games.

Quite simply, I said to Olly, 'How much is he on?' He
said about £120 a week. So, I said, 'Send him over, he fits
our bill perfectly.' I signed Zamora before I had seen him
play, although Dick Knight, the old chairman at Brighton,
said publicly that we'd been to a game and seen Zamora,
which we hadn't.

I took him blind. Zamora came into the building,
skinny, six-foot-one-plus, a kid with a baby face and you
thought, 'What we got here?' I think he had six games on

loan for us, scored six goals. So, we decided to sign him. Zamora cost us £100,000 in the end. A fantastic bargain. That was the start of his progress and Brighton getting back to where they wanted to be.

Zamora was a very clever player. He had a great understanding. To be fair he was one of the first centre-forwards who could play on his own up there, he understood the role. Technically very good, right and left foot, good in the air. What I liked about him was he could take a bollocking at half-time as well. If there was something to be said you could say it to him, he didn't sulk, he took it on board and then he'd go out for the second half and try and prove me wrong. I have to say, though, it was very infrequent I'd have to do that with him. Very intelligent and good to manage, knew where he wanted to go.

When we first got him, we were told he wouldn't score goals on a regular basis in the old Third Division. But he did. Then the year after when we got promoted from the Second Division to the First Division it was, 'Oh, well maybe that's his level.' In the First Division, the Championship as it is now, he got his goals there as well and got his move into the Premier League. I wouldn't say Zamora was prolific in the Premier League with Spurs, West Ham, Fulham, QPR, but looking at his record, there was a season at Fulham for instance where he played 48 games and scored 19 goals. It's a decent record.

Zamora scored goals at all levels and made his England debut as well so I'm proud of the boy. It was a gamble for us in the first place, not in terms of the money, not when he was on £120 a week, if he failed it didn't matter too much. We took the gamble on him for £100,000, Dick Knight did a fantastic deal with Bristol Rovers, and to see Zamora progress like he did, it's fairytale stuff really from where he came from.

THE ONE THAT GOT AWAY

Muzzy Izzet: Chelsea to Fulham on loan in 1996

The one that got away from me was Muzzy Izzet, early on when I was manager of Fulham. He was playing for Chelsea reserves and I'd seen him a lot. As a manager at that level I took great care and attention about who was playing in the reserve leagues, in London especially, so I used to go to Chelsea a lot.

Izzet was one of the standout candidates. We'd actually agreed a deal with Chelsea to take him on loan to Fulham. But come the Thursday afternoon he goes and signs for Leicester. Martin O'Neill pipped me. Steve Walford, one of the coaches at Leicester, had been down a couple of times to look at Izzet and they were at a game I was at. This would have been maybe the February.

I think what we did is make Leicester move [quicker] when they heard Izzet was coming to us on loan. Chelsea would have used that against Leicester and said, 'Listen, we've agreed everything with Fulham for Izzet to go on loan for the rest of the season unless you act now.' Leicester bit on it, took him on loan there instead, then bought Izzet and look what a career he had.

It was frustrating because we'd done a lot of homework on him. I'd been badgering Chelsea about taking him. They thought he was probably better than Fulham were at that time in the old Third Division, so it was back to square one for me.

Good pro, worked hard, could do some fantastic things with the ball. There was a doubt about his pace at times but he outweighed that with his ability on the ball. He could see a pass and physically, too, he could tackle. I suppose that was par for the course for anyone who played for Martin O'Neill.

But eventually I did manage him when I went to Leicester. I remind Muzzy of that. He didn't know anything about it though. Players often don't.

GRAHAM ALEXANDER

*Managed: Preston North End (caretaker 2011–
2012); Fleetwood Town (2012–2015); Scunthorpe
United (2016–2018); Salford City (2018–2020);
Motherwell (2021–)*

MY BIG DEAL

Josh Morris: Bradford City to Scunthorpe United on a free
transfer in 2014, after he had already played for Graham at
Fleetwood Town on loan previously from Blackburn Rovers

It's very close between Josh and Nathan Pond. I signed Josh
twice, and he was part of our promotion-winning team after
I brought him in on loan from Blackburn to Fleetwood.
He came in the January and played on the left side of the
diamond and helped us go all the way through to the play-
off final at Wembley, where we beat Burton to move up to
League One.

He was fantastic for me and we then signed him again
on loan for the following season and he played all through
the campaign. His parent club was Blackburn at that time
and he moved away at the end of that season when he signed
for Bradford.

In that time, I changed jobs and became the Scunthorpe
manager. I went back in for Josh and was able to secure him
on a free transfer despite him having another two years left
on his contract, which we took over.

He scored 20 goals for us in his first season and you felt
that he was going to score every time he got the ball. He
was one of the highest scorers in the country that year and
all from midfield. He's got a great attitude, loves training
and loves playing games and there was a trust between him
and me, which is why managers go back and sign players

again. He knew what I expected of him and I knew what to expect from Josh.

Josh did brilliant for me at both clubs. Ironically, I also tried to sign him when I was at Salford, but I left the club beforehand. But once I left, he did then join Salford. I also tried to bring him to Motherwell in my early days here, but that never panned out.

I couldn't finish this interview without talking about Pondy as well. I inherited him at Fleetwood where he was a club legend, but it hadn't been working out for him and he was on loan at Grimsby when I joined. I brought him back and he was great for me.

I respected Nathan a lot on and off the field. I later signed him for Salford as I knew what he could give me to get us out of the National League – he was a great leader of men, terrific professionalism, knew what it took to win promotion and he's right up there on a similar pedestal to Josh as my best signings.

THE ONE THAT GOT AWAY

CHÉ ADAMS: Ilkeston Town to Fleetwood Town for £30,000 in 2014

The club had sold Jamie Vardy just before I got there and not only did they make some money from that move, but they also decided as a club they were keen to find the next Jamie Vardy at that non-league level.

Ilkeston at the time were playing 18-, 19-year-old players in their first team and our chief scout Steve Davis had highlighted Ché as a very good player. We did our homework, I watched him and we decided we wanted to make a move for him. He was a bit raw at the time, but was quick, powerful and he had really good movement and appeared to be a player who was playing at a level beyond his years.

We were about 24 hours from signing him when Sheffield United received a tip-off about him and effectively blew us out of the water.

I believe it was Steve Chettle who had a role at Ilkeston and he obviously gave his old Nottingham Forest team-mate Nigel Clough the warning that Ché Adams was soon to be sold to Fleetwood and urged him to sign him for Sheffield United instead because Ché was destined for the top, which has been proven fairly accurately.

We didn't know then he would later move to Birmingham City for £2m and play international football for Scotland. We played it right and didn't do anything wrong. Unfortunately, the contacts network can help you in the game but on this occasion it went against us as it was difficult for us to compete with Sheffield United.

SAM ALLARDYCE

*Managed: Limerick (1991–1992); Preston North
End (caretaker 1992); Blackpool (1994–1996);
Notts County (1997–1999); Bolton Wanderers
(1999–2007); Newcastle United (2007–2008);
Blackburn Rovers (2008–2010); West Ham United
(2011–2015); Sunderland (2015–2016); England
(2016); Crystal Palace (2016–2017); Everton
(2017–2018); West Bromwich Albion (2020–2021)*

MY BIG DEAL

Jay-Jay Okocha: Paris Saint-Germain to Bolton
Wanderers on a free transfer in 2002

There's more than one actually. But the two world-class
signings, without a doubt, were Jay-Jay Okocha and
Fernando Hierro. Both were when I was managing Bolton
and are the two outstanding signings. What makes it even
more remarkable is they were both free transfers.

I would have to say that Youri Djorkaeff came close to
those two as my best signing, because he was a World Cup
winner and a European Championship winner. But Jay-Jay,
on the world stage and his ability as a footballer and the
fact that he captained Bolton for three years, just pipped it.

I got Jay-Jay when he had finished at PSG. He had been
to Germany, he'd been to France. Everyone wanted to come
to the English Premier League and Jay-Jay was one of those.
So, we met him in Charles de Gaulle Airport before he flew
out to the 2002 Japan and South Korea World Cup. I didn't
think we would be in with a chance really.

But as soon as Jay-Jay got back from the World Cup we
rang him to meet him again and, because we were first in
and nobody else had actually made a jump for the talent that

he was, we persuaded Jay-Jay to come and sign for us before anybody else expressed their interest.

That was one hell of a signing at the time. Everybody thought Jay-Jay would go to somewhere like Manchester United or Arsenal, somewhere like that, a club of that ilk. And he turned up at Bolton!

With Hierro, it was all about the Premier League again. Having fallen out with Real Madrid after many years as their captain, having fallen out with the club president as well, he had come back from Qatar, which wasn't a move he had enjoyed too much.

We gave him the chance to not just experience the Premier League, which he wanted, but also it was the opportunity for his children to experience England, to learn English, so it was a double-barrelled situation for him.

It was great for him and absolutely magnificent for us. This guy was the best passer in the Premier League by a million miles.

It was Bolton, I know. But we were Premier League and it all started with Djorkaeff. Once everybody thought, 'Why is a World Cup winner playing at Bolton? What's happening there?' he was the inspiration for many who came to us.

Ultimately it led to Nicolas Anelka playing for Bolton, one of the best goalscorers we've ever known. Happy days.

THE ONES THAT GOT AWAY

Samuel Eto'o: Real Mallorca to Bolton Wanderers for £8m, possibly 2002

Robert Lewandowski: Lech Poznań to Blackburn Rovers for £7m in 2010

They were the two that got away.

It was Bolton again with Samuel Eto'o. The club said they couldn't afford it, which was ridiculous. Bolton, typical tight so-and-so's they were, but there you go.

There was also Robert Lewandowski when I was at Blackburn Rovers. It was just seven or eight million Euros [£6m–£7m], as he was still at his club in Poland [Lech Poznań].

This is a good story because he got to the airport to fly over to meet with us and you remember the Icelandic ash cloud of 2010? Well because of that he couldn't get on the plane!

That ash cloud crisis lasted for a few days and it meant that Lewandowski never arrived from Poland. He ended up signing for Borussia Dortmund instead of us. He tells the story himself these days.

I could have been a God bringing Lewandowski to Blackburn Rovers. He could have got us in the top half of the league with the goals he went on to get.

We wouldn't have held on to Lewandowski long, though, before selling him, that's what Blackburn did once the owner, Jack Walker, had died. There was no funding of the club anymore, so Lewandowski would have been a success and sold on. But at least it would have been a nice problem to have had, having managed him first!

JIMMY ARMFIELD

Managed: Bolton Wanderers (1971–1974);
Leeds United (1974–1978)

MY BIG DEAL

Tony Currie: Sheffield United to Leeds United for £250,000 in 1976

A few players from the Don Revie era were coming to the end and one or two of them had to move on and I was at a stage where I had to see what there was available in the youth team and find out where we needed strengthening. I had replaced Brian Clough after his short spell at Leeds so it was important I got things right after what had been a rocky time at Elland Road for quite a number of weeks. It wasn't an easy time to come in as we were 19th in the league and even though they had won the league the season before, it was clear that the squad needed some freshening up. I added the likes of Ray Hankin to play alongside Joe Jordan, Arthur Graham from Aberdeen, and I also bought Brian Flynn, who was a workhorse midfielder. They were good players and the team was doing all right but when I bought Currie things started to click a little better.

Currie was available and several clubs could have gone and got him and I don't know why that didn't happen. But I watched him a couple of times and eventually I agreed the deal myself with Sheffield United, where he had been very successful for many years, before I even spoke to my chairman. The chairman asked me, 'What if he's no good?' I said, 'Well let's see how he goes on Saturday and then we can take it from there.' But there was no need to worry, he was wonderful for us and just did something different to everyone else. He was a playmaker but had goals in him as well. You need that balance in a team. Currie had an inbuilt talent and a lot of flair even though he was a big man. He was your typical gem that needed polishing. I brought him into my office one day and told him that if he kept playing as he was he would be back in the England team by the end of the season – and he was, after I gave him a glowing report when Ron Greenwood called me. I told Ron that Tony was our best player and subsequently he returned to the England team. He liked to be 100 per cent fit all the time and in peak physical condition so occasionally he would come to me and say, 'Boss, I have this strain, or niggle,' but I'd just walk away and tell him to get on with it. I knew how important he was to us and that we always needed him to play. That's the greatest compliment I can give him.

I bought Peter Thompson from Liverpool when I was Bolton manager and he is another I would single out. We had just won the old Third Division and I knew we needed more experience to cope with life in the higher league as I was getting by with six or seven under-21s in the team. I spoke to Bill Shankly and commented that I noticed he wasn't picking Thompson in his team. Shankly, seeing where I was going with my thread, quickly came back to me and said, 'Forget it, he's too valuable for us.' But I kept talking to Shanks and offered all the money the club had to spend, which was about £18,000. Eventually he agreed to sell him to us and he added the experience and quality I was looking for. Peter remained at Bolton for five or six years so he proved a good buy, as I knew he would be.

THE ONE THAT GOT AWAY

No one

No one especially that I can recall. I was fortunate in that whenever I really wanted a player I usually managed to persuade my chairman to help me get our man!

LEN ASHURST

Managed: Hartlepool United (1971–1974); Gillingham (1974–1975); Sheffield Wednesday (1975–1977); Newport County (1978–1982); Cardiff City (1982–1984 & 1989–1991); Sunderland (1984–1985); Al Wakrah (1988–1989); Pahang (1991–1992); Weymouth (1992–1993)

MY BIG DEAL

John Aldridge: South Liverpool to Newport County for £2,500 in 1979

Aldo has to be classed as my best signing in terms of value for money, pure quality and considering what he went on to achieve. I paid his non-league club South Liverpool just £1,500 straight away and then a further £1,000 a year later. I can't take all the credit, though, as I have my brother Robin to thank for discovering him. Robin worked at Ford Motor Company and that's where John worked also, on the lathe. He told me there was this lad at his place who was playing for South Liverpool and was scoring lots of goals and creating some interest.

I went along to have a look at him. I knew after 15 minutes that I wanted to sign him. He led the line, he held the ball up, he was sharp around the box, he could drop off and create space for himself or he could run at the centre-half and push defenders going forwards. He was just very impressive in a number of ways. And as a Scouser like myself he was down to earth and he lifted the dressing room with his attitude and his humour.

In terms of value for money, I also signed Tommy Tynan for Newport from Lincoln for just £1,500. He became a legend there with all his goals. I signed him in the boardroom at Liverpool with Bob Paisley and Bill Shankly there.

THE ONE THAT GOT AWAY

Dave Bennett: Cardiff City to Sunderland

When I was manager of Cardiff City, the backbone of my team was Dave and Gary Bennett, Jeff Hennerman, the centre-forward, and a stalwart already at the club, Phil Dwyer. I then signed Gary Bennett after I moved to Sunderland in 1984 because we needed a centre-half. He became one of my best-ever signings actually and remained an integral part of the team long after I departed. But my regret is that I should have signed his brother Dave as well because they were close brothers and signed from Manchester City to Cardiff as a duo and I should have kept them together because they were both terrific players.

Dave was at Coventry City by this time, where he ended up having five great years. But at this stage I am confident he would have joined his brother at Roker Park. I liked the fact he could play striker or right wing, though I found he was happier on the wing with space ahead of him to run into rather than space behind him. Aside from the football, Davie was also a great character in the dressing room, and he would have added a lot in that sense at Sunderland also.

The reason I didn't sign him, though, was partially down to race grounds. I still remember the chairman Tom Cowie's words. He said, 'It would be a risk to sign two black players – and also, I haven't got the money,' so he wriggled out of the signing of Dave Bennett on financial grounds. But the real reason was fear of a backlash from the fans, as in those days, the late 1970s and even into the 1980s, it was still quite unusual to see a black person around the north-east. Thankfully that is all changed.

But it's as if racial tolerance started in London and slowly crept northwards as we saw the likes of Mark Walters having problems in Scotland deep into the 1980s when he was at Rangers. Even Gary [Bennett] was only the second black player to play for Sunderland after Roly Gregoire. I pushed Tom Cowie as hard as I could to sign Dave as well and he was adamant, he was not going to bend for those reasons on a 50-50 basis, on both financial and racial grounds.

I was prepared to offload a few players to recoup the money so that we could accommodate Dave, but it wasn't to be, which is a shame as he would have made a big difference to us.

RON ATKINSON

Managed: Kettering Town (1971–1974);
Cambridge United (1974–1978); West Bromwich
Albion (1978–1981 & 1987–1988); Manchester
United (1981–1986); Atlético Madrid (1988–
1989); Sheffield Wednesday (1989–1991 & 1997–
1998); Aston Villa (1991–1994); Coventry City
(1995–1996); Nottingham Forest 1999

MY BIG DEAL

Bryan Robson: West Bromwich Albion to Manchester
United for £1.5m in 1981

Bryan Robson was my best signing in terms of the finest
player I ever signed. We broke the [British] transfer record
for him so it wasn't like he was a bargain buy, but I didn't
have any qualms about it as I knew what we were getting.
I knew 'Robbo' well from when I managed him at West
Bromwich Albion and as soon as I became United manager
I wanted to sign him straight away. But funnily enough it
wasn't like I told him when I left West Brom, 'I'm coming
back for you.' He sounded me out and said, 'Don't forget to
come back for me!'

The centre of midfield was an area we were particularly
weak in so it was a no-brainer for me. I told the directors
at Old Trafford that while we were breaking the record it
wasn't even a gamble. But if anyone at Man United was
slightly nervous about the price those fears soon quelled
as 18 months later Juventus offered to double the fee we
paid. But there was no way we were selling as he was a
United great in the making, as he proved to be in time.
Bryan had everything you would want from a midfielder.
He was dynamic, he could tackle, he could kick with both

37

feet, he would work up and down the pitch and do the ugly things, and he could score goals, with his head also. He was the complete midfield player – pure gold. There was no other manager in football then who would not have wanted him in their team.

I made so many signings over the years and unfortunately I can't name all of the good ones but others who I would single out would be Mark Bosnich [a free transfer from Sydney Olympic to Aston Villa] and Ugo Ehiogu [£40,000 from West Bromwich Albion to Villa], who were both signed for little or no money. And Paul McGrath was a great signing from St Patrick's in Dublin for £40,000, when I brought him to United. My scouts sent him over and I had a look at him for a month. He was a late developer but he was one who you knew was always going to make it. I was glad to work with him again at Villa some years later.

THE ONE THAT GOT AWAY

Gary Lineker: Leicester City to Manchester United for £800,000 in 1985

The one who I would like to have taken would have been Gary Lineker from Leicester to Man United. I was told I needed to get rid of one or two strikers before I could sign him and, while all that was going on, Howard Kendall came in and nicked him from under our noses and took him to Everton; fair play to Howard and Everton for being aware enough to have taken him while we were sorting our own house out at United.

He scored 40 goals in his one season at Goodison before his move to Barcelona, so they did well out of him. It nearly happened for us but we couldn't get it done in time.

We were in the 1985 FA Cup Final and his contract was up at Filbert Street. It was a transfer we were looking to get done in that summer. But Howard got wind of it and he sold Andy Gray and quickly bought Lineker. Nowadays we would never have lost him because the bigger clubs like United are so powerful we would have just bought him and offloaded the others at our leisure. But in those days even United had to wheel and deal, which is what cost us.

Who knows, if we had have signed Lineker we might just have won the league. Frank Stapleton and Mark Hughes were great for me, but we just needed someone with that extra pace who was capable of banging in 25 or 30 goals a season like Liverpool had with Ian Rush. Unfortunately it is a case of what might have been.

JOHN BARNWELL

Managed: Peterborough United (1977–1978);
Wolverhampton Wanderers (1978–1982); AEK
Athens (1983–1984); Notts County (1987–
1988); Walsall (1989–1990); Northampton
Town (1993–1994)

MY BIG DEAL

Emlyn Hughes: Liverpool to Wolverhampton
Wanderers for £90,000 in 1979

I could have nominated Andy Gray as he was comfortably
my 'biggest' signing in terms of money at just shy of £1.5m.
Andy paid us back in his first season with a winning goal
in the 1980 League Cup Final and sixth place in the league
to see us through to the UEFA Cup. But Emlyn shades it
on the value for money aspect. Admittedly he was at the
opposite end of his career to Andy and was winding down
what had already been a spectacularly successful career, but
for the two seasons he was with us Emlyn was superb and
gave the team everything I had wanted and more.

Both Andy and Emlyn were strong characters and each
had a significant effect in the dressing room and on the pitch
in terms of leadership and influence, especially Emlyn with
the winning mentality he was bringing from his trophy-
laden spell at Liverpool.

I actually tried to sign Roy McFarland initially and met
him twice but he wasn't sure if he wanted to leave Derby so
after our second meeting I moved on and the Emlyn deal
happened pretty quickly, over a few days. I spoke to Bill
Shankly about him so I knew what I was getting. Shankly
felt Emlyn still had another couple of years in him and
told me, 'He won't let you down.' I knew he was available

because there were rumours he wasn't happy at being switched between defence and midfield, and Alan Hansen was coming through with Phil Thompson there too, so there appeared to be the opportunity to sign him.

Emlyn had a selfish and focused nature on what he wanted to achieve and anything that got in his way he just dismissed. Is it coincidence that the only trophy he hadn't won when he came to Wolves was the League Cup and then he won that very trophy in his first season with us? My decision to bring in this added experience and leadership was no slight on the senior players already at the club as the likes of Derek Parkin, Willie Carr, Kenny Hibbitt and John Richards, who were all at the backend of their careers, were fine players and good pros. But Wolves had been relegated a couple of seasons back and, although they were promoted straight back up, Wolves were just about surviving in the top flight so I felt we needed this extra knowhow. I made the decision to break up what had gone before by bringing in Emlyn as captain, though retaining John Richards as club captain. Emlyn's arrival raised a few eyebrows at the time but it didn't deflect him from being the leader that I thought he was.

THE ONE THAT GOT AWAY

Michel Platini: Saint-Étienne to Wolverhampton Wanderers

I needed a midfield player of quality because I had Kenny Hibbitt and Willie Carr and both were at the backend of their careers. They were both very good players and I knew I might have got another couple of seasons out of both but I felt we needed strengthening there because if either of them got injured we had no real quality underneath. So would you believe it but I had agreed a $200,000 deal with Saint-Étienne to sign Michel Platini after he helped them win the French league in 1981. But unfortunately I could not get my board to agree to it and it kept going on and on. It dragged on for about three weeks and in that time Platini sustained a leg injury and was out for a few months so that transfer was put to one side. When he came back he was sold to Juventus and soon became the world star we all soon got to know about.

He was a huge missed opportunity for us. I saw him play several times, I had him watched and he was magically gifted technically. Whether he would have handled the more aggressive game in England, I am not sure. But it would have been nice to have found out!

The other big one was Zbigniew 'Zibi' Boniek. I sent my chief scout over to Poland to watch him play for Łódź. He even stayed at his place and Boniek agreed to come over and sign for us but my chairman reneged on the deal when he had indicated to me that we could sign him. That was hugely disappointing because the lad had been in the Poland side for about five years by then and would have added something different. Like with Platini, he ended up going to Juventus instead.

I also went for Peter Reid and it went to a tribunal. I should have pulled out of that deal but because of the freedom of contract rules he was allowed to speak to other teams whoever came in. It took about three or four months and in that time he signed a new contract with Bolton and ended up at Everton!

I identified all three of these guys and I felt they would have made a big difference to Wolves. I am not saying we would have signed all three but at least one, maybe two of them, could have added something dynamic to what we had already. They were all highly talented players. I ended up converting Mel Eves from striker to a deeper role but throughout my time at Wolves we always lacked some strength in depth as once one of my first-teamers got injured the depth just wasn't there. The club was building a new stand around that time and that sucked up all of their money and put them on the edge of bankruptcy hence we missed out on these fine players that were ready to come to Molineux.

DAVE BASSETT

Managed: Wimbledon (1981–1987); Watford
(1987–1988); Sheffield United (1988–1995);
Crystal Palace (1996–1997); Nottingham
Forest (1997–1999); Barnsley (1999–2000);
Leicester City (2000–2002 and caretaker 2004);
Southampton (caretaker 2005)

MY BIG DEAL

Brian Deane: Doncaster Rovers to Sheffield United for
£30,000 in 1988

I could nominate a number of players such as Dennis
Wise, who we got for nothing from Southampton and sold
to Chelsea for £1.6m; Vinny Jones, who we bought from
Wealdstone from the non-league for £10,000 and sold for
£660,000; Nigel Winterburn, who cost us nothing and made
us £350,000 from Arsenal; John Fashanu cost £150,000 and
went to Villa for £1.5m; but I just think Brian Deane tops
them all for a few reasons.

He was the one signing I made that generated the most
money but there was so much more to him than the money.
We were in the [old] Third Division when he joined us and
he scored 30 goals in his first season when we were also
promoted, then 24 goals the season after when we were
promoted again, to the First Division, when he scored 17
goals. So he was prolific for us. The irony was that when
I signed him he was far from prolific for Doncaster. I only
saw him the once before I signed him and he didn't even
have a great game, but a guy whose opinion I respected a
lot called Keith Mincher, our youth team coach, had seen
him more and liked him. What I did see straight away
was that he was a good athlete, had good control and was

quick, who worked hard out wide as well as centrally, so I signed him.

His manager then was Dave Mackay and Joe Kinnear was the assistant, who I dealt with. Joe told me that the player had potential but he wasn't sure how far he would go because he needed to toughen up a bit. Everyone I spoke to said he wasn't ready – and I needed him to be ready. But while nobody raved about him, no one slagged him off either.

No other club was in for him as far as I'm aware so eventually I took a punt and offered 20 grand. They asked for 40, but we met in the middle. In the end he was a revelation and hit it off up front with Tony Agana. He was our top scorer every season, until our chairman agreed to sell him to Leeds for £2.9m, so we made a huge profit. Brian was magnificent for us and we comfortably avoided relegation in our first year in the top flight but as soon as he went we were relegated. That's how much of a difference he made to us and I'm sure if we had kept him we would have stayed up longer.

THE ONE THAT GOT AWAY

Chris Coleman: Swansea City to Sheffield United

Chris was a solid defender who I would have liked to take to Bramall Lane. We met the player and I thought he was going to come, but quite simply he went to Crystal Palace instead. Similarly, I was hoping to sign Iain Dowie at Sheffield United and again was hopeful he would join and link up with Tony Agana and Brian Deane in attack. But we were outbid. In both cases we got a phone call saying they wouldn't be joining because they were getting more money elsewhere. That's football.

Other than those two I don't ever recall losing out on a major deal. I was linked with Duncan Ferguson once when he was still at Dundee United. I inadvertently encouraged a journalist's story when he asked me about Ferguson as a replacement for Brian Deane. I said something like, 'I appreciate the player but don't think we could ever afford him.' Next thing I know I have his manager Jim McLean on the phone giving me a bollocking for tapping up his player. I explained to him how it happened and told him how we couldn't afford him anyway, but couldn't resist adding, 'Unless you would take £1m?' His answer ended in 'off'! Big Duncan ended up going to Rangers for [a then British record] £4m.

BILLY BINGHAM

*Managed: Southport (1965–1968); Northern
Ireland (1967–1971 & 1980–1993); Plymouth
Argyle (1968–1970); Linfield (1970–1971); Greece
(1971–1973); Everton (1973–1977); PAOK
Salonica (1977); Mansfield Town (1978–1979)*

MY BIG DEAL

Bob Latchford: Birmingham City to Everton for
£350,000, including the exchange of Howard Kendall
and Archie Styles to Birmingham as part of the
package, in 1974

I actually saw Bob in a reserves game first, though when
he signed for me he was a very established member of
Birmingham's first team at age 23. In fact he had scored
consecutive hat-tricks against Ipswich and Leicester a couple
of months before he came to Goodison so it was not like he
wasn't on anyone's radar. He was a very good centre-forward
and could have signed for better teams than we were at that
time but I think he knew he would grow with us as I shaped
the team. The fact he went on to score over 100 goals for
the club would suggest I got that one right (138 goals in 289
games). It was quite hard to get him from Birmingham. I
seem to remember their manager Freddie Goodwin was not
all that keen to sell Bob at all, for obvious reasons, because
he knew how good he was, but maybe he knew he would
achieve a lot more at Everton than he would at Birmingham?
Plus he got two of my players and some cash off us!

As soon as Bob arrived he looked a player. He was very
strong and powerful, which was what I liked about him most
at first. It was unusual for a young player to have that kind
of power. He also had frightening pace. He became one of

my best players, comfortably. Bob had a few assets but his greatest has to be the ability to know where the goal was, with a ratio of about one goal every two games, which is quite something. I would look at goals to games ratios a lot when looking at players and I always felt that any striker, or midfielder, who gave you a goal every two or three games was in the top bracket. Those who scored every four or five games less so, though they might give you something else like creativity.

I subsequently had to bring in players who were right to play around Bob as he soon became the cornerstone of my team and I knew I needed something different to both bring out the best in him but to also add balance to the team. Duncan McKenzie was another of my best signings. He could be frustrating and wasn't always consistent but he did things I liked. He was different to Bob and he blended into what we were doing nicely.

THE ONE THAT GOT AWAY
No one

I enquired about a lot of players but generally I got what I wanted, especially at Everton where John Moores backed my judgment on just about any player I wanted, which was some responsibility, but I like to think I didn't let him down too often. He usually gave me the funds that I wanted but then he did own half of Liverpool! [Moores founded the retail outlet Littlewoods, which spawned the Football Pools.]

TONY BOOK

Managed: Manchester City (1973, 1974–1979, 1989, 1993)

MY BIG DEAL

Dave Watson: Sunderland to Manchester City for £175,000 in 1975

We were looking for a centre-half and we had Dave watched a few times and I also spoke to Ian MacFarlane, who was coaching at Sunderland and he gave a glowing tribute on Dave as a player and as a character. So we made our move and thankfully managed to sign him. He had just broken into the England team before he joined us so his pedigree was right up there. Dave slotted in nicely alongside either Mike Doyle or Tommy Booth at the back. He was great in the air, a good team man, was always committed and was the type of player who really put in as much hard work on the training ground as in the games. Dave commanded respect from his fellow players and even though he ended up with 65 England caps he wasn't the type to carry an ego, he was a down-to-earth lad – the model professional who put it in game after game.

Asa Hartford was another lad that did well for me, performing week after week, a box-to-box player and was a good passer of the ball. He arrived before Dave [in 1974]. I took him from West Brom for £210,000 after Don Howe had placed him on the transfer list. He was supposed to have had a hole in his heart, having failed a medical at Leeds a few years earlier. My chief scout Ken Barnes used to come to me every week and say even if that lad has got a hole in his heart, he will do for me! I think Asa had his best years with us from 1975 to 1979, winning the League Cup in 1976 and missing out on the league championship by a point to Liverpool in 1976/77. I drove across to meet Brian Clough before we sold him to Nottingham Forest for half a million pounds. But strangely he only played three games there.

THE ONE THAT GOT AWAY

Graeme Souness: Middlesbrough to Manchester City for £350,000 in 1978

Liverpool were in for him at the same time as us and ultimately it appeared the player fancied going to Anfield more than he did us. I hadn't seen much of Souness then but I trusted the opinion of Ian MacFarlane, as I did with Dave Watson's signing. He would have made a fantastic addition to our team for £350,000 but their success in the late '70s coupled with the fact they had a couple of Scots there like Kenny Dalglish and Alan Hansen, so I guess that move was more attractive to him than City. It was obviously a shame given what he went on to achieve in his career as he was a top-performing midfielder. He was one of the best midfield players of his generation.

I also tried hard to sign Alan Ball from Arsenal before he went to Southampton, as I had Colin Bell injured at the time. With his quality and experience, he would have been a perfect replacement for Colin but the board wouldn't sanction the move, which was a blow. Without doubt, though, Souness would have been the better signing purely because he had a more years on his side.

KEN BROWN

Managed: Norwich City (1980–1987); Shrewsbury
Town (1987); Plymouth Argyle (1988–1990)

MY BIG DEAL

Steve Bruce: Gillingham to Norwich City for
£135,000 in 1984

I spotted Steve at Gillingham because I was always
wandering around the country watching games, which was
something I learned from my predecessor John Bond. I
employed Mel Machin when I replaced John and Mel and
I would also travel round together. Steve was one of those
players who stood out for obvious reasons. He was strong
on the field and a strong personality in the dressing room
also, which is a clear reason why Alex Ferguson made him
his captain at Manchester United later. With a player like
Steve, you know what you are always going to get. If he had
a bad game I didn't need to say anything to him because
nobody would have been more upset than himself, as he set
himself very high standards, which the younger lads would
learn from.

Normally I liked to promote from the youth team if
we had the talent available and the kid was ready for his
opportunity. I saw it in my own playing days at West Ham
when they gave chances to Bobby Moore, Geoff Hurst and
Martin Peters. But at Carrow Road I identified the fact we
needed a player like Steve so I bought him for just £135,000
– after a tribunal – and went on to sell him for £800,000. I
was pleased I took him on as there were about a dozen other
clubs looking at him but they hesitated.

A few months after Steve signed I returned to
Gillingham and their chairman had a real go at me about

the price. I said, 'It's no problem, you can have him back because he's useless.' The chairman was taken aback until I added that it would cost him another £100k on top! Although I don't see Steve as much these days, we remain good friends and it was pleasing to hear him say that without Norwich the rest of his career would not have happened.

THE ONES THAT GOT AWAY

Neil Ruddock: Millwall to Norwich City

David Beckham: Apprentice to Norwich City

I had a very strong interest in Neil 'Razor' Ruddock. I badly wanted him when he was a youngster at Millwall and I worked hard for a long time to get him before finally losing out to Spurs. There were actually quite a few clubs chasing him and I was optimistic for a short time of getting him as Norwich was a step up for him, but as soon as Tottenham started sniffing we had no chance.

At this particular time at Norwich we didn't have Neil's type of player as I knew Steve Bruce was going to leave and I had to find someone to replace those leadership skills and strength at the heart of the defence. Neil was very consistent and managers knew that he would always give everything to the cause. His career went a bit wrong in the end but at his peak he was the type of towering centre-half everyone would have in their team.

Another time, when I was a player assessor with the FA, I was lucky enough to travel to Japan for the World Cup with the team. I met David Beckham there and on the return flight I got talking to David and his father about his career. David's father asked me if I remembered David having trials with Norwich City as a boy as he recalled taking David to Norwich and watching him play a trial match when I was manager of the club.

Unfortunately, I didn't remember. It seemed I missed out on signing a future great but I had absolutely no recollection of it, which doesn't make it any better but these kinds of things do happen in football if a lad doesn't show up as much on the day of that particular trial.

Apparently, they were pleased to see that I was watching the boys from the sidelines. I said to David, 'Son, you should have tried a bit harder, you missed your chance – you could have come to us and been a Norwich legend!' I don't think he was too unhappy, though, with how his career turned out.

STEVE BRUCE

Managed: Sheffield United (1998–1999);
Huddersfield Town (1999–2000); Wigan Athletic
(2000); Crystal Palace (2001); Birmingham City
(2001–2007); Wigan Athletic (2007–2009);
Sunderland (2009–2011); Hull City (2012–2016);
Aston Villa (2016–2018); Sheffield Wednesday
(2019); Newcastle United (2019–2021);
West Bromwich Albion (2022–)

MY BIG DEAL

Christophe Dugarry: Bordeaux to Birmingham City on loan in 2003

It took me 24 hours to think over this question but, in the end, there was only one answer.

I got a phone call when I was Birmingham City manager: would I like Christophe Dugarry? Just a call, out of the blue really. Would I? You bet I would! A World Cup winner with France at St Andrew's playing for us in our first season in the Premier League after getting up by beating Norwich in the play-off final the previous year. It was gold dust. Too good to be true, eh? But it wasn't.

Dugarry was magnificent for us and kept us up. I had him at my house, my wife wasn't in, so I brought him a Rich Tea biscuit and said welcome to England. 'What is this?' he said. 'A Rich Tea,' I said. 'It is what we have in England.' I think that down-to-earth approach appealed to Christophe and helped get him to the club.

He was the most fantastic, talented footballer. He changed us. After Christophe had been with us a while, Geoff Horsfield came to me and went, 'Bloody hell, gaffer.' He was in awe of him. Dugarry had been with Milan,

Barcelona, Marseille and Bordeaux before us. He'd won the 1998 World Cup and the 2000 Euros with France. For his first six months at Birmingham Dugarry was out of this world. He kept us up. He had a run of five goals in four matches and that took us from relegation to I think it was 13th in the table.

I'd got Dugarry on loan initially when we'd looked to strengthen the team in the January transfer window of 2003. He soon became the best player I ever had the privilege to manage. He was sensational – difficult as well, don't get me wrong. We signed him on a permanent contract at the end of his loan and he left very quickly afterwards. But for those six months, he was sensational. We finished higher that season, with Dugarry in the side, than Aston Villa, which was the first time that had happened I believe since the 1970s.

His ability, his talent, got people off their seats. He was different: a World Cup winner playing for Birmingham City! People say Christophe Dugarry is the best player the club has ever had and it is certainly a fair debate between Christophe and Trevor Francis to this day as to who is the best-ever Birmingham player.

THE ONE THAT GOT AWAY

John Terry: Chelsea to Huddersfield Town

When I was managing Huddersfield, I was so close to signing John Terry – I thought it was going to happen, pretty certain actually for £750,000. But then Gianluca Vialli, who was manager at Chelsea, changed his mind. John had done well out on loan with Nottingham Forest for five or six games and because of that they decided to keep him.

The deal had some legs at the start and I really thought I was getting him, but all of a sudden it didn't happen. It would have been a straight deal, no loan. JT was only a kid then. The course of history would have been changed wouldn't it? One of the most successful captains ever, with five Premier League wins, five FA Cups, a Champions League and nearly 80 caps for England. Instead, he'd have been at Huddersfield Town!

It was kind of ironic, I guess, that I ended up signing John at the end of his career at Aston Villa instead. He was great for me and so nearly helped to get us back to the Premier League but the play-off final loss to Fulham ended our dreams, sadly.

ALAN BUCKLEY

Managed: Walsall (1978–1986); Kettering Town (1986–1988); Grimsby Town (1988–1994, 1997–2000 & 2006–2008); West Bromwich Albion (1994–1997); Lincoln City (2001–2002); Rochdale (2003)

MY BIG DEALS

Paul Futcher: Halifax Town to Grimsby Town for £10,000 in 1991

Garry Birtles: Notts County to Grimsby Town on a free transfer in 1989

'Futch' had been around for quite some time before I signed him as he had already played for the likes of Luton, Manchester City and Derby. I first became aware of him when I heard he had gone to Man City for £350,000 to replace Tommy Booth when he was still in his early 20s. So, he'd always been on my radar. Futch also played with my brother, Steve, at Derby so I knew him well.

I was in my third season at Grimsby and at this time Paul couldn't get in the side at Halifax. Around that time, we had sold Andy Tillson to QPR for half a million pounds, so we needed a replacement – Garry Birtles used to play there now and again but I needed a permanent centre-back. I called Halifax up because I knew he wasn't in the team and we got him for a nominal fee. He came to us as a 34-year-old and was brilliant for three or four years. Value for money and for his ability he's comfortably my best signing. He couldn't run but he didn't need to – he read the game that well. Nobody ever got past him even though his legs had gone because his football brain was absolutely brilliant.

Garry would be my equal best signing after we snapped him up from Notts County, for nothing. I couldn't reach him at first and kept trying this number and wasn't getting anywhere. So, I put it on the back burner and went on holiday to Menorca. When I came back, I tried this number again and he picked up. He said, 'Sorry you couldn't reach me before, I was on holiday in Menorca.' How ironic; I could have signed him on the beach! He came to us and was our highest earner at around £400 a week, but it suited him as I only expected him to train a couple of days a week so he could travel from Nottingham.

Everybody knew about him of course after his achievements at Nottingham Forest and when you hear his name that he might be available you have to be interested. He had some back trouble at Notts County, might even have had surgery on it, but I thought he could do a great job for us. Nottingham wasn't that far from Grimsby so I hoped he might be interested. I spoke to him and told him the style of our football was like how his great Forest team played under Cloughy so he was keen to join us.

The two seasons Garry played with us coincided with consecutive promotions from the Fourth Division to the Second. People couldn't believe that he would come and play at Grimsby. He was such a good lad, totally grounded and the only reason he packed up was because of his ongoing problems with his hamstrings.

Another one I pursued and eventually signed after he had played in America was Steve Daley, for Walsall for nothing. He was great for me as well. We were playing Port Vale in a pre-season match and I actually thought Vale had stolen a march on us for Steve's signature, but he had a think about it and came to us thankfully. He had a year with us and, like with Birtles and Futcher, was absolutely brilliant.

You couldn't wish to meet a more down-to-earth lad than Steve and considering he was once the record transfer when he moved to Man City from Wolves that's a quite a thing. Even after I left Walsall, I signed him again – for Kettering.

THE ONE THAT GOT AWAY

Robin van der Laan: Port Vale to West Bromwich Albion for £300,000 in 1995

Normally I got pretty much everyone I tried to sign. Even Steve Daley, who I just mentioned there, I almost missed him to Port Vale, but we got him in the end.

Generally, the clubs I managed had quite strict financial structures, so you tended not to go after too many for fees that were out of our financial capabilities, but I obviously scouted and signed a lot of players within budget.

The main one who springs to mind who I did really want to sign was Van der Laan. I had signed another Dutchman, Richard Sneekes, from Bolton, and Van der Laan would have complemented him wonderfully well. He was playing for John Rudge at Port Vale and was out of contract, but this was a time when the club who held his registration could still demand a fee.

He came and trained with us at West Brom for a couple of weeks and looked every bit the player you would have wanted in your squad and would have fitted in perfectly to what I had then. He had fantastic strength, power, was box-to-box, could tackle, pass, get in the box late and score a goal. He would have been absolutely flipping brilliant for us. If I could have had him and Sneekes they would have been like [Arnold] Muhren and [Frans] Thijssen for me.

Unfortunately, Derby manager Jim Smith got wind of his availability and they were on the up, heading for a promotion to the Premier League and he went there. We probably took too long trying to get a deal done because we didn't want to get our fingers burned and were hoping to go to a tribunal to pay a smaller transfer fee. But Jim came in and paid the money that Port Vale were asking for.

We definitely had the time to do a deal because he was training with us when nobody else knew he was on offer. We offered about £300,000 and Rudgey was asking for something like £350,000. But I think they got even more than that in the end from Derby.

It was disappointing but I understood our financial situation and if you can't afford it, you can't afford it, you just have to get on with it. But Robin would have been a brilliant signing for us.

KEITH BURKINSHAW

*Managed: Workington (1964–1965); Scunthorpe
United (caretaker 1966–1967); Tottenham Hotspur
(1976–1984); Bahrain (1984–1986); Sporting
Lisbon (1987–1988); Gillingham (1988–1989);
Pahang (1991); West Bromwich Albion (1993–
1994); Aberdeen (caretaker 1997)*

MY BIG DEAL

Tony Galvin: Goole Town to Tottenham Hotspur for
£3,000 in 1978

The biggest signings I ever made in terms of glamour and
prestige were the two Argentines, Ossie Ardiles and Ricardo
Villa, but purely for value for money my best would have
to be the hard-working left-winger Tony Galvin. When
I was playing for my final club Scunthorpe, I struck up a
good rapport with one of the directors there and we became
golfing buddies. That friendship continued over the years
and when I was at Tottenham he phoned me up and said
there was a lad he had seen playing for Goole Town and
he thought he would make a player at a higher level. Tony
was studying Russian at the University of Hull at the time,
which was pretty unique in itself for a footballer. I sent my
chief scout Bill Nicholson up there to take a look at him. Bill
came back with a good report and he felt he could do well
for us so I spoke to Goole about signing him. They wanted
£5,000 but I ended up paying £3,000.

That money was the best I ever spent in my career as a
manager when you think about how many years he played at
Tottenham and also for the Republic of Ireland. Tony wasn't
your typical glamour player like Glenn Hoddle and Ossie
Ardiles but he was priceless to the team; he never stopped

running. He was also a terrific lad who was very popular in the dressing room. Our left-back Chris Hughton liked to get forward so, when he went on a run, Tony was clever enough to drop back and fill the space and cover for Chris. And when I bought the two frontmen who made such a difference to us in the early '80s, Steve Archibald and Garth Crooks, Tony created so many of their goals with his crosses – after Glenn had pinged those balls inside the full-back for Tony to run on to. Glenn could find a sixpence from 50 yards so Tony had plenty of service down the flanks to run on to. Glenn was obviously another great player for me but he was already at the club when I reached White Hart Lane.

Ossie and Ricky were two of my best, also. Again it took a phone call to tip me off. Harry Haslam was manager at Sheffield United at the time and he called me and asked if I would be interested in signing an Argentine World Cup winner and he mentioned that a lad by the name of Osvaldo Ardiles was available. He said he couldn't afford him but still felt he wouldn't cost that much money for a club the size of Tottenham. Harry was going over there to sign another player for a fraction of the price. I was aware of Ossie because he had been one of the best players of that 1978 World Cup so I was quite excited. I spoke to my board and they gave me their backing to fly to Buenos Aires to meet Ossie.

Harry mentioned that he was leaving on the Friday with Terry Neill [the Arsenal manager], who was going out there to sign Ricky Villa, the lesser-known of the two players. Come Friday Terry had pulled out of the Villa deal as his board were apparently not keen to sign a foreigner, so I went out with Harry. I arrived on the Saturday and was shown around by the former Argentina defender Antonio Rattín, who was sent off against England in the 1966 World Cup quarter-final. He introduced me to Ossie and his wife on the Sunday and he signed for us an hour later.

Ossie asked me while I was out there whether I would also be interested in Ricky Villa. I was aware of Ricky but he was more of a gamble for me as he had been on the bench more for Argentina in that '78 World Cup. But I was willing to take a punt on him so I made contact with the Tottenham board back in England about whether we had the money to sign Ricky as well. They gave the go-ahead and we signed them both for £620,000.

I threw them both straight into the team and neither won a game for their first six matches! We lost 4-1 to Aston Villa after a ticker tape parade before their home debuts and were then beaten 7-0 at Liverpool – all in their first month at the club. Thankfully both adjusted to the English game and were huge successes. Of course Ricky will always be best remembered for his great goal in the 1981 FA Cup Final replay. It was ironic though as I subbed him in the first game as he wasn't very good!

THE ONE THAT GOT AWAY

Alan Hansen: Partick Thistle to Tottenham Hotspur

I went up to Scotland to watch a centre-forward. It turned out that player wasn't all that good but while I was there I noticed Alan Hansen playing in midfield for Partick Thistle. He looked a real player but I felt that he wasn't playing in his best position. When I came back to Tottenham I asked Bill Nick to go and have a look at this guy and give me his opinion. Bill also felt he was a good player but didn't think he would be effective for us in midfield. We let him pass and about three weeks later he signed for Liverpool!

We now know what a great player he turned out to be though in the heart of their defence. I am pretty sure that we could have signed him when we looked at him because we were not aware of any other clubs in for him at that stage. But in football you win some and you lose some. It was a shame to miss out on Hansen but I did, though, eventually end up with my Scottish centre-forward, albeit a different name to the first one I targeted when I noticed Hansen; for I signed Steve Archibald from Aberdeen in 1980.

GEORGE BURLEY

Managed: Ayr United (1991–1993); Colchester
Town (1994); Ipswich Town (1994–2002); Derby
County (2003–2005); Hvveart of Midlothian
(2005); Southampton (2005–2008); Scotland
(2008–2009); Crystal Palace (2010–2011);
Apollon Limassol (2012)

MY BIG DEAL

Matt Holland: Bournemouth to Ipswich Town for
£800,000 in 1997

Matt became my best signing for qualities both on and off
the field. One of my old coaches used to say you can tell
a player's personality from the way they play on the field
and that was Matt – a 'hundred percenter' from start to
finish who always gave everything. He was an all-round
quality player who started out as a young lad at West Ham
where it didn't quite work out for him. He then went to
Bournemouth and became captain there when he was 21,
22, which also speaks volumes for his character.

I went to watch him a few times and really liked him.
The hardest part was persuading Bournemouth and their
manager Mel Machin to agree to sell him because they
didn't want to, which was understandable as Matt was an
inspirational player with a great attitude, work ethic and
personality who loved his football.

I still remember how he impressed me when I first
went to watch him play for Bournemouth at Dean Court.
He was a full-back at West Ham but by the time I saw
him he had moved into midfield, which suited his game. I
can't remember who Bournemouth were playing but I took
my chief scout along, Charlie Woods, and we were both

very impressed with Matt and especially his work ethic and felt he was someone we really needed to make a move for. Thankfully we were able to do the deal with Bournemouth.

Matt was great for us. He helped take us into the Premier League, when we finished fifth in our first season back in the top flight in 2001, which remains a highest position for a promoted team into the Premier League. He subsequently became an international with us who ended up playing and scoring at the World Cup [2002], so he was a top player.

Marcus Stewart was another of my best signings from Huddersfield but we paid a lot more for him, but he repaid us as he helped us get promoted and then scored 19 goals the following season when we finished fifth in the Premier League. Tony Mowbray was an inspirational leader who I signed from Celtic when he wasn't getting a game there. And Mark Venus and Jim Magilton were others who would have to be up there with my best signings. With Venus, Wolves took Steve Sedgley off me and still paid £100,000 – they're the nice deals!

THE ONE THAT GOT AWAY

Kevin Phillips: Watford to Ipswich Town on a free transfer

This is easy for me. I had watched Kevin and really liked him. I found out that he was nearing the end of his contract so I subsequently moved quickly on it. I got him in my office, everything was agreed. He was a lovely lad and he was keen to come to Ipswich. But what did for me was the fact we were told Watford were unhappy with him going for free and the deal would have to go to a tribunal. My chairman then, David Sheepshanks, wasn't prepared to go to tribunal as he was worried he was going to have to pay too much money so the deal was off. Sunderland moved in and they ended up paying about £325,000 which probably increased with add-ons. So, we didn't need to find too much money to get him but our finances were very tight at the time so I guess paying anything would have been too much.

It was a bitter pill to swallow because there's no doubt he would have scored lots of goals and won games for us. I knew Kevin had it in him to be a top striker, as it proved when he played for Sunderland and scored all those goals alongside Niall Quinn. Every time I saw him score another goal for Sunderland it was painful and was hard not to think what might have been if we had managed to pull off that deal!

TERRY BUTCHER

Managed: Coventry City (1990–1992);
Sunderland (1993); Motherwell (2002–2006);
Sydney FC (2006–2007); Partick Thistle
(caretaker 2007); Brentford (2007); Inverness
Caledonian Thistle (2009–2013); Hibernian
(2013–2014); Newport County (2015);
Philippines (2018)

MY BIG DEAL

Scott McDonald: To Motherwell after a trial in 2004

Scott came to us on trial at Motherwell and, at the time, he was going from club to club trying to earn a contract somewhere. On the recommendation of an agent I knew, we agreed to take a look at him. First impressions were a bit mixed because he was fat, stocky, cheeky, a bit arrogant, over-opinionated and wasn't fit enough. He certainly needed taking down a peg or two, which I was happy to do. Everyone told me he's got no chance of making it, but while he was all those things, I just saw something in him that I liked. Most notably, he scored goals and that's not a bad habit to have in your locker. Sometimes you have to follow your gut instinct and I did with Scott as I thought he had qualities we could work with. When we got him fit he was a real handful for defenders, though it was hard to get him fit because he was quite lazy and hated training, or let's just say he was economical with his running.

On the plus side, he was a great finisher and always seemed to produce goals when we needed them most. You always felt there was a goal in him – at any time. I guess the best example of that was 'Helicopter Sunday' in the 2004/05 season. We were playing Celtic on the final day of the season and they would have won the league if they beat us. Rangers were at Hibernian and were also in with a chance of the championship. With five minutes to go, we were 1-0 down and then from nowhere Scott scored two goals in the dying minutes, scoring the winner when he should have passed, but that was Scotty. Rangers won at Easter Road so they won the title. Obviously I was delighted to win the match and being an ex-Rangers player it meant a lot more to me. Ironically, Scott was a massive Celtic fan so he upset his own club. But it made him and he ended up signing for Celtic two years later and as we now all know he became a Parkhead goalscoring legend.

THE ONE THAT GOT AWAY

Victor Wanyama: Beerschot to Inverness Caledonian Thistle for £10,000

When I was at Inverness, Steve Marsella was my chief scout and my goalkeeping coach. Steve had been talking to some agents and he was told there was a guy called Victor Wanyama who we should take a look at. The talk was that he was a real player in the making and he would be a terrific signing for someone. Victor was about 20 at that time. The deal on the table was relatively small in modern football terms as a payment of just £10,000 was needed to buy him out of his Belgian club. Unfortunately, we didn't have that amount of money to buy him as to us that equated to a player's (annual) wage.

I wouldn't say we were very close to signing him but Steve spoke to his agent, who in turn spoke to the player, so we certainly had the opportunity to bring him into the football club. But that fee, which might be nothing to many clubs, was a big deal to us and was too much, sadly. It's one of those instances where I cannot help thinking 'what might have been' if we had found that money from somewhere and took him. He has gone on to enjoy a wonderful career with Celtic, Southampton and Tottenham so he was clearly a bargain at the time.

FRANK CLARK

Managed: Leyton Orient (1983–1991);
Nottingham Forest (1993–1996); Manchester City
(1996–1998)

MY BIG DEAL

Stan Collymore: Southend United to Nottingham Forest for £2.75m in 1993

It would have to be Stan – 50 goals in 78 games is pretty good going. I saw him play quite a lot for Crystal Palace reserves while I was still manager of Orient. I used to watch a lot of reserve team football as that was the level at which we could compete financially. A good friend of mine called John Griffin was chief scout at Palace and he kept telling me about this lad Collymore, who he felt would be a terrific player but wasn't getting a chance at Palace where he apparently wasn't fitting in after moving down from the Midlands.

He then moved to Southend United for £150,000, which we could never have afforded. He did well there and in the meantime I got the Forest job. As soon as I arrived people told me we needed a striker. We had just banked a fair bit of money from selling Roy Keane, Nigel Clough and Gary Charles and so I was allowed to spend some of that. I had barely spent any money in almost a decade at Orient as we never had any, so it was a big deal for me to spend this kind of money.

Within two days of arriving at Forest I paid £1.5m for Colin Cooper and then £2m [rising to £2.75m] on Stan, and I never regretted it. He really hit it off up front with another signing I made, Brian Roy, who I brought over from Foggia. They were terrific together for 12 months. It wasn't always easy to manage Stan, but it was worth the trouble. He could be a bit of a loner, argumentative, was suspicious of everybody, didn't make a lot of friends in the dressing room, but the players knew what he was capable of and what a match-winner he could be come Saturday, so they were prepared to put up with his moods and idiosyncrasies.

We ended up selling Stan to Liverpool for £8.5m, so it was good business to make a £6m return on our investment in just two years. We would have loved to keep him but the club didn't handle the situation very well and should have secured him on a longer and better contract much earlier than when we tried to do just that. By the time the Forest board offered him improved terms, he had already had his head turned by a few of the big hitters at Liverpool. I am not accusing the club of anything – it was more players in his ear. So from there it was difficult to keep him. We tried very hard but couldn't compete with Liverpool.

The only one who would push Stan close in terms of value for money would be a lad called Kevin Hales, who I signed for Leyton Orient from Chelsea. We paid him £200 a week and I told him we couldn't afford a signing-on fee and we were not in a position to haggle. I said if that's not enough we will have to leave it. But fortunately he was happy to sign and he played for over ten years at Orient. Initially, it came out in the media that he had got a bad knee. Maybe that was true in the top division with Chelsea but he was fit enough to play in the lower divisions and he played over 350 league games for Orient.

THE ONE THAT GOT AWAY

Ian Woan: Runcorn to Leyton Orient

A friend of mine who was scouting in the north-west spotted this midfield player in the non-league and he recommended him to me. I went to watch him play a midweek cup match on a cold and windy evening in November and I really liked the look of him. I tried to sign him and actually invited him down to Orient for a chat. But on the day he was due at the club I received a call from Ron Fenton, who was then Brian Clough's assistant at Forest. He said, 'Now then Frank, Ian Woan, tell me about him?' I said, 'He's going to be a good player Ronny but you're a bit late as he's coming down to sign for me now.' To which Ron replied, 'I'm sorry to tell you Frank that he is actually coming here to sign for us!'

Somebody had obviously tipped Forest off and he ended up there and I lost him. But ironically I inherited Ian when I became Forest boss. He had a wonderful left peg and was a quality player but initially Ian and I had a few battles because I felt he could be lazy; I needed more work rate from him. A player of his ability should never have been playing at Runcorn, so something clearly wasn't right with his game. But to be fair to him he did work at his game and by the time I left he was on the fringes of the England squad.

ALLAN CLARKE

Managed: Barnsley (1978–1980 & 1985–1989);
Leeds United (1980–1982); Scunthorpe United
(1983–1984); Lincoln City (1990)

MY BIG DEAL

David Seaman: Leeds United as an apprentice in 1981

I had my ups and downs in management but the one thing I always believed in was youth. When you sign lads from school, they need four or five years for them to develop into your first team, but I wasn't given that time to nurture them at Leeds. However, the lads I signed as apprentices were David Seaman, Denis Irwin, who I spotted playing for the Republic of Ireland Schoolboys at left-back, Terry Phelan, John Sheridan and Scott Sellars at Leeds, and Carl Tiler and John Beresford for Barnsley.

David was a talented kid and I could tell that he had something. But it's funny that my first real memory of him was when I had to give him a rollicking. We were on the training ground with the first team and I saw him leaning against these five-a-side goalposts. I stopped the session and went over to him and asked, 'What do you think you are doing?' He didn't really know what I was referring to so I told him that when you come out to train you must always have the same mentality as if you are playing a game and I didn't like his body language – it was lethargic and suggested he didn't much care. I learned a great deal from Don Revie, who I still refer to as The Gaffer, and the one thing he was big on was discipline and I picked that up off him.

It's easier to drill these habits into players while they are young than when they are older. David took my message on board and never did it again. Football is all about good habits. He was learning under a good goalkeeper in John Lukic, though, who I inherited, so that helped. David was still very young then but he just looked like a proper goalkeeper and with a perfect build for the position. I was very surprised when Leeds let him go for almost free after I had gone. It was unbelievable and I couldn't understand it. Seaman was sold for just £4,000 [to Peterborough United] when Eddie Gray was manager. That was a shame as he was a gem.

I also signed John Beresford when he was playing in Manchester City's reserves as a midfielder. He was 20 when they released him and I got him to come and see me. I told him I wanted him to join us and advised him that if a bigger club came in for him, I wouldn't stand in his way. I put him on £200 a week – the same he was on at City. He couldn't get in the team and he was knocking on my door every week and I told him his chance would come. When it did come it was as left-back and that's where he stayed. I sold him a year later to John Gregory at Portsmouth for £350,000!

THE ONES THAT GOT AWAY

Frank Arnesen: Ajax to Leeds United

Garry Thompson: Coventry City to Leeds United

I was so close to landing Frank Arnesen – I even had him and his wife round my house in Leeds. When Johan Cruyff signed for Barcelona, Frank became the Ajax captain and was already a star for Denmark. He would have improved us tremendously and would have been our general in midfield. He ended up going to Valencia after they offered him all kinds, like a free villa. I couldn't compete with them but I was *that* close to signing him.

At Leeds, I also wanted to sign a striker and a winger but the problem is as a manager that you can't always control what order you sign your players in. I wanted the big striker Garry Thompson from Coventry City but I knew he needed good service from wide so I signed Peter Barnes from West Bromwich Albion.

If I was given the choice I would have signed the striker first because I liked him. He was a big, strong lad who led the line well and could score goals – a good target man. I like to think he would have learned a lot from me, though he wasn't the same kind of striker as myself; he was more of a Mick Jones. But in the end, after I signed Barnes, I didn't have enough money to sign Thompson even though I had arranged it with his manager Gordon Milne.

NIGEL CLOUGH

Managed: Burton Albion (1998–2009 & 2015–
2020); Derby County (2009–2013); Sheffield
United (2013–2015); Mansfield Town (2020–)

MY BIG DEAL

Craig Bryson: Kilmarnock to Derby County for
£450,000 in 2011

It's unbelievably difficult to pick your best signing. I'm into
24 years as a manager. If you sign ten players a year that's
a lot of players to think about. I had to spend a few days
talking to Simon [Nigel's brother and chief scout] until we
came up with this decision. I'd like to talk about a few more
before we get to the number one.

There was Chris Martin. He was a free transfer from
Norwich, when I was manager at Derby. A few years ago, I
think Derby turned down £10m for him. Still playing, still
scoring goals, so to get a striker of that quality on a free,
wow. He was on loan from Norwich at Swindon in League
One when we went to watch him. Gary [Crosby, assistant
manager] and Simon did most of the watching. He was sub
most of the time. I'd say, 'How was he?' and they'd say, 'He
was sub.' Martin didn't really play. Norwich had an option
on him and didn't take it up. So, we took him and look at
the goals he scored at Derby since.

Then there's Jake Buxton, also on a free transfer. We got
adverse publicity when we signed him for Derby because he'd
come from non-league at Burton and all that sort of thing.
And he'd been at Mansfield before that. But Jake got very
close to the Premier League with Derby, their player of the
year and everything. We knew what Buxton could do and the
influence he could have on the team as we knew him from

when he was playing for us at Burton. For a free transfer player, he gave great service to Derby. He came back to us when I returned to Burton and we were in the Championship. Then he's taken over from me there as manager.

Another one is Shaun Barker. He had the potential to be right up there. He could have played for Derby for ten years. He'd have been the captain and the leader. It was such a tragedy that his career was cut short by injury [severe knee problems]. He later worked for the academy at Burton.

There's another couple who come to mind: Ché Adams. Signed him from Ilkeston Town when I was Sheffield United manager. I think he cost £20,000 or something like that. Years later he's playing in the Premier League and cost Southampton £15m.

We got Chris Basham on a free from Blackpool and took him to Sheffield United. He played every week in the Premier League and was highly rated in the stats. Jackson Irvine as well. We took him to Burton for a quarter of a million from Ross County and sold him for about a million and a half profit in a year.

So, you can see how difficult this choice is, but the one I've come up with is Craig Bryson. Pound-for-pound, we reckon he's the one. Paid £450,000 for him from Kilmarnock and he was one of those we were all convinced about, Gary, Simon and me. We all tried to watch players in those days. Kilmarnock was a long trek from the Midlands, but Bryson was one of those we all said straight away, 'Yes, he's the one,' and came back positive about it.

He ran miles and miles. I think he was voted Derby's player of the decade by the fans – and there were some good Derby players over that decade. He was a bit of a throwback in that he ran beyond the midfield, like a Steve Hodge, that sort of player. He scored goals from midfield and those players are very few and far between.

We watched him on separate trips, with Simon and Gary up first, individually, and they would come back and say, 'You've got to see this lad.' If we all ticked the box then that would be it. After 20 minutes of me seeing Bryson I could have come home. He made about ten runs into the box – didn't always get the ball, but he just kept making those runs. I just thought, 'Yep, he's the sort of bloke for us.'

It wasn't hard to persuade him to join us as he wanted to come down and was very good to deal with. He's one of those lads that you keep in touch with over the years. He's very unassuming and a good team player. Scored important goals over the years for Derby. So, he's the one.

THE ONE THAT GOT AWAY

John McGinn: St Mirren to Sheffield United in 2015

Again, from Scotland, I didn't see him, but Gary and Simon went up when we were at Sheffield United and came back raving about John McGinn.

We saw McGinn at St Mirren before he went to Hibs. Gary and Simon both said, 'Listen. There's a good midfielder there. Go and have a look at him.' Similar to Bryson they'd said straight away, 'That's him!' I had a look on DVD but we found out it was all set up for McGinn to stay in Scotland and go to Hibs.

We still had a little pursuit of him. We were interested but it didn't get to the stage where we talked to McGinn. I think it was already done for him to go to Hibs. Then Aston Villa took him, didn't they? Paid £2.5m, something like that. We were at Burton by then and it was beyond us to get McGinn.

There were a few others. We had Gary Hooper in the building at the Derby training ground but couldn't get that one done for financial reasons. We were desperate for a goalscorer at the time. He went from Scunthorpe, to Celtic and then Norwich and scored a lot of goals. I think he played for Grays Athletic against us as well, that's where he started, when we were non-league at Burton. He was always one we liked and missed out on.

When we were going up to Scotland we saw the two lads at Hamilton, James McCarthy and James McArthur, who I think was 16 when we first saw him when we were at Derby and we agreed he was going to become a very good player. But again, financially, we couldn't do it.

We also liked the lad at Ipswich, Cole Skuse, and he was also at Bristol City as a holding midfielder. He was our kind of player but couldn't get him over the line.

Every signing is a gamble. You have to miss out on a few. You can be put in a position where you have to pay this money and you have to do it NOW. We were never in a financial position to do that.

Clubs with a lot of finances can afford those mistakes, but it's very difficult when you can't afford to make mistakes like that. You have to be certain.

It's a mixed bag that makes up a good player. You try and assess his character on the pitch, how he goes about it, interacting with his teammates. The ability has to be there, his attitude and whether he fits in with how we play. Then the research into his character, injury record, things like that, comes later.

But first you are looking for that spark on the pitch that makes you think, 'Hold on a minute.'

I get quite excited about signing a player if I'm sure about him. I get nervous if I'm not that sure. In that instance you have to back your instinct, no matter what you're a being told about him, and be prepared to walk away.

JOHN COLEMAN

Managed: Ashton United (1997–1999);
Accrington Stanley (1999–2012 & 2014–);
Rochdale (2012–2013); Southport (2013–
2014); Sligo Rovers (2014)

MY BIG DEAL

Paul Mullin: Radcliffe Borough to Accrington Stanley for
£15,000 in 2000

Paul had the biggest impact of any player I ever signed. He
had played against us the season before we brought him
in, when we were both vying for the UniBond [Northern
Premier League] First Division, and he actually scored a
couple of goals against us.

The fee we paid, £15,000, was actually a lot of money
at the time for a club at that level. But it was a bargain as
he got fitter as he got older and he really embraced being a
full-time footballer and being a professional, when we got
promoted. He's a great character and is still a good friend
of mine.

It wasn't a hard deal to get done as Radcliffe were very
much a selling club and their manager was a good friend of
mine, Kevin Glendon. He was brilliant for us, scored a lot
of goals and led the line brilliantly, though I never classed
him as a prolific striker. He was just so reliable and very
rarely missed a game. He cracked a bone in his toe and
missed a couple of games once and I absolutely hammered
him for it because he was just so durable. He worked his
socks off for us. The amount of games we got out of him
was a testament to his character as we worked him into
the ground. I don't have a bad word to say about him as a
player or a man.

If I had to compare him to someone from the upper echelons I would have to say a player like Emile Heskey, because of his work rate, he was good in the air, led the line so well and was physically strong. These types of players might not receive the amount of credit they deserve from the wider football community but they are always appreciated by their team-mates as they know what they do for the team. Paul was like that. Selfless and hard-working.

It was a great wrench when we had to sell him. We were having financial problems at the time and were in danger of going bust so he signed for Morecambe. It was heartbreaking for me when he left and that says everything about his contribution to Accrington.

Kayden Jackson is another considering we got him on a free from Barnsley and managed to sell him for £1.6m with a 30 per cent sell-on clause. That was the best business I have probably ever done, from a pure financial angle. But he was another good player for me, with pace, power and strength and he could finish. I was pleased for him when he got his big move to Ipswich.

THE ONE THAT GOT AWAY

Craig Dawson: Radcliffe Borough to Accrington Stanley in 2009

I had a good relationship with Radcliffe and had arranged to buy Craig off them for £3,500, which was a cut-price fee, but our chairman didn't want to pay a fee so we missed out and he went to Rochdale. I think he ended up getting sold to West Bromwich Albion for a couple of million! It was frustrating because everything had been agreed, but you just don't know what was going on in the chairman's life at the time, or what his or the club's finances were so it's tough to criticise him. That's how our club was, struggling to stay afloat. I'm sure the chairman had a valid reason why he couldn't spend that money.

I think Craig actually played a friendly for us. He ticked every box for a centre-half. He was capable in the air, could score lots of goal for a defender. He attacked every ball like his life depended on it and that was the attitude we wanted to instil in our team.

He was a top pro and is continuing to be a top pro in the highest league. I believe there are quite a few more players in the lower leagues who can make it in the Premier League. Some managers are buying players from abroad when good, capable players are already here in the lower leagues under their own nose. I have bought players from abroad myself but some come over and struggle to adjust to the English game, whereas some of the quality players in the lower leagues are already accustomed to our game.

There was another as we [Accrington] were close to signing Glenn Murray from Carlisle but he went to Rochdale [in 2006] because our chairman wouldn't pay the wage that he wanted. He was on his way to us but we wouldn't pay the extra £100-a-week difference that Rochdale were prepared to pay.

STEVE COPPELL

Managed: Crystal Palace (1984–1993; 1995–1996; 1997–1998; 1999–2000); Manchester City (1996); Brentford (2001–2002); Brighton & Hove Albion (2002–2003); Reading (2003–2009); Bristol City (2010); Crawley Town (2012-2013 director of football); Portsmouth (2013–2014 director of football); Kerala Blasters (2016–2017); Jamshedpur (2017–2018); Atlético de Kolkata (2018–2019)

MY BIG DEAL

Ian Wright: Greenwich Borough to Crystal Palace on a free transfer in 1985

We used to make our training ground a place where local non-league managers could drop in and say hello, watch us train or maybe have a chat. One such manager whose opinion we respected was Billy Smith. He was telling us about pre-season training and said, 'We've got a black kid who's training with us and he's different gear.' I asked how old he was and whether he had been a reject from a league club. He said he was about 21 or 22 and thought he had trained with Brighton but was now labouring. I was sceptical because I heard those types of stories all the time and knew that generally players that good never slipped through the net so I thought there must be something wrong with him.

Anyway, I was persuaded to send our liaison officer Peter Prentice along to watch him train, but I never expected much to come of it. He came back and said this lad has really got something about him. I was encouraged enough to invite Ian along to train with us during pre-season and you didn't have to be a super-scout to see that he had a lot going for him. Within a few days we offered him a contract because he had it all: left foot, right foot, quick, good in the air, hungry, enthusiastic. I said to my chairman at the time, Ron Noades, 'This is going to sound stupid, but this kid has the ability to play for England.'

He had the raw talent and earned the nickname in his first season of 'super-sub'. He still had a lot to learn then like keeping his emotions in check and staying focused but the best thing to happen to his development was the fact we then signed Mark Bright from Leicester City. Brighty was of course another of my best signings. Brighty taught Ian how to be a pro, how to hone his skills and stay behind after training to improve himself further. The combination of Wright and Bright not only sounded good but was fantastic for our club and very fruitful for Ian given what he went on to achieve.

The signing of Brighty was a reward for me and Ron Noades driving hundreds of miles up and down the motorways because we didn't have the money to just sign the best players around, so we had to be creative. We went to Crewe a lot and we had been tipped off about Mark Bright. We understood that Leicester had to pay Port Vale a fee as soon as he played a certain amount of games and, as he got nearer to this figure, they began to leave him out to avoid paying the fee.

This became known and I went to see him play for Leicester reserves against Man City reserves at Maine Road. He scored a hat-trick. I couldn't help looking around the stands to see which other scouts were there to see if we would have any competition for his signature. We agreed to sign him for £30,000.

Just when we thought we had a bargain there was a problem with his medical as he had a condition called symphysis pubis; put simply it was a groin problem. It meant we ended up signing him on a pay as he played deal, but I don't recall him missing a game because of a groin injury. He was such a dedicated trainer; we couldn't get Brighty off the training ground. Wrighty saw this and followed his example. They became a great strike partnership and good friends, too.

Still, if I was asked at that time if it was obvious Wrighty would go on to greater things like he eventually did with Arsenal and England, I would probably have said 'no', because he still had much to learn. But he did learn those things and became a huge asset to our club. I remember in the promotion-winning year of 1988/89, he signed a new contract with us in the October while we were about 12th in the league. He didn't have to do that as there were other clubs sniffing around by then, but he felt like he hadn't quite completed the journey. I was still disappointed when he told me he wanted to move after we had finished third in the top flight, because I hoped he would want to stay having finished so high up in the league. But as soon as I knew Ian wanted a move, I then knew we had hit a glass ceiling.

There was no animosity, though, and I was as proud as punch when I saw him scoring all those goals for Arsenal and when he played for England. We don't see each other that often but when we do it's as though we're still in the dressing room together. He was never that eloquent in his days at Palace and now to see him on *Match of the Day* talking so well on the game also makes me feel very proud at how far he has come in his life and career. He's bright as a button and, understandably, is a hugely popular TV personality.

THE ONE THAT GOT AWAY

Joleon Lescott: Wolverhampton Wanderers to Crystal Palace for £2m in 2006

The only person I looked at for many years and thought he'd be ideal for Crystal Palace was Joleon Lescott. I tried to sign him after his Wolves career – and I thought I had him at one stage. We were having talks about him and I really thought we had him, then the next minute I read that he had gone to Everton. It was a blow because I thought he would have been perfect for us. He's the only one I remember being disappointed about and can't think of any other player I bust a gut for and ended up with nothing.

In hindsight I don't blame him as he clearly saw Everton as a bigger club than Palace and I think David Moyes was manager then, of a club that was going in the right direction. But I did think we had him. We were quietly getting the deal done with no other club in for him to my knowledge and then I read in the newspaper he had gone to Everton. But I had no bitterness as that happens in football. Fortunately, those disappointments didn't happen to us very often as we were usually dealing in the bargain basement.

At Palace we weren't prolific in the market because we never had a great deal of money, so it wasn't as though we were chasing lots of players every summer. At times we didn't make any purchases and went with what he already had. Our model was to sign young players and try to develop them.

Joleon was a bit different to that as he was a more mature player who had had knee problems and I empathised with that so would have handled it. I liked everything about him. He was a mountain of a defender. I don't mean that in a derogatory sense that he was a lump; I mean he was so powerful and able to deal with anything thrown at him, while also being quick enough to compete with the sharpest of forwards. His character was also outstanding.

ALAN CURBISHLEY

Managed: Charlton Athletic (1991–2006);
West Ham United (2006–2008)

MY BIG DEAL

Clive Mendonca: Grimsby Town to Charlton Athletic for £700,000 in 1997

I think I've got to go for Clive Mendonca as my best signing. Charlton had done 18 months playing at Selhurst Park and then gone to Upton Park. Then we sold Robert Lee and a couple of other players to help fund us going back to The Valley. It was a bit tough for a couple of years not being able to sign anyone, while we seemed to be selling everybody. But after that period, the first time we bought anyone was 700 grand on Clive Mendonca, which was massive for us.

Mendonca had scored against us the previous season and then the Grimsby manager was leaving. My chairman said to me, 'Listen, we can put up a million pounds.' Which was unheard of. He wanted me to spend it on three or four players and I said no, as I wanted Mendonca because we needed a goalscorer. Matty Holmes became available as well – he wanted to come back to London having gone from West Ham to Blackburn. So, we got the two of them [Mendonca and Holmes] for a million quid.

Mendonca just changed the way we played. He came in that season, hit the ground running, everybody got on board and we went up. He was a fantastic finisher and got the hat-trick at Wembley against Sunderland in the 4-4 First Division play-off final and scored one of the pens in the 7-6 win that got us promoted to the Premier League.

Every year players were sold to pay the wages for the summer, so to bring a couple of quality guys in made a bit of a statement that the club was back on track. And Mendonca was a major part of it – not just the hat-trick, but reconnecting us with the fans. When we went back to The Valley, all the seven-year-olds when we left were now 14 and supporting other clubs. We lost a generation of fans. And if we had lost at Wembley, I am sure we would have sold Mendonca, Richard Rufus, Mark Kinsella, Shaun Newton. They would have all gone because people were sniffing around and we wouldn't have been able to keep them. The promotion, therefore, was a massive thing and Clive Mendonca was a major part of it.

Mendonca is from Sunderland, it's his club. Apparently Peter Reid, who was managing Sunderland then, was interested in him. We got him down to London and Alan Buckley had just taken over as Grimsby manager and he wanted to talk to Mendonca to persuade him to stay. I'd got Mendonca in my car and his phone kept going off. It was Alan Buckley, so the pressure was on.

But I got Mendonca off to the medical, he didn't have a clue where we were. I explained to him I was driving him to Woodford for the medical and I'm saying that this was east London and Charlton was in south London and you had to go through a tunnel. He just didn't have a clue. He didn't know much about us. And I'm driving through Chigwell and I'm saying, 'Clive, this is Chigwell,' and he's not saying a word, really quiet, and I'm thinking, 'This isn't going well.' I'd picked him up from King's Cross and I drove all through the West End, Buckingham Palace, all the sights and we've got to Chigwell and I said, 'Look, this is Chigwell. Spurs have got their training ground here. A lot of Spurs players live round here, West Ham players. You could live here if you want. I live round here, but I have to go through the tunnel every morning.' And he goes, 'Chigwell?' And I go, 'Yeah.' And he went, 'OK, that's good. Sharon and Tracey come from Chigwell.' He's thinking *Birds of a Feather*!

The Charlton fans took to him. He changed everything. Took us up. Unfortunately, we got up and he got an injury, a hip injury, and had to retire. We went back down on the final day and then we came straight back up. Clive was gone by then with his injury, but he'd put us back on the map.

I know Geoff Hurst got the hat-trick at Wembley, great and everything, but Mendonca's three goals in that 4-4 draw were fantastic. Mendonca just changed Charlton forever.

He never did live in Chigwell, though!

THE ONE THAT GOT AWAY

Tim Cahill: Millwall to Charlton Athletic for £1.5m in 2004

In 2004 we were invited out to China, if you can believe that, pre-season. Shanghai. Claus Jensen, unbeknown to me, had a clause in his contract that if he got to his final year and someone bid £1.5m then he could go. So he wasn't on the trip, apparently because of an injury. The chairman phones me up and says he's got some bad news, Fulham want to sign Claus and what do I want to do? There's a time difference so I told him to leave it with me, to have a think. Then I heard about Tim Cahill possibly leaving Millwall for a similar fee so I got back to the chairman and said, 'Let's get hold of Millwall – I want Tim Cahill, he's scored loads of goals, he's an attacking midfield player and is exactly what I want.'

My chairman then tells me that Theo Paphitis, the Millwall chairman, said we were in the lead for Cahill because we had Claus's money and we could pay up front whereas the other clubs that were sniffing wanted to do it on bits and pieces. I thought it was done. Cahill's girlfriend was from the south so I thought that was great, he might not want to move out of London. But then Cahill goes and signs for Everton and was a fantastic signing for them as we all now know.

I could bring some sexy names up that I might also have got, but Cahill is the one that gave me the hump most. I thought we had him. At a later date I found out, though I don't know how true it was, we lost him over wages. It wasn't a fantastic difference. If I'd have been in London I think I'd have got him. But because I was in China he went to Everton, and scored loads of goals and was a great success.

We had a good side. Being next door to Millwall, I knew what Cahill was about. Cahill would have complemented Scott Parker. That was the season we finished seventh in the Premier League, just missed out on Europe. We fell right at the end, we should have finished higher but didn't and part of the reason was Parker got sold as well.

I could have named Mathieu Flamini who I had in the office and he decided to go to Arsenal. There are loads, but Cahill would have been the perfect signing for me. If I'd have known it was over money I'd have made sure we got him. I was on a TV programme with Cahill and he said it was because Everton were more established, but I don't know. Because I was in China I couldn't even meet him to get our point of view across. When I was at West Ham I thought I'd got Ashley Young and I didn't. If you get them into a room you feel you've got a chance.

When West Ham stayed up and Sheffield United went down, I drove to Sheffield and stayed with Phil Jagielka for four or five hours because I knew he was going and I wanted to sign him. But he wanted to stay up north and decided to go to Everton. Again! I didn't get that opportunity to get in a room with Cahill and we suffered because of it. Like Mendonca, I knew Cahill would have fitted seamlessly into the team and was exactly what we wanted. It still bugs me.

KEITH CURLE

Managed: Mansfield Town (2002–2004); Chester City (2005–2006); Torquay United (2007); Notts County (2012–2013); Carlisle United (2014–2018); Northampton Town (2018–2021); Oldham Athletic (2021)

MY BIG DEAL

Nicky Adams: Northampton Town to Carlisle United on a free transfer in 2016

The pressure on you as a manager in the lower leagues is that the clubs don't have much money to spend, so when you do invest money on a player you have to be prudent and make sure it's well spent. I bought Nicky for Carlisle when I was there and, because I knew what he would bring having worked with him before, I signed him again for Northampton when I went into that job. He's a winger who does what it says on the tin; he puts balls in and supplies crosses that often lead to goals, which is why he is always high up in the assists charts. He is just a reliable player who has a real hunger for the game and that attitude is infectious in the dressing room.

Nicky still had a year left on his contract when I signed him for Carlisle but Northampton allowed him to move. Like with any player I sign, I always try to meet them twice beforehand so they get to know me and I get to know more about them. In doing so I get to understand more about the player's character and I can then assess whether I see them fitting into the environment that I am trying to create. I get to know their interests and what their family ties are. I don't always sign every player I meet because sometimes the fit isn't right.

In lower-league management it's so important to create the right environment and then to find the right players to fit into that to help the team grow and improve. I met Nicky twice at De Vere Mottram Hall in Manchester, which is an area he would have known being a Bolton lad. We never talked finance on those occasions but we met again for a third time when the deal was pretty much done to agree terms.

He's one of the best I've worked with and he might have played a higher standard if he just had a bit more pace, as he struggles to get away from people. But give him the ball and he manoeuvres it perfectly with his ability to play the right pass into the strikers at the right time. He is very reliable in that regard, which is why I have always appreciated what he brings to the teams he plays in.

I also signed Charlie Wyke from Middlesbrough for £20,000 before he later became a £400,000 player for Sunderland. He was a good striker for me.

THE ONE THAT GOT AWAY

Clint Hill: Free transfer to Northampton Town

There are not too many players that have got away from me. Usually in Leagues One and Two you have to develop players from scratch. If you've not identified a player from the potential you have seen and are relying on waiting for them to first make his name, it's usually too late then. But I would probably say Clint Hill, a solid, reliable defender I had with me at Carlisle after I signed him on a free from Rangers.

When I came to Northampton Town I thought, why not go back for Clint, even though he was 37 at the time. But unfortunately for me he decided to take a coaching job at Fleetwood instead, under the management of Joey Barton. I wanted Clint because he was an experienced player, a winner and an infectious character who can set the right tone in the dressing room and on the field.

He was an honest player who put demands on other players around him, which I appreciated as manager. I gave him the opportunity to extend his playing career but he opted to take the coaching route to further his career and I understood that.

TOMMY DOCHERTY

Managed: Chelsea (1961–1967); Rotherham
United (1967–1968); Queens Park Rangers (1968
& 1979–1980); Aston Villa (1968–1970); Porto
(1970–1971); Manchester United (1972–1977);
Derby County (1977–1979): Sydney Olympic
(1981 & 1983); Preston North End (1981);
South Melbourne (1982–1983); Wolverhampton
Wanderers (1984–1985); Altrincham (1987–1988)

MY BIG DEAL

Peter Osgood: Signed as a youth player at Chelsea in 1964

I signed him from the Chelsea youth team. We held trials
and he impressed me immediately and I thought to myself,
'I have to sign him,' so I signed him at half-time during
that game actually. His skill and technique impressed me
straight away and those qualities became more evident the
more he played for us. He scored goals for fun as well and
not just any goals but spectacular goals. I remember one
game in particular when we won 2-1 at Burnley [in January
1966] and he scored them both; and that was only his first
full season as a professional.

Peter had everything. He was over six feet tall, was
good in the air and was very elegant with his long strides
while running with the ball for a tall man, not a loping
clumsy tall player, but graceful. He was a great pro and
always full of the joys of spring. He was such a lovely lad
that he never really grew up and I mean that in the nicest
way as he was as cheery in his latter career as he was as a
young lad. Peter was unlucky not to win more than his four
caps for England but they had a lot of good centre-forwards
in those days and maybe Peter wasn't Alf Ramsey's type,

I don't know. But I thought the world of him. For me he was just like the Hungarian great, [Nándor] Hidegkuti, a deep-lying centre-forward of the highest calibre, which is as good a praise I could heap on him.

Charlie Cooke is a close second behind Peter. He really was a terrific winger. I had a lot of good contacts in Scotland and I knew the Scottish scene very well. I used to drive up to Glasgow quite often and watch a game if there were no games going on in England, especially if I received a recommendation on a player from someone whose opinion I respected. I saw Cooke myself and was impressed with him so we paid Dundee a club record £72,000 for him. I picked him for Scotland when I was the Scotland team manager as well.

THE ONE THAT GOT AWAY

Peter Shilton: Stoke City to Manchester United in 1976

Around about 1976, I wanted to sign Peter to replace Alex Stepney, whose form, I felt, had gone backwards quite a bit. I was a fan of Stepney's and I actually signed him for Chelsea from Millwall, though I also sold him to Man United. But as time went on I didn't feel he was the same keeper so that was when I tried to bring Shilton to Old Trafford.

I had agreed the deal with Stoke City manager Tony Waddington but Man United wouldn't pay the fee, which was a little over £200,000. Nor would they pay him the couple of hundred pounds a week wages he wanted. Matt Busby [who was on the board] said they weren't paying that kind of money for a goalkeeper. United were a huge club in those days also but they could be a bit tight with money. They are obviously not so tight with their money now, but they were then.

I was very angry about the situation as I knew what type of keeper we would have been getting. It wasn't a gamble in any way, he was an England international by then and was a goalkeeper approaching his peak years. Unfortunately Nottingham Forest reaped the rewards for our refusal to pay the money and Cloughy [Brian Clough] bought Shilton instead and they went on to win the league and two European Cups!

ALAN DURBAN

Managed: Shrewsbury Town (1974–1978); Stoke City (1978–1981 & 1998 caretaker); Sunderland (1981–1984); Cardiff City (1984–1986)

MY BIG DEAL

Mike Doyle: Manchester City to Stoke City for £50,000 in 1978

I picked Mike up for hardly anything for a player of his experience. I needed a central defender and he was playing in midfield at Man City but I did what Cloughy did at Derby with Dave Mackay. Admittedly, Mackay was the best I played with by a mile and the likes of Jimmy Greaves and Alan Mullery would agree with me. So, he would probably show up well in most positions, but it showed me how a good, experienced pro could adapt from midfield to defence. So I converted Doyle and stuck him next to Denis Smith at the back.

I always preferred young forwards and older defenders and therefore I had no issue putting Mike and Denis together at the back even though they were both over 30. Mike played 46 games for me in his first season in 1978/79 and helped us get promotion to the top flight so he was a success in all kinds of ways. He never had the same character as Dave Mackay, but still fitted into our team nicely and struck up a great partnership with Denis at the back. Denis was my Dave Mackay in the way that he helped Mike settle in at the heart of the defence as Dave had done with Roy McFarland when he came in from Tranmere.

I am equally proud of Kevin Phillips signing for Sunderland from Watford on my recommendation to manager Peter Reid when I was his chief scout. We needed someone to play off Niall Quinn and I watched Phillips three or four times and thought he would be ideal. His early movement impressed me, he missed that many chances I couldn't believe it, but I thought he would improve as was the case. He got better and better.

Other honourable mentions would go to Ally McCoist, who I brought to Sunderland from St Johnstone but it was just too early for him at that level then at 18. He later proved to us all at Rangers that he was good enough, but I should have sent him out on loan somewhere first to let him learn his trade. Brendan O'Callaghan, who I signed from Doncaster in my first month at Stoke, was another of my best signings. He was very consistent and chipped in with a few goals.

THE ONES THAT GOT AWAY

Mick Mills: Ipswich Town to Sunderland

Michael Laudrup: Brøndby to Sunderland

I had agreed a fee with Ipswich manager Bobby Robson for Mick as I wanted to throw the young lad Nick Pickering further forwards into midfield from full-back, as Ian Munro had disappointed me in that position. I also felt that I never had a decent captain at Roker Park and knew that Mick's experience and leadership skills would make him the perfect captain. He had played over 700 games at Ipswich, hardly ever got injured and I thought he would do a good job for us.

I was so confident that it was a done deal I called a press conference to announce it. The player was on his way up to Sunderland to complete the move and then, unfortunately, Lawrie McMenemy got involved. He wanted to speak to Mick so they diverted his trip and before I could catch my breath he was a Southampton player. I don't know how they did it but Mick never did come up to Roker Park. He had a good career at Southampton as well – they finished second one year.

I also tried very hard to sign Michael Laudrup before he became the legend we all knew at Juventus. I went over to Denmark to meet him and his father while he was playing for Brøndby. They were a Copenhagen-based club but I seem to remember meeting him at a coastal location so maybe he was preparing for an away game? Anyway, I was reasonably confident he would come and join us at Sunderland but he was voted the Danish Player of the Year in 1982 and that brought him a lot of attention. Juventus ended up signing him for a lot more money than we had planned to pay and I think even Liverpool had hoped to sign him by that stage so it never worked out for us.

SEAN DYCHE

Managed: Watford (2011–2012); Burnley
(2012–2022)

MY BIG DEAL

Tom Heaton: Bristol City to Burnley on a free
transfer in 2013

It's hard for me to go beyond Tom Heaton because he came
to us not earning a fortune having just been relegated at
Bristol City and a few seasons later he won England caps,
so the story speaks for itself.

Granty [Lee Grant] left us and went off to Derby after
winning our Player of the Year so for my first signing I went
and signed Tom on a free transfer from a club that had just
been relegated from the Championship! I got slaughtered for
making a relegated goalkeeper my first signing and allowing
Granty to go, which wasn't really the truth as he turned
down a contract.

Tom was on my radar because I was on the cusp of
signing him for Watford just before I got a tip-off that I
wouldn't be at Watford for very long, if you know what I
mean. I had spoken with Tom and his agent and the deal
was agreed, but around the time I found out I was getting
the sack, Watford pulled the plug on it. I told his agent,
'Don't worry, I will find a way to come back for him.' It was
an honour thing for me, and I obviously kept my promise
and took him to Burnley instead.

It wasn't a shot in the dark; we'd known about him
for a number of years and knew he was the right signing
to make. I'd seen a lot of him in the Championship and I
spoke to Malky Mackay, who had him at Cardiff, and he
always spoke very highly of him. I've been in the game a

long time and spoke to a few goalkeeping coaches who all rated him highly.

Similar with Nick Pope, he's a top-class professional and very strong in his belief about what he can do as a goalkeeper. It was his mentality that most impressed me before I signed him. When his team were getting pelters from supporters and the goals were flying in, from watching DVDs on my laptop I could see that he was doing everything he could to keep his team in games. You need to have a very strong mentality to be like that.

There are a few signings I would mention like Joey Barton, just because nobody thought that move would work. Dave Jones and Scott Arfield are other great stories for this club. Scotty was on his way to either MK Dons or Southend, but we stepped in and he ended up playing for years with us in the Premier League and is still doing well. Michael Keane and Tarky [James Tarkowski] were others but they cost good money and were already on the radar, but Tom Heaton was free and was just relegated so he's a clear choice.

THE ONE THAT GOT AWAY

Harry Kane: Tottenham Hotspur to Burnley for approximately £6m in 2013

There are quite a few that get away from you, for various reasons, but when we first got into the Premier League, I remember phoning Tottenham about signing Harry Kane. He would definitely be the most high-profile one that got away.

I know it sounds mad but at the time he'd had a couple of loan spells that hadn't worked out, like at Norwich. But I'd had good reports about him from my mates at Millwall. That's a tough place to play as I know from my own time there. But Harry handled it very well, worked hard for the team, playing off the striker and linking play very well.

I still knew people there and they all said he was a brilliant lad and was very professional, so all the boxes were ticked.

After those reports and having met him myself, I thought, 'Yep, you're definitely the type of player for us.'

In fact, around that time, I met him and his family randomly in Portugal. He was with his parents and I said to him, 'What do you think?' He said he wanted to give Tottenham a proper go, which I thought was fair enough.

Anyway, when I got back, I still gave [then Tottenham manager] Tim Sherwood a call to see if we could nick him. I spoke to my board, who made the relevant phone calls, but it soon became clear that at that time the board were never going to give me the money because of the big numbers they were putting on his head.

At the time, it was hard to fathom because he'd had a couple of loan moves that hadn't worked out but fair play to Tottenham for standing by him and valuing him so highly. The rest is history.

They wanted something like six or seven million, which doesn't sound much now but at the time was a lot, especially for a club like us! We were prepared to pay two or three, but our board couldn't go any higher.

I've bumped into Harry many times since then and he always speaks and says hello. I'm a supporter of a kidney charity and he's helped me out a few times with signed shirts and he even sent my lad a message for his 18th [birthday]. He really is a terrific fella, the real deal. I can't speak highly enough of him and his family. He is a fantastic player and is an equally fantastic guy.

SVEN-GÖRAN ERIKSSON

Managed: Degerfors IF (1977–1978) ; IFK
Göteborg (1979–1982); Benfica (1982–1984);
Roma (1984–1987); Fiorentina (1987–1989);
Benfica (1989–1992); Sampdoria (1992–1997);
Lazio (1997–2001); England (2001–2006);
Manchester City (2007–2008); Mexico (2008–
2009); Ivory Coast (2010); Leicester City (2010–
2011); Guangzhou R&F (2013–2014); Shanghai
SIPG (2014–2016); Shenzen (2016–2017);
Philippines (2018–2019)

MY BIG DEAL

Roberto Mancini: Sampdoria to Lazio on a free transfer in 1997

My best signing? Well, that's very, very difficult. But when I left Sampdoria and went to Lazio, I took with me Mancini. I had Mancini with me for five years at Sampdoria. He was a certain age, 32 or 33, so I got him to Lazio for very little money. The transfer fee was very small; in fact I don't think Lazio paid anything.

At that time, I had agreed to sign for Blackburn Rovers as manager and the first thing I said was I want to bring Mancini. And Mancini wanted to come. But Blackburn said no because his salary was too high. Then Lazio came for me and I changed my mind and Mr [Jack] Walker, the Blackburn owner, was kind enough to cancel the contract I'd signed. I went to Lazio and Lazio said, 'Yes, you can have Mancini.'

Mancini became an extremely important player in the dressing room and on the pitch. For me he played three-and-a-half years at Lazio and we won seven trophies. Not only because of him, we had an extremely good football team, probably the best team in the world at that time. We had players like Juan Sebastián Verón, Alessandro Nesta, Pavel Nedvěd, Hernán Crespo and Christian Vieri – an incredible team.

Mancini was my captain at Sampdoria but when he came with me to Lazio, no. It was Nesta, who was a boy when he joined Lazio, so he was the captain. But Mancini still acted like a captain. Mancini had some defects, of course, a hot temper. He was very angry on team-mates when they didn't do what he thought they should do. And he was very angry at referees.

Mancini wanted things to be perfect, everything from the kit man to cleaning ladies in the dressing room, all had to be performing well when the Sunday game came. He had something special because people liked him. His passion for football was something very, very special. He didn't come to get the money or to have a nice time in Rome. He came for winning.

When Mancini was at Sampdoria and I went there, Mancini was everything – he and Gianluca Vialli, but then Vialli left. Mancini then did everything, he was with the kit man, the bus driver, the cleaners, the chef, everything. I told him, 'How is it possible that you can play? You are doing the work for everyone in the club. You must be tired.'

He became my assistant manager with Lazio and was learning. When I managed Leicester City I brought Mancini to play. He was maybe 37 by then and he played a few times, not so many, before saying he was going into management with Fiorentina. Mancini liked English football and he remembered that when he became Manchester City manager, less than two years after I had been there.

THE ONE THAT GOT AWAY

Torbjörn Nilsson: IFK Göteborg to Benfica

He was a striker, the best in Europe at that time [1982]. Liverpool wanted him. I had joined Benfica as manager from Göteborg and the first signing I wanted to do was Torbjörn. And he came, we were looking at the club, we were looking at a house, we were looking at the training ground and discussing a contract. At the end Torbjörn changed his mind and he went instead to Germany, to Kaiserslautern.

If he had come to Benfica, Nilsson would have become the white Eusébio. He wasn't good, he was the best. Torbjörn was the best striker I had in all my life and I had a lot of good strikers. He had everything, which is why Liverpool wanted him, he said no. Roma also wanted him, he said no. He went to a small club, Kaiserslautern. I asked him why he did that and he admitted he didn't know why.

With him at Benfica I think we would have been fantastic. We were very successful for two seasons, we won the league twice, we played a final in the UEFA Cup, lost to Anderlecht, we played the quarter-final in the European Cup, lost against Liverpool, and we won the Portuguese Cup. We were good, but I think with him we would have been better, one of the best club sides we have seen. We would have won that UEFA Cup Final against Anderlecht for sure.

He was one of these wonder boys. I think he was 17, 18 when he joined Göteborg and then he signed for PSV Eindhoven. Very young to leave Sweden and there was no success at all, so he came back. Torbjörn was at the club when I went to Göteborg from a lower club and what I saw in him was absolutely incredible. But in the games, he was afraid, he was nervous, he was mentally not strong so I fixed a mental coach, a sports psychologist from Norway. I said to Torbjörn, 'I can't really help you to take the last step. Are you interested in this psychologist?' Six months after that, the whole of Europe wanted Torbjörn Nilsson.

He was the best in Europe. I remember we played a friendly game against Southampton. It was winter-time, in February. That was the week before we went to Valencia and beat them in the quarter-final of the UEFA Cup on the way to winning the cup. The result of that friendly game was 4-4. And when I left the pitch at the end to go into our dressing room, in the dressing room already was the coach of Southampton, Lawrie McMenemy, and he said, 'Boss, what's the price? Whatever you ask for him, I will buy him.'

Torbjörn had scored three or four goals. I said simply, 'He's not for sale.'

Nilsson was top scorer in the UEFA Cup that season and then he went to Germany and no success. He didn't like it. He went back home to Göteborg, won the UEFA Cup again, beating Dundee United. I would have taken him when he went back to Göteborg, but I had too many foreigners at Benfica so I couldn't do it. Torbjörn never went out of Sweden again.

Today, he is travelling around the Nordic countries, especially Sweden, giving speeches on sports psychology. Yes. Can you imagine? We keep in touch and when we meet I still ask him, 'Why did you not come with me to Benfica?'

He still does not know.

ROY EVANS

Managed: Liverpool (1994–1998); Fulham (co-manager 2000); Swindon Town (2001)

MY BIG DEAL

Stan Collymore: Nottingham Forest to Liverpool for £8.5m in 1995

Stan was certainly my most expensive signing; it was an English record transfer fee at the time. He might not have totally delivered on his potential, and there are reasons for that, but he was still my best signing because we did get a lot of goals out of him while he was at the club – something like a goal every two games, which is a very good return.

There were a few big clubs interested in Stan at the time and I told him what we were trying to achieve at Liverpool and didn't mind guaranteeing him a place in the team because my view was you don't spend that amount of money for them to sit on the bench.

I knew about Stan at the time, but we still went and watched him and what we saw was pace, power and strength, qualities that you fear when someone like that is playing against you. At his best he was unplayable. We were a very attacking team at the time and Stan was a good addition to that. It wasn't just about his goals, he was hugely powerful when running with the ball, he brought people into the game.

The main thing that let Stan down was the fact he wouldn't move from his home in the Midlands and that caused us some problems occasionally when he was late for training or such like, so that was the biggest disappointment. Those occasions happened too often. On the occasions he wouldn't be there or was late, some players would say,

'Where's Stan today?' or, 'Where was he yesterday?' and that stuff didn't do him any favours.

I think he could have been even better if he had settled in the area. These are the reasons why he ended up going back to the Midlands with Aston Villa after two seasons at Anfield. He was clearly happier in the Midlands.

Nonetheless, we were exciting to watch and were always in the top four, qualifying for Europe, but, unfortunately, we couldn't challenge Manchester United at that time when they were particularly strong. When you're manager of Liverpool you're expected to win trophies and we just won a League Cup [1995, before Collymore arrived] and made an FA Cup Final [lost to Manchester United in 1996]. The fact we didn't win more trophies was not Stan's fault, we were just too far behind United at that time.

Some of your best signings are not always players that you buy but the ones you develop from the youth team or reserves. The likes of Steve McManaman, Robbie Fowler and Jamie Redknapp were already in the first team when I took over as manager, but I tried to develop them further in the first team and their development was pleasing to see through their careers.

THE ONE THAT GOT AWAY

No one

There would have been a few players we tried to bring into the football club and it never worked out but I don't remember any particular player too much. And it wouldn't be fair on them to mention their name at this stage. One of the benefits of managing a club like Liverpool is that you tend to sign most of the players you go in for.

BRIAN FLYNN

*Managed: Wrexham (1989–2001); Swansea City
(2002–2004); Wales U21 (2004–2012); Wales
(caretaker 2010); Doncaster Rovers (2013)*

MY BIG DEAL

Roberto Martínez: Walsall to Swansea City on a free
transfer in 2003

I had been aware of Roberto since he signed for Wigan
in 1995 as our reserves would play their reserves regularly.
It seemed like we were at Springfield Park every month!
Roberto came over from Spain after Dave Whelan spotted
him on a business trip there, along with Jesús Seba and Izzy
Díaz. All three came over.

Roberto was the only one who made it really and
I followed his career from those early days at Wigan, to
Motherwell and then to Walsall.

Anyway, fast forward to 2003 when I was manager of
Swansea, just before I was about to set off from my home in
Burnley to drive down to Swansea for training on Monday,
I had a call from my assistant saying that Walsall reserves
were playing at Hednesford and I should drop by and have
a look at Roberto, as he was still on our radar. I thought it
was a great idea and did just that.

I watched this game and knew straight away that Roberto
was just what I needed. He stood out. I had not long signed
Leon Britton from West Ham and Lenny Johnrose from
Burnley and thought if I could place Roberto in between
those two that would be the perfect midfield combination
for Swansea. I had a word with Walsall manager Colin Lee
and asked if I could take Roberto on loan. He said if I could
persuade him, I could have him.

He came down on the Tuesday and I spent the whole day selling the club to him and explaining our targets, how he would fit in and he agreed to join us. He spoke very good English, was an intelligent man and he did his homework and got to know how well Swansea had done previously under John Toshack a few years earlier, so he was aware we were a big club but on hard times.

The last match he played for us in his first season, a 4-2 win over Hull, meant we survived relegation. If we had lost that game, we would have dropped into the non-league. I have no doubts that without Roberto's influence on our team we would have been relegated that season. If that had happened, I could see happening to us what had happened to Newport County – we might well have struggled to get back up for 20 years.

That was how significant Roberto's impact was on the football club.

He was a cultured midfielder – he didn't know what a big ball was. Everything went to feet, played through the midfield. I like to think the image Swansea have now of being an attractive footballing side emanated from what we started then.

But it wasn't only Roberto's football skills that had a positive effect on the team. His character and personality was also so important for morale and confidence. Once he went into town after training and arranged with a Spanish restaurant for all the lads to go there for a meal after training. They all went along for a pasta meal that cost no more than £2.50 a head!

I'm not surprised Roberto has gone on to be a top manager because he always had that potential.

I would also like to mention a couple of other key signings I made: Darren Ferguson [see below] and Tony Humes, who was great for me at Wrexham after I took him off Ipswich. They told me they would be pleased if Tony could have a good career but it was unlikely to be at Ipswich as he was too committed in the tackle to the point that he was prone to injuring himself. I was happy to take him. He was brilliant at Wrexham in the centre of our defence.

Gary Bennett was another terrific signing for me at Wrexham. He was a winger at Chester City when I signed him, but I saw something in him to know he would make a good striker. I told him I didn't want to see him on the wing or helping out in defence. I made it clear I wanted him in the middle of everything when we were in the opposition box. He scored over 100 goals, before we sold him on to Tranmere for £300,000 – not bad for someone we paid nothing for.

THE ONE THAT GOT AWAY (sort of)

Darren Ferguson: Wolverhampton Wanderers to Wrexham in 1999

Darren is one of my best signings, as well as being my one that got away, but then came back again! Is that clear? Let me explain.

I needed a midfielder at Wrexham and I was fortunate in that I was close to Alex Ferguson. I called him up and asked him, 'Do you think your Darren would play for me on loan at Wrexham?' He said he didn't think so as he wouldn't want to drop a division. It was common knowledge at the time that Darren wasn't getting along with the Wolves manager Mark McGhee so I thought I'd try my luck. But it never worked out and he went to Holland instead.

I followed his path and soon learned that it hadn't worked out for him over there and he was now training at Wigan, out of contract. I phoned Alex up again and asked if Darren would come and train with us with a view to signing. This time, Sir Alex said, 'I'm sure he would, Bri.'

I told him how keen I was to sign him, but explained the money wasn't so good compared to what he would have been on elsewhere. I told him he could name his own contract, whether it's one year, two years or three years. Or even one month and see how it goes, see if he liked us.

But before he could sign it was looking like he was my one that got away again. He called me and said he had been offered a load of money to play in Japan and he couldn't turn it down. I tore up the contract he had just signed and let him go. Darren went out there at the weekend, but before he was able to sign, he was back home. The manager of the Japanese club had been sacked and his deal was off. Therefore, I was finally able to properly sign Darren. He ended up playing over 300 games for Wrexham, long after I had left, so he wasn't a bad signing was he.

GERRY FRANCIS

*Managed: Exeter City (1983–1984); Bristol
Rovers (1987–1991 & 2001); Queens Park
Rangers (1991–1994 & 1998–2001); Tottenham
Hotspur (1994–1997)*

MY BIG DEAL

Nigel Martyn: St Blazey to Bristol Rovers on a free
transfer in 1987

It's funny how some of these deals transpire as I had just
lent Bristol Rovers £10,000 of my own money to buy Ian
Holloway, as they didn't have any money and were in
financial difficulties. But then I picked up Nigel Martyn
for free on the back of a tip-off from the tea lady! She came
up to me and said, 'Gerry, there's a great goalkeeper down at
St Blazey, please go and take a look at him.' I told her that I
had zero money to spend but would try to look into it. The
next time I went into the canteen for a cup of tea she refused
to serve me because I hadn't checked out her goalkeeper. So
I promised her I would go and take a look at him and I did.

When I saw him I thought, 'Blimey, we have to do
something.' I only had to watch him for 45 minutes and
it was clear he was more than a rough diamond – he had
such great natural ability. His team was under the cosh so
I managed to see a lot of him and his talent was obvious. I
rang the chairman and insisted we did everything we could
to sign him. Nigel was working in a warehouse earning
£100 a week and wanted £150 to sign for us. Even that was
too much for us at the time and we eventually paid him
£125 a week. Within two years he was the first million-
pound goalkeeper in English football when he signed for
Crystal Palace.

I had no hesitation throwing Nigel straight into the first team. I was privileged enough to play with some great goalkeepers like Peter Shilton, Gordon Banks, Ray Clemence, Phil Parkes and people of that ilk and Nigel was similar to all those guys. He was totally unflappable, was a terrific shot-stopper, was quick coming off his line for a big man – he had to work on crosses like all good goalkeepers – but he never had any weaknesses. I was devastated when they sold him as we were top of the league and, within a week, they sold my goalkeeper and my centre-forward, Gary Penrice, and got £1.5m for the two of them. Fortunately we still managed to get promotion.

There are a few others I am pleased about on reflection. I signed Peter Crouch for QPR from Tottenham for 50 grand and gave him his first game in professional football. After selling Andy Sinton for a load of money to Sheffield Wednesday, I bought Trevor Sinclair from Blackpool to QPR for £650,000, which was the most I had ever spent on a player then but they ended up selling him to West Ham for over two million quid. Both Crouch and Sinclair went on to play for England.

And I signed David Ginola for Tottenham from Newcastle when nobody wanted him and he ended up being Player of the Year. David was already a big name and had been amazing for Kevin Keegan but then things went stale for him and he was available for ages before I took a chance on him. These are all signings I'm proud of but because of the romance of the story Nigel Martyn would be the pick of them.

THE ONE THAT GOT AWAY

Emmanuel Petit: Monaco to Tottenham Hotspur

I worked on the Petit deal for nine months and was gutted when it never materialised. I saw him play for Monaco at the back after he had already been in and around the France team but he had been discarded. He was a player I admired and had earmarked as soon as David Howells sustained a bad injury and I wanted him to replace David in midfield because he was strong, talented, had great ability on the ball and was obviously versatile because he was a midfielder playing at centre-back.

I was ready to sign him after they played Newcastle in the quarter-final of the UEFA Cup but they didn't want to sell him until their UEFA Cup run was over with. Unfortunately for me and Tottenham, Arsène Wenger had moved to Arsenal in that same season and he used to be Petit's manager at Monaco so they had a longstanding rapport, which eventually proved my undoing.

That deal was so close to being done. He had already taken his medical with us and on the night we all went out for a dinner along with the chairman Alan Sugar and his son Daniel. He was due to come in the next morning and sign on the dotted line. But Daniel's driver, who was driving him over London, told us the next day that he had asked if he could take him to Arsène Wenger's house, where he then agreed to sign for Arsenal instead of us! That was one of my biggest regrets.

Not only did he become a great player for Arsenal along with Patrick Vieira in midfield, he went on to win the World Cup in 1998. We did well at Tottenham and finished as the top London club in my time there but who knows what we might have achieved with the addition of a quality player like Petit?

TREVOR FRANCIS

Managed: Queens Park Rangers (1988–1989);
Sheffield Wednesday (1991–1995); Birmingham
City (1996–2001); Crystal Palace (2001–2003)

MY BIG DEAL

Chris Waddle: Marseille to Sheffield Wednesday for
£1m in 1992

I heard Chris was looking to come back from France so I
thought, 'I'll speak to his agent and see what our chances
are.' It quickly became clear he was keen and said if we
were fair with him he would be fair with us and that's how
it panned out. I went across to Paris to negotiate the deal
with Marseille chairman Bernard Tapie. We agreed the
fee pretty quickly and also the contract for Chris. We had
finished third in the [old] First Division behind Leeds and
Manchester United before he arrived, so it wasn't as though
he was taking a step down at that stage of his career. We
were on the up and I was looking to improve. He had great
experience then in his early 30s but he just loved playing the
game. His desire was infectious.

I played him on the right of midfield and he was
always a threat, especially when cutting back in on to his
left foot with the accuracy of his shooting ability. He had
this stepover too, which was a skill that proved to be very
effective. Quite simply he was outstanding and would
almost certainly go down as one of Sheffield Wednesday's
greatest-ever players.

Chris took us to another level in his first season at
Hillsborough. Opposing managers always knew the man
they had marking him had to be fully on his game and often
they doubled up by putting two defenders on him, which

117

created more space for us elsewhere on the park. He was instrumental in getting us to two cup finals in 1993 and was rightly named Player of the Year and really should have regained his England position also – I'm not sure why he didn't. It was a signing that gave me enormous pleasure.

In terms of other signings, when I took over at Birmingham in '96 the team had just finished 15th in the second tier of English football and I told the board when joining the club that I wanted to sign a high-profile player to generate some interest and enthusiasm to lift the club. I was looking at free transfers and the player I signed was Steve Bruce. I always regarded Steve as a top player and one of the best never to play for England. His experience and leadership added a great deal to our dressing room.

Initially, I spoke to Sir Alex Ferguson and he told me Steve had a year left on his contract and was due a testimonial so when we signed him we had to compensate him for that loss of earnings, which made him Birmingham's most expensive signing. I managed to bring in Ray Wilkins and Peter Reid as free transfers in my first managerial job at QPR but times had since changed and bringing in a household name like Bruce was not as easy seven years on so I was very pleased to get that deal done. Steve had two good years with me and the fact he came back to do well for Birmingham as manager gives me a lot of satisfaction.

Another signing I'm proud of was that of Andrew Johnson, who I had from a 16-year-old at Blues. When I was Crystal Palace manager and Steve Bruce wanted to take Clinton Morrison off me to Birmingham I insisted that Johnson was part of the deal. Fortunately he became a huge success at Selhurst Park, scoring lots of goals [74 in 140 league games] and winning eight England caps. When I think of the club's history and their best and most effective strikers I would rank Andrew just behind Ian Wright.

THE ONE THAT GOT AWAY

Christian Poulsen: FC Copenhagen to Birmingham City

I was alerted to Christian while he was at Copenhagen so my assistant Mick Mills and myself went to watch him play for Denmark under-21s. We also watched him play against Lazio at the Olympic Stadium in the Champions League [in August 2001], as well as looking at several videos. So we decided he would add something to our midfield and agreed a fee with his club, which was about £1m.

He came over to St Andrew's with his parents to have a look around and hopefully sign after agreeing personal terms. We were ready to talk money and get him signed up when a call came through from Karren Brady who asked if we could wait until she arrived. So there was a delay of about an hour. Then, when she arrived, she made what can only be described as a derisory offer, which was rather embarrassing, and the deal collapsed. It was obviously disappointing for me after putting a lot of time into it.

Myself and Mick knew we had a player of great potential. You only have to look at the clubs he ended up playing for and the transfer fees involved to fully understand the type of player we missed out on here: he played for Schalke (€7m), Seville, Juventus (€9.75m), Liverpool (£4.5m) and Ajax, not to mention the 92 caps for Denmark. I left Birmingham City shortly afterwards.

BARRY FRY

Managed: Dunstable Town (1974–1976);
Hillingdon Borough (1976–1977); Bedford Town
(1977–1978); Barnet (1978–1985 & 1986–1993);
Maidstone United (1985–1986); Southend
United (1993); Birmingham City (1993–1996);
Peterborough United (1996–2005, caretaker 2006,
director of football therefater)

MY BIG DEAL

George Best: Manchester United to Dunstable Town on loan in 1974, and later Barnet

I don't have to think twice about my biggest or greatest signing, as it was George Best by a country mile. It was my first managerial role, taking over in March 1974 after the club had struggled for years. My first gate was 37 – with not even a dog in sight. It was obvious we needed to improve the club's profile and image so I went to see George. We knew one another from our Manchester United days. I had been there a year when Matt Busby brought a few lads over from Belfast and he asked me to look after George Best. Clearly I didn't do a very good job!

So I went to see Bestie at his nightclub in Manchester, Slack Alice's. I asked him, 'Will you play for me in two pre-season friendlies?' He said, 'Yes, but Tommy Docherty holds my registration so you need to arrange it with him.'

Fortunately, when I arrived at The Cliff my old mate Paddy Crerand was in the car park and he offered to introduce me to The Doc as an old United player. The Doc couldn't believe that Bestie was willing to play for Dunstable when he couldn't get him to play for United. Tommy asked me who we were playing and I told him I hadn't even gotten around to organising the opposition. So Tommy kindly offered to bring a Manchester United XI to Dunstable Town with Bestie playing for us and we beat them 3-2!

It even made *News at Ten*! We were being talked about everywhere and it brought some much-needed cash into the club and gave us some profile. I was then able to put a great team together, bringing in Jeff Astle and he scored 34 goals to help us win the Southern League.

Then after I had been manager at Barnet for five years, the club was facing some financial problems. The players had not been paid for two months and I knew that something had to be done. So I called in another favour from Bestie and asked him if he would play for a Barnet XI against a Tottenham XI managed by Keith Burkinshaw with Steve Perrryman. Again, he never let me down, there was a capacity crowd and every single player was able to get what they were owed.

I have lots of George Best stories and they are all stories of him doing good deeds, but you never get to hear about those. I asked him to do an after-dinner speech when I was owner of Peterborough – he filled the place. I owe George big time. When he was on *This is Your Life* I got speaking to him in the green room and I asked him, 'Why did you always help me out when I asked, why did you come and play for me at those shit holes when you were way above that?' He said, 'Baz, I never forget how you looked after me when I first came to United.' He explained that he remembered how I always bought his two complimentary match tickets off him whenever he needed to send money back to his family in Belfast. I looked after him in my own way and he never forgot it.

THE ONE THAT GOT AWAY

Jamie Vardy: Fleetwood Town to Peterborough United

We agreed to pay Fleetwood one million quid for Jamie

Vardy. I spoke to his representatives and our manager Darren Ferguson spoke to Jamie at the same time. We knew Cardiff and Leicester were in for him as well but our pitch to players we wanted was, 'Come to the Posh and play every week. If you go to those bigger clubs too soon you may well be sitting on the bench.' Unfortunately, Leicester still nicked him off us.

I was not surprised to see his sudden rise for Leicester and then England, because I saw him play at Halifax prior to him going to Fleetwood so I knew all about him. He impressed me in the same way that Craig Mackail-Smith impressed me. He never stopped running or putting the opposition's back four under pressure. I wanted to know where he got his energy from, but he had it. I'm a great believer that if you are a natural goalscorer in the non-league you would be a goalscorer in the Championship or even higher.

JOHNNY GILES

*Managed: Republic of Ireland (player-manager
1973–1980); West Bromwich Albion (player-
manager 1975–1977); Shamrock Rovers (player-
manager 1977–1983); Vancouver Whitecaps (1981–
1983); West Bromwich Albion (1984–1985)*

MY BIG DEAL

Peter Beardsley: Carlisle United to Vancouver Whitecaps
for £275,000 in 1982

I brought him in not long after I took over at Vancouver. It
was during the winter when I asked my old Leeds United
mate Peter Lorimer, who came with me as player-coach, to
have a look around the English leagues to see if there was
any talent around. He went to look at somebody at Doncaster
when they were playing Carlisle and Peter caught his eye
instead and he asked me to have a look at him. We were
training in London anyway so I went down the road and
watched him in a match at Brentford a few weeks later. He
didn't play particularly well but I liked him and signed him
as I saw enough in him that I thought I could work with.

When you are scouting a player I always felt you
shouldn't judge him on how well he plays on the day but on
the all-round potential and the little things you think you
can work with to make him better, which was the philosophy
that helped me with Peter. It was a little surprising there
was not one club in for him; no Arsenal, Spurs, Manchester
United or any of the bigger clubs so we didn't have to pay
a fortune.

Peter had more pace than he was often given credit
for; he was strong, well-balanced, had a great attitude and
terrific ability on the ball. The main thing I needed to work

with him on in those early days was trying to get him to do less on the ball as soon as he received it. He was thinking what skills he could do before he even had the ball under control, so I gave him the example of Kenny Dalglish. I said Kenny has all the skills in the world but he doesn't do anything until he has that ball totally under control. Peter listened and he learned.

We didn't have him all that long before Big Ron [Atkinson] came in for him and took him to Manchester United, where it didn't really work out for him. He needed to go back to Newcastle before the English footballing public really saw the best of Peter.

Other signings I was proud of would be Paddy Mulligan for West Brom from Crystal Palace. I had played with him for the Republic of Ireland. He wasn't getting on well with Malcolm Allison so I was pleased to take him on a free and he ended up playing a significant role in our promotion-winning season back to the top flight. Mick Martin would be another I'd single out as I took him from Manchester United for just 25 grand and he was another important player in our promotion-winning team at West Brom.

THE ONE THAT GOT AWAY

Paul Mariner: Plymouth Argyle to West Bromwich Albion

I went to see him down in Plymouth and he more or less promised to sign for me at the Albion. We agreed to pay something like £200,000. But somehow, after that verbal agreement, Bobby Robson came in late and took him from me to Ipswich Town. Fair play to Bobby and whoever tipped him off, but I was very disappointed because I thought I had him, but those kinds of things do happen.

Mariner was a good old-fashioned centre-forward who I liked a great deal. He was strong, scored goals and had a real good attitude. I guess he would have been like Harry Kane in his own day. He ended up being a big success at Ipswich and was an integral part of Bobby's team which won the FA Cup in 1978 and the UEFA Cup in 1981.

BOBBY GOULD

Managed: Chelsea (caretaker 1981); Bristol Rovers (1981–1983 & 1985–1987); Coventry City (1983–1984 & 1992–1993); Wimbledon (1987–1990); West Bromwich Albion (1991–1992); Wales (1995-1999); Cardiff City (2000); Cheltenham Town (2003); Weymouth (2009)

MY BIG DEAL

Stuart Pearce: Wealdstone to Coventry City for £30,000 in 1983

I was at Coventry working with a guy called Brian Eastick who I took from Chelsea to come and work with me with the first team. His strength of player knowledge was the London area and I told him that I was struggling with the left-back position and asked if he could recommend anyone.

At the time I had Brian Roberts, soon to be sold to Birmingham City, but Brian was mostly a right-footer and I always preferred a right-footer at right-back and a left-footer at left-back for balance. Straight away Brian told me there was a guy called Stuart Pearce at Wealdstone who had been released by Terry Venables at QPR.

It just so happened they were playing at Yeovil that night so I told my wife I would be picking her up and taking her to Yeovil. She said, 'That sounds nice; are we going for a meal?' I said, 'No we are going to watch a left-back play.' It was at the old Huish Athletic Ground and within the first five minutes I saw this number three hit the right-winger with a tackle I hadn't seen for years. Their number seven nearly landed on my lap in the directors' box. I turned to my wife, Marg, with a big smile on my face and said, 'I've seen enough, we can go home now.' She pointed out the game had only been going seven minutes and suggested we at least stayed until half-time, so we did.

Stuart was a real physical specimen. I arranged to speak with him through the Wealdstone manager and subsequently went to his house when he was still living with his mum and dad. We had to wait for him to come in from work as he was a sparky. We chatted and he agreed to come to Coventry.

I remember in his first training session George Curtis, a stalwart of the club who was then a director, said, 'What a find! I presume he is going straight into the first team, Bob?' I resisted that temptation and gave him a few reserve games first. I threw him in for his debut at Highfield Road against QPR, who were still managed then by Terry Venables. It was one of the best debuts I have ever seen, especially for a non-league player going into the top division.

I experimented on a pre-season tour of Sweden and played Stuart on the left-hand side of midfield and the best compliment I can pay him is that he reminded me of Duncan Edwards. But I went back to my original idea of a 4-4-2 with Stuart at left-back.

Other signings I am especially proud of would be Terry Gibson from Tottenham to Coventry and again for Wimbledon after he had an awful time at Manchester United, where he went for £600,000. I approached the chairman Sam Hammam and told him I was looking for someone to play off John Fashanu and felt Gibbo would be perfect. As chairmen do, he said, 'How much?' I told him it would cost us a quarter of a million. He nearly fell off his chair as he was used to paying five or ten thousand. But he softened and said, 'OK, meet me at this Lebanese restaurant in London.' He then presented before me 12 sheep testicles and said, 'If you can eat all of those I will give you the money for Terry Gibson.' So I soaked them all in vinegar and downed every last one of them. He then knew how serious I was about Gibbo and gave me the money!

Steve Ogrizovic from Shrewsbury was another, after he failed to break through at Liverpool. Oggy was brilliant for me, though that transfer went to a tribunal because I wouldn't pay the money they wanted. We paid about £75,000 in the end. I signed Cyrille Regis from West Bromwich Albion and he was a big success. Keith Curle, Terry Phelan and John Scales were also players I took from the lower leagues for not very much. But I didn't get all of them right. Paul Williams didn't work out at Coventry and one name I left with Sam Hammam as a recommendation after I left was Robbie Earle, but it didn't work out for him either.

THE ONE THAT GOT AWAY

Ian Wright: Crystal Palace to Wimbledon

He would be the only one that got away from me. I went to watch him a few times at Crystal Palace while I was looking for someone to play alongside John Fashanu at Wimbledon. I liked Wrighty a lot but hand on heart I went for Terry Gibson because I knew what he would give me having worked with him before at Coventry.

I never got as far as putting a bid in for Wrighty but he was on my mind and I thought about going for him for quite a while. I saw his pace, he was a free spirit and I was a bit like that in my own playing career so I appreciated the job he did. He read the knock-downs and was just a very special centre-forward, but my instincts led me towards Gibbo instead.

HARRY GREGG

Managed: Shrewsbury Town (1968–1972);
Swansea City (1972–1975); Crewe Alexandra
(1975–1978); Carlisle United (1986–1987)

MY BIG DEAL

Joe Corrigan: Manchester City to Shrewsbury Town on
loan in 1968

Joe Corrigan was my best recruit but you could also say he
was my 'one that got away' too as it was such a short-term
move. I plucked him from the Manchester City reserves
when he was having a bad time there. Although Joe never
did make his debut with us, I always had it in mind that he
would replace John Phillips, who I sold to Aston Villa and
who then became Peter Bonetti's replacement throughout
the 1970s. While I was delighted to take Joe and work with
him, it was equally disappointing not to manage him on
a permanent basis, but he was clearly destined for greater
things than what we could offer him at Shrewsbury.

He soon returned to City and made the big time. Joe
had terrific potential in those days and I saw it immediately
but he went back to City and made the mistake of telling
everyone that Harry Gregg made him, which Malcolm
Allison didn't like too much. I had to tell him to stop talking
about me because he was being crucified by the manager.
So I am nominating Joe as my best signing purely because
I was pleased to have identified his talent and potential at a
time when few were that aware of him.

I'm also pleased with many other players I signed like
goalkeeper John Phillips at Shrewsbury when he was still a
teenager, before he went on to have a long career at Chelsea.
Then there's Jim Holton at Shrewsbury. 'He's six-foot-two,

eyes of blue, big Jim Holton's after you!' He went on to play for Scotland and Manchester United but I signed him from West Bromwich Albion where he was a rookie in the youth team. At Swansea I brought in Dai Davies, Jimmy Rimmer on loan, Robbie James, Alan Curtis – they were all my kids, I signed them all.

One final name I'd like to mention who I didn't sign but who I had some influence on was the great George Best. When he was training with United as a rookie, I happened to play against him because I was recovering from an injury at the time and playing with the kids. I played outfield for a bit of fitness and this kid on the wing slipped the ball through my legs and I thought, 'That was lucky, he won't do that again.' Then he did it again and I thought, 'This lad can play but he was starting to embarrass me so I told him, 'Son, if you do that again I'll break both of your f****** legs.'

Bestie could have done it all day if he wanted, he was magical and we became close friends. But before he signed I had a word with the manager Matt Busby. I asked him, 'You should take a look at the wee Irish boy at The Cliff.' He came back to me and said, 'He's good, just a shame he's too small.' Thankfully, he soon came round.

THE ONE THAT GOT AWAY

Bruce Grobbelaar: Vancouver Whitecaps to Manchester United

Dave Sexton was the manager of Manchester United at the time and he asked me back to Old Trafford, as the goalkeeping coach. Gary Bailey was then starting to establish himself as the number one keeper, though I thought he was a legend in his own mind. The guy I brought in who would have been much better than Bailey was Bruce Grobbelaar.

So how did I get to know about Bruce? Well I managed Crewe Alexandra for three years up to 1978 and just happened to go back and watch my old club playing a game when Bruce was there on loan for them [in the 1979/80 season]. I thought to myself, 'Christ, this guy can play!' He wasn't a liner, he came off his line to deal with situations and I liked that as I was the same in my day at United. I then spoke to the Crewe manager Tony Waddington and asked him if I could borrow Bruce for a couple of weeks, which was of course an unofficial trial for Manchester United.

I had Grobbelaar with me at Old Trafford for two weeks and for some reason he and I really hit it off. He happened to be a terribly nice fella and was very intelligent. On the Friday before his trial ended, I said to him, 'Has he [Sexton] spoken to you yet?' He said, 'No, H.' Bruce was only playing for Vancouver Whitecaps at the time and was very gettable but Dave Sexton wouldn't sign him. We lost him and it was a huge mistake by the manager.

He went on to sign for Liverpool, of course, for just £250,000. Even then, when he was Liverpool's regular keeper he called me to ask if I could work with him. I had too much respect for Bob Paisley to agree to that request and besides I told him, 'We'd both be sent to jail if we did that!' However, I did agree to watch him a few times and I would mentor him privately. But I wouldn't want to take any credit for his great career as you can only teach from what ability they have and he had bucket-loads. It's just a shame Dave Sexton didn't agree with me!

BRYAN HAMILTON

*Managed: Tranmere Rovers (1980–1985); Wigan
Athletic (1985–1986 & 1989–1993); Leicester
City (1986-1987); Northern Ireland (1994–1998);
Norwich City (2000)*

MY BIG DEAL

Mike Newell: Luton Town to Leicester City for £375,000
in 1987

Michael was a fantastic pro who worked hard and always
gave you everything. You knew what you were getting with
him. He was a loyal, hard-working player who listened to
what you wanted from him and he did everything he could
to carry out whatever it was I asked of him. I had him at
Wigan before I sold him to David Pleat at Luton so I knew
what I was getting, having worked with the lad previously.
He did tremendously well for me at Wigan, helped me win
the Freight Rover at Wembley in 1985, scored there in fact,
so he was someone I knew I could rely on.

From Wigan he then advanced his career by going to
Luton because David was building a fabulous team and
he was a great football man. I never wanted to sell him
nor did I ever wish to lose my best players, but because he
was such a great lad who deserved to progress his career,
I allowed him to go. I never stood in a player's way from
doing that.

I imagine, with all due respect to Luton despite the
great job that David Pleat had done there, Michael would
probably have felt that joining me at Leicester from Luton
was another step up in his career. There is no doubt that
Leicester is a bigger club than Luton so this move showed
the upward curve in his career that continued after Leicester.

He made the most of all his talents and is why he had a very good career. I take some satisfaction out of the fact that Michael's next two moves after Leicester were for more than £1m to Everton and then Blackburn, where he played with Alan Shearer.

THE ONE THAT GOT AWAY

David Platt: Crewe Alexandra to Leicester City

Myself at Wigan and then Leicester, John Rudge at Port Vale, Dario Gradi at Crewe and Joe Royle at Oldham – I'm sure there were more but these are the names I know for sure – used to scour the leagues looking for those gems who had slipped the net, or not managed to make it through the ranks at the bigger clubs.

I tried to sign David Platt from Crewe when I was at Leicester. Platt had started at Manchester United but didn't make the grade there. It never went too far, though, as I couldn't make a deal work. Dario Gradi, who was a good friend of mine and who had a great eye for a player, wanted more money for Platt than I was able to pay. We offered them £90,000 but Dario was holding out for £100,000 and we really could not stretch to pay another penny – that's how tight finances were then.

It was obviously disappointing at the time to miss out on a promising player like David Platt for the sake of another £10,000 but I can't say it has been paining me ever since because these types of things happened a lot in football, and you move on. I have no regrets about my playing or managerial career. I am only grateful for the opportunities I had and I am pleased that the likes of Platty was able to make the most of his ability and enjoy a terrific career. Crewe ended up selling him to Aston Villa for £200,000 so Dario was right not to sell him to us for that money because he made a hell of a lot more from Villa.

Leicester City was the biggest managerial job of my career but I never had much money to spend so the player targets I would often look out for were mostly young lads who I tried to sign before they made their name. I also looked into signing Gary Pallister and Tony Mowbray at different times when they were at Middlesbrough but I just didn't have the money to bring these lads in, which was so often the case. I scouted and explored the possibility of signing many players throughout my management career but there's not much you can do if you don't have the transfer budget to make them happen.

DAVID HAY

Managed: Motherwell (1981–1982); Celtic (1983–
1987); Lillestrøm SK (1989); St Mirren (1991–
1992); Livingston (1993–1994 & interim manager
2009); Dunfermline Athletic (1994–1995)

MY BIG DEAL

Mo Johnston: Watford to Celtic for £400,000 in 1984

Mo was my best signing, though people might find that
strange because of his time at Rangers later in his career.
Mo has never been allowed to forget his move to Rangers
but I personally feel, because of that, he never received the
credit he deserved for what he did for us at Celtic. He was a
real hero at Parkhead and his goals, along with those of his
strike partner Brian McClair, were a significant factor in our
winning the Scottish Premier League in 1986.

I first knew of Mo when he was banging the goals in for
fun at Partick Thistle [41 goals in 85 league games]. I then
considered going for him as soon as I arrived at Celtic but I
signed Jim Melrose instead from Coventry City. A year or
so later, after Mo had gone south of the border to Watford
and performed so well there [23 goals in 38 games], he
became available again. These were the days when Scottish
clubs could compete with English clubs in terms of transfer
fees and wages, which is obviously no longer the case. So I
brought him back up to Scotland. Watford didn't want to
lose him but they also never wanted to keep an unhappy
player so we signed him for £400,000.

Mo was terrific for me. He had a reputation for being
a playboy but I don't think that was fair on Mo. He never
missed a day's training while I was manager, he was always
fit and always gave his all and that is all you can ask of a

player. Mo was a great goalscorer as the statistics will tell you but what they don't show is just how well he dovetailed with Brian McClair as a strike partnership. Brian was signed by Billy [McNeil] as an attacking midfielder but I pushed him further up the pitch and he never let me down [99 goals in 145 games before he moved to Manchester United]. The goal that Mo scored, which helped us seal the Premier League in 1986, summed up how well those two combined, with a pass from Brian to Mo after a great team move.

Mick McCarthy would be another signing I was especially pleased with, but it was just unfortunate that I was sacked a week after he arrived so I never got to work with him as much as I had hoped. We needed a strong, commanding centre-back and we spent some time looking at Steve Bruce at Norwich City but, when it became clear that Manchester United were in for him, we switched our attentions to Mick. He was perfect as a reliable, solid defender and was just what we needed.

THE ONE THAT GOT AWAY

David Dodds: Dundee United to Celtic

It's ironic that one of those who got away was Dundee United player David Dodds yet in a strange twist of fate – and no disrespect meant to David – it turned out to be a very fortunate outcome. I bid £250,000 for David but Jim McLean wanted more, which I was unwilling to pay. And in the time while we negotiated about David, Mo became available so I went and signed him instead.

If Jim had not requested that extra money we would have signed David Dodds and I would not then have gone for Mo. And as mentioned above, Steve Bruce was another who got away but I was more than happy with Mick McCarthy, who we signed instead. Steve, like Mick, was a powerful centre-half and we spent some time watching him.

KENNY HIBBITT

Managed: Walsall (1990–1994); Cardiff City
(1995–1996; 1996 & 1998 caretaker)

MY BIG DEAL

Martin O'Connor: Crystal Palace to Walsall for £40,000 in 1994

My best signing was the central midfielder Martin O Connor, who we managed to buy from Crystal Palace for £40,000 – the most the club spent on a player in my time there. He was superb for me and the club ended up selling him for half a million after I left so they did well out of him financially as well as his contribution on the park.

At the outset I needed a midfielder and Martin was a name I was familiar with after a Bromsgrove Rovers fan recommended him to me previously. I never forgot about him and asked others around me what they felt about him. Quite often fans will give you names but you'd rarely act on the recommendations. I did my own research also and by the time I was ready to move he was at Palace. I guess I should have acted earlier on the word of the Bromsgrove supporter!

I went to watch him play for Palace reserves against Southampton reserves at The Dell. I took my wife along with me as it was only about an hour and a half from where we were living. After 20 minutes she asked me what I thought. I said, 'I will be making a move for him.' She wondered why because he hadn't done much. I told her to watch him and the work he does off the ball and then she understood. He had pace, power and a great work ethic.

It wasn't an easy negotiation as Alan Smith, the Palace manager, wanted 100 grand for Martin, which was too much for us. After a lot of talking we eventually agreed on

40 grand that included a lump sum and some incremental payments. I never regretted signing Martin as he was terrific for me. I loved him as a player and so did the Saddlers supporters.

I also signed an old team-mate of mine from our Wolves days, Wayne Clarke, for Walsall from Man City. He was great for us and did well until he left for an extra £50 a week to go to Shrewsbury Town, which was a real disappointment for me and my plans for the season had gone out of the window as he was a quality goalscorer.

I signed Kyle Lightbourne on a free form Scarborough. Kyle became a reliable goalscorer for the Saddlers and scored 27 goals in the 1994/95 season when Walsall were promoted, just after I left. And he scored another 24 and then 25 goals in the next two campaigns, which unsurprisingly earned him a £500,000 move to Coventry City, who were in the Premier League at the time. Walsall, therefore, didn't do too badly from my best signings. For me, it was just disappointing I didn't get the chance to work with these players a bit longer.

THE ONE THAT GOT AWAY

Roger Milla: JS Saint-Pierroise to Walsall

In 1990 I was appointed manager of Walsall, taking over from of one of my ex-managers, John Barnwell, who had a bit of a lean time there and they were relegated from the [old] Second Division to the Fourth Division in consecutive years so the club was more or less on its knees and needed a big lift to instil some kind of inspiration to lift the gloom that surrounded the club.

Well my first season there was World Cup year and we had a player come in for treatment with a groin injury that kept him out of the Cameroon team and the tournament. His name was Charlie Ntamark. I asked him if he knew Roger Milla and he did – very well – so I asked him if he could have a word after the World Cup as to whether he would be interested in joining us.

He was 38 at the time but knew where the goal was and had been around the game a long time, playing in France for many years. The odds were high but worth a chance. Charlie spoke to him and Milla said he was interested. I thought, 'Great, this is just what the club needs to give everyone a boost, especially the fans.' Until he said he wanted $1m, that was it then, the dream had gone! I do sometimes wonder whether we might have snapped him up if we had approached him before the World Cup when he had no club and it was prior to all his goalscoring exploits in that Italia '90 tournament.

I also tried to sign Micky Adams, a former team-mate of mine at Coventry City, and the experienced centre-back Derek Mountfield. Both players still had a lot left in them but I missed out on them, though Mountfield ironically did play for the Saddlers later in his career.

GLENN HODDLE

Managed: Swindon Town (1991–1993); Chelsea
(1993–1996); England (1996–1999); Southampton
(2000–2001); Tottenham Hotspur (2001–2003);
Wolverhampton Wanderers (2004–2006)

MY BIG DEAL

Ruud Gullit: Free transfer to Chelsea in 1995

Robbie Keane was a great buy for me at Tottenham, but I just think to get a legend like Ruud on a free was a great deal. We knew he had a slight problem with his leg, but we were happy that could be managed. I wanted to do at Chelsea what I had done at Swindon and play three at the back. I had been playing there but I was finishing as I'd had a dodgy left knee since leaving Monaco. Not many teams played three at the back in England and I was wondering who I could get that would fit my plan – and I wanted a footballing defender to bring the ball out and play as opposed to a purely defensive player. Then I heard on the grapevine that Ruud was possibly available and, as my mother used to say, 'If you don't ask, you'll never know!'

We spoke to Ruud's agent and arranged a meeting. I went over with [chief executive] Colin Hutchinson and met with Ruud. I reminded him of how he couldn't go anywhere in Italy without being mobbed and, although he would be known in London, he would regain some freedom. He liked the sound of that and he also liked the idea of playing at the back.

English football would probably have been frowned upon by many top Dutch players around that time, but he knew I wanted to get the ball down and play. I had played against him when he was a youngster at Feyenoord as well as in England v Holland matches so he knew how I liked to play and we probably had a similar philosophy. That was a big part of him coming to England.

We were in transition as a club and I even told him that signing him was part of trying to take us to another level. Chelsea hadn't won a major trophy in over 20 years [since the European Cup Winners' Cup in 1971] and I was keen to improve the club in a number of ways from the playing side of it, which is what we did with the signing of Ruud, to improving the training facilities and other aspects. There was no transfer fee with Ruud, but his contract was obviously high, so it showed the club's intentions to improve and expand.

Ruud was excellent, his application, his example to the players, his attitude, everything was spot on. He made my job easier in the way that he raised standards because other players looked at him and wanted to follow his example. Ruud got on great with the players and I'm sure he loved the new challenge and probably never realised how big a move it would be for him given that he ended up managing the club when I got the England job.

I was just so excited when we signed him and I couldn't wait to see the reaction of the Chelsea fans because at that time it wasn't the Chelsea that we know now. It was a huge deal and along with the likes of Mark Hughes and Dan Petrescu it was probably the start of when things took off for the club in terms of their ambition and just thinking bigger.

THE ONE THAT GOT AWAY

Samuel Eto'o: Real Mallorca to Tottenham Hotspur for approximately £8m in 2002

The deal that got away from me was Samuel Eto'o – he was the one I really hoped to get but couldn't get it over the line.

He was only about 21 at the time and it was before the days when he was a huge star, which came later at Barcelona.

Eto'o wanted to come to us and the fee wasn't astronomical, even for those days. It might have been something like eight million, but I can't remember exactly. Behind the scenes, though, the owners [ENIC] had heard a few stories from Madrid, where he had been playing, that they didn't like and it put them off him. He was a young lad then and young lads make mistakes. I'm sure I would have handled him, but I didn't get the chance. I was very annoyed we didn't get him, but ultimately it wasn't my money we were spending and as a manager you have to respect an owner's decision and move on.

Samuel had been at Real [Madrid] and then moved to Real Mallorca after a loan spell there, which was when he started to score quite freely. I went over to Madrid to watch him play for Mallorca against his old club. I had only been watching for about five minutes and I'd seen enough. He went on this amazing run when he ghosted past three or four Madrid players and was fouled on the edge of the area. The reaction he got from his old crowd was incredible, for an away player. It was no surprise to me that he ended up having the kind of career that he had.

We also looked into Fernando Morientes when he was at Real Madrid and he was also keen to come, obviously a couple of years before he ended up going to Liverpool. But Samuel was the one we really went after and it was disappointing we didn't make it happen.

I never really had great finance behind me at any of my clubs as manager and in this instance at Tottenham, when we didn't get Samuel, we had to go for Gus Poyet on a much smaller fee from Chelsea and ended up bringing Teddy Sheringham back from Manchester United on a free. It was a frustrating time.

Another one I missed was Dennis Bergkamp. When we did the Gullit deal at Chelsea, we also had an outside chance of getting Bergkamp at the same time as we'd heard he would be interested in joining us. But we didn't pursue it or get to the stage of speaking to the player because Chelsea made it clear that we couldn't afford the two of them. They didn't have the money, and that was before he went to Arsenal. It was a shame, but I understood the situation.

BRIAN HORTON

*Managed: Hull City (1984–1988); Oxford United
(1988–1993); Manchester City (1993–1995);
Huddersfield Town (1995–1997); Brighton &
Hove Albion (1998–1999); Port Vale (1999–
2004); Macclesfield Town (2004–2006 & 2012)*

MY BIG DEAL

Uwe Rösler: FC Nürnberg to Manchester City for
£350,000 in 1994

I've got three good signings to single out. The first one was
at Hull, Richard Jobson, just 40 grand from Watford and he
went on to play for Oldham, Leeds, Man City and England
B. So he was a good signing. Jim Magilton at Oxford United;
he cost me 100 grand off Kenny Dalglish at Liverpool. He
went for £600,000, I think, when Alan Ball took him to
Southampton. And my third signing of note is Uwe Rösler
at Man City and he'd be my best.

We were struggling for a striker. Quinny [Niall Quinn]
got injured and I got a phone call from the agent Jerome
Anderson saying I've got an East German international
player who has had a broken ankle, I think it was. Jerome
said you can have him for a week on trial. At that level
you rarely get a player to come on trial. He came in on the
Monday, played a reserve game on the Tuesday night at
Maine Road. Francis Lee was Man City's chairman then
and we watched him play. There were lots of scouts there
and I said, 'Get him off quick! Do a deal with Jerome.'

He was that good. We got Rösler off, Francis did a
short-term deal with the agent, Jerome, and he played at
QPR on the Saturday in the first team, straight away. He
went on to have a fantastic career with Manchester City.

Rösler formed a great relationship with Paul Walsh and when Niall Quinn was fit I played the three of them and we absolutely murdered Blackburn and almost stopped them winning the league, winning 3-2 at Ewood Park in the April.

Uwe and me, we made friends and we are still friends to this day. When he's back in England, and not working in Germany as he has been recently, he lives a couple of miles from me, so we've always kept in touch. When he moved to England he lived in the same apartment block as I was living. He was upstairs, used to come down and watch the football on Sky with me. He was a good player, a great team man. Players loved him, his work rate was unbelievable, and he scored goals.

He had a great attitude, he was fit as he looked after himself, was a good mixer, got on great with the lads. It's a hard choice, though, because Jobson and Magilton were good signings, both went on to play in the top division in the Premier League. But I'm going with Uwe. We speak regularly and I've seen Uwe's son play at Manchester City. His lad's name is Colin – Uwe said he named him after Colin Bell. His lad plays right-back, centre-back and I've seen him play in midfield as well, seen him a lot. He was in City's under-23s and then moved on.

THE ONE THAT GOT AWAY

Mark Bright: Leicester City to Hull City for £45,000 in 1986

I'm going to plump for Mark Bright. He'd gone from Port Vale to Leicester and I'd heard he was available from Leicester. I went to watch him play in a night game when I was at Hull. Bryan Hamilton was manager of Leicester. As managers and scouts usually do, they left the game with ten minutes to go. But I didn't, I stayed behind. I was that impressed. I stayed behind to speak to Bryan and he said, 'Yes, you can have him, he's available for 45 grand.'

I went back to my chairman and it was, 'Yes. We can pay that.' And I spoke to Mark, we met on the A1, can't remember where now, and he wanted a signing-on fee. It wasn't a fantastic signing-on fee to be fair but the chairman wouldn't do it. Hull had been in trouble, they'd almost gone to the wall when the owner Don Robinson took over and he wouldn't go past what he thought was the cut-off point. He was very cautious.

I wouldn't want to say what the signing-on fee was. It would look like I'm having a go at the chairman, but it wasn't fortunes by any means. Today you would think it was pocket money. We were in the equivalent of the Championship at the time and, no, the chairman wouldn't budge. I said to him afterwards, 'See what Mark Bright is worth now?' and he said, 'I don't care. That was the rule, that's what it was.' I understood that as well.

So, Mark Bright went to Crystal Palace and the rest is history. Didn't he do well with his career. I've met Mark many times since, he's a good football person.

GÉRARD HOULLIER

Managed: Le Touquet (1973–1976); Nœux-les-Mines (1976–1982); Lens (1982–1985); Paris Saint-Germain (1985–1988); France (1992–1993); France U18 (1994–1996); France U20 (1996–1997); Liverpool (joint manager 1998 & sole manager 1998–2004); Lyon (2005–2007); Aston Villa (2010–2011)

MY BIG DEALS

Sami Hyypiä: Willem II to Liverpool for £2.6m in 1999

Dietmar Hamann: Newcastle United to Liverpool for £8m in 1999

Emile Heskey: Leicester City to Liverpool for £11m in 2000

I would say they are the three players who stand out as my best buys and I have to put them together, it's too hard for me to separate them. My three 'Hs'.

Didi won a lot of medals in his career, which says a lot about him as a player. He won two Bundesliga titles and a UEFA Cup with Bayern, and he came to Liverpool and we won quite a lot of trophies. He even played in an FA Cup Final while at Newcastle. In his total of seven years at Liverpool, Didi won two FA Cups, two League Cups, the Champions League and the UEFA Cup. He stabilised the midfield for me in my time at Anfield. His eye for the pass, his experience, he gave a balance to the team.

Hyypiä was a good signing because we bought him for just over £2m and when you think he played ten years at Liverpool and won a Champions League, UEFA Cup, FA

147

Cups, League Cups, he won everything. OK, everything but the league!

Heskey made the team better. I'm glad that Michael Owen acknowledges that it was thanks to Emile he had more freedom on the pitch, more assists. Emile was very good and did more than people think. With Heskey in the team, our strike force was different. He was young when he came from Leicester to us [22], a good personality, a good team-mate. I was the first foreign coach for Liverpool and they all bought into the project and we were successful together.

We are talking about players brought in who added something to the team. Those three, I can't separate, they were different, one a defender, one a midfielder, one a striker. Those are the best that I bought from outside. Steven Gerrard was already at Liverpool when I went there. He was a youth player and I picked him out of the academy to come with us, to play with the first team.

So, I think that helped him too.

On a different topic, actually the worst buy you make is more on your mind than the best ones! My worst was El Hadji Diouf from Lens for ten million [in 2002]. He was good player, but it was his attitude. I mean, he spat on a Celtic fan when we played a UEFA Cup game up there and we were 1-1. A good game, it was a fantastic atmosphere and a few minutes before the end when Diouf overran and went into the crowd, a fan wanted to touch him. Diouf was running back to the field of play and then he turned and spat on the Celtic supporter. Why he did it, I don't know. So that was the end of it, the end of Diouf. His performances for the team were not as good as they could have been, but his attitude was absolutely disgusting. He was a nice person deep down, but you can't do something like that. I couldn't change him. You can't change the stripes of a zebra.

THE ONES THAT GOT AWAY

Cristiano Ronaldo: Sporting Lisbon to Liverpool

Rio Ferdinand: West Ham United to Liverpool

Everything was agreed for us to sign Ronaldo but then Manchester United played Sporting in a friendly match in Lisbon and Ronaldo was so good that afterwards all the Manchester players asked Alex [Ferguson] to sign him. And he did just that. How did I feel then? Well, you can imagine. I was devastated.

I've always had a good relationship with Cristiano because of that, because of how close we were to signing him for Liverpool. He would have been our player. The fee was agreed, everything was settled. But at the last minute it changed.

Manchester moved quickly but they had private things with Sporting before. They played this game, he was good, and that is how it is. The fee that we agreed was different from the fee that Manchester United paid. Manchester bought Cristiano for £12.5m. Our fee was far less than that. The one who knows is Rick Parry, who was the chief executive of Liverpool at the time. I couldn't do anything without him.

I also tried to sign Rio Ferdinand for Liverpool when he was at West Ham. It was before I found Hyypiä and Stéphane Henchoz. When I came to Liverpool they told me I could have only £12m to reinforce the team. We got in touch with Ferdinand's agent, who was Pinhas Zahavi and he said the price was £18m. We tried everything to get it down and I think we may actually have got it down to £15m. But anyway, I needed more than one player. It is merely a souvenir now. But I do think occasionally of the times Rio and Cristiano almost signed for me!

They are not the only United legends I almost signed for Liverpool. There was also a game that Rick Parry and

I went to see and the player we liked was Robin van Persie. But sadly that didn't materialise either as he went from Feyenoord to Arsenal.

MARK HUGHES

Managed: Wales (1999–2004); Blackburn (2004–2008); Manchester City (2008–2009); Fulham (2010–2011); Queens Park Rangers (2012); Stoke City (2013–2018); Southampton (2018); Bradford City (2022–)

MY BIG DEAL

Vincent Kompany: Hamburg to Manchester City for £10m in 2008

There's been quite a few good signings. I signed Craig Bellamy twice [Blackburn and Manchester City] and he did great for me. I remember Ryan Nelsen and Aaron Mokoena. We got them in on a week's trial when we were struggling at Blackburn, just to have a look at them, didn't know anything about them.

We got them for buttons as there was very little money and we stayed up. Chrissy Samba, we paid £300,000 for him and he did very well too. Marko Arnautović, a bit of a maverick to say the least, but we paid £2m for him at Stoke and sold him for £25m!

But the best one for me would be Vincent Kompany.

When I was with Blackburn we played away to Hamburg in a pre-season friendly. He was about 20, 21 then, stood out and was impressive, but we couldn't afford the money to bring him to Blackburn, which was about five or six million. So, I filed him away in my mental Filofax. He was clearly a big, big presence.

It was just that initial observation that he'd be one that I'd want if I had the opportunity. When I then got the Manchester City job, it was different, not that all the money I thought I'd be getting turned up. The owner, Thaksin

Shinawatra, had his financial assets frozen and there were a few white lies to be told when I was talking to players. But I did get Kompany in.

I got a call that he might be available and I went over to see him in a hotel. It wasn't easy to get him. When the big money came in to Manchester City, if I'm honest, I don't think many people knew there were two clubs in Manchester! It was a case of you had to sit down and say this is how it's going to be. People had to take you at your word that what you were saying was going to happen. We were a little bit of a hard sell because we didn't have too much of a European standing. If you are going for top European players they are thinking, 'Why should I go there?' We had the money and we had the resources but we still had to get the players in.

But I sensed with Vinnie all along that he was thinking, 'This is the place for me, I want to go into the Premier League and show what I can do.' He'd convinced himself he was a midfield player in those days. I felt I couldn't afford to play Kompany in midfield because we were lacking a bit of presence in defence, so that was my thinking.

So, I played him first game. I always remember, he was in midfield still, received the ball, turned quickly and then his first pass was 50 yards to the left wing on to somebody's toe and I'm thinking, 'We haven't got anybody here who can do that.' So, I left him where he was and he played mostly in midfield for me. But Kompany always had the potential to play at the back because that's where I initially saw him. Unfortunately for me he got an injury in my second season and he was out for a number of games. Maybe if he had been fit and well, then I might have lasted a bit longer at Manchester City.

Vinnie was outstanding. He has always been very grateful to me, he's always said if you hadn't given me the opportunity I wouldn't have had the success that I've had since, which is very nice but it's not really true because Kompany's success is a result of how he's approached the game and how he's conducted himself as a player and as a person. What little input I've had, he's surpassed that with his own input.

We kept in touch after I left the club as his kids went to my grandchildren's school so I came across him quite often. He invited me to his testimonial game as well, which was nice. He's a good guy, very focused. He knows what he wants. Kompany is very much a leader. He wasn't the captain when he came to the club but he was the captain in the dressing room, so to speak. He always had questions and needed a valid answer. Vincent didn't have the armband but he was very much the captain of the dressing room.

THE ONE THAT GOT AWAY

Adama Traoré: Barcelona to Stoke City

There weren't too many really. I was of the view once you got them in the room or in your office, then, until the deal was done, you didn't let them out. For the most part that was always the tactic and mostly it paid off.

One that's unknown, and obviously he's doing well now, is Adama Traoré. I'd been over to Barcelona and had seen him as a young kid, watched Traoré play for the B team there two or three times. I felt I'd never seen anyone as quick over the first five yards, ever. So, I'm thinking he's got the power and the physique for the Premier League and he's quick as well. I was Stoke manager at the time and we had a distinct lack of pace up top. We needed more so I felt he'd fill that role for me.

So, we got him over. I actually had my player, Bojan [Krkić], on the phone to Traoré telling him he needed to come and sign for Stoke, to convince him to leave Barcelona to come to Stoke. Getting players to come to Manchester City was hard. This was even harder. But we eventually got Traoré and his agent over and I was thinking, 'He's in the office, he looks enthused, excited by it,' and then there's the bombshell from the agent, 'Oh, we are just going to speak to Aston Villa after this.' Well, you didn't tell us that!

We thought we were the only ones in for him. Basically, the agent was finding out how much we were going to give Traoré and then say to Villa you top this and we'll come to you. Traoré was only 17, 18 years old. He was showing up in senior football with the Barcelona B team. He was outstanding. A bit erratic, not quite sure what to do with the ball at times, but at Wolves he's improved in that regard and has made progress.

When Traoré was at Villa I think the manager there, Tim Sherwood, didn't fancy him at all. Whether it was Traoré's attitude or his decision-making in games, he would pass when he should shoot and shoot when he should pass, I don't know. But he's through that now. He has so much power and a low centre of gravity; very difficult to contain.

KENNY JACKETT

Managed: Watford (1996–1997); Swansea City (2004–2007); Millwall (2007–2013); Wolverhampton Wanderers (2013–2016); Rotherham United (2016); Portsmouth (2017–2021); Leyton Orient (2021–2022)

MY BIG DEAL

Kevin McDonald: Sheffield United to Wolverhampton Wanderers for £250,000 in 2013

He was a very good player who always seemed to have a major influence on matches. He'd been at Sheffield United for a couple of seasons and was often played as a number ten, but I thought he was perfect to play deeper. He had a few top years for Wolves playing just in front of the back four.

He was the life and soul of our dressing room and he absolutely loved football. I know that might sound like I'm stating the obvious, but it is not always the case. Some players prefer to be in the gym than on the football pitch. But with Kevin, he genuinely loved the game and loved his training. He was a great lively personality.

I think it's fair to say he matured later in his career after a difficult time earlier on at Burnley. He was more mature physically and mentally by the time he joined us at Wolves. Although he did well for us at Wolves he was probably even better after he left us at Fulham, who he helped get promoted into the Premier League a couple of times. So, I like to think the Wolves move springboarded his career for better things that also included a handful of caps for Scotland as well.

Sheffield didn't want to sell him when I went in for him, but they were in League One at the time and we came to know that he had a £250,000 buyout clause in his contract.

He was great for Wolves, dictating terms in front of the back four. I later ran into quite a few Sheffield United fans and they said, 'Thanks a lot, Ken, for taking our best player off us,' though there were a few other words involved as well that I had better not repeat! I saw one of them while I was on holiday, so I did get a bit of stick from Blades fans, but it was usually in good humour.

I signed Benik Afobe at Wolves and he came low and went high, fee-wise; Steve Morison did well for me at Millwall after I signed him from Stevenage in the non-league. He ended up moving on to Norwich when they were in the Premier League. The central defender Tom Naylor also gave Portsmouth some fantastic service, as did goalkeeper Craig MacGillivray.

THE ONE THAT GOT AWAY

Jamie Vardy: Fleetwood Town to Millwall

We had Jamie Vardy on our list at Millwall, but it seemed at the time that everybody had Jamie on their list. I did go as far as driving down on a scouting mission to watch him play for Fleetwood at Yeovil. But it soon became clear he was at a level beyond Millwall, he was that good.

He played up front on his own in a 4-5-1 and his work rate and his pace shone through like it does now at Leicester. How he plays now, was exactly what I saw that night; he always looked like he was going to get in from any ball put through to him.

I never actually spoke to Jamie, but I did have a casual conversation with his agent. He made it obvious to me that from the phone calls he was having, he had bigger fish to fry than Millwall. I had to accept it and move on.

It's been great to see him come through from the non-league in the way he has, but those stories are few and far between now.

There is also a lad called Sammie Szmodics who is playing at Peterborough now. I tried quite hard to sign him for Portsmouth from Bristol City but couldn't get it done. Peterborough were prepared to pay the money and we didn't get him.

DAVE JONES

Managed: Stockport County (1995–1997);
Southampton (1997–2000); Wolverhampton
Wanderers (2001–2004); Cardiff City (2005–
2011); Sheffield Wednesday (2012–2013);
Hartlepool United (2017)

MY BIG DEAL

Denis Irwin: Manchester United to Wolverhampton Wanderers on a free transfer in 2002

It sounds big-headed, but I've had good deals at many different clubs I've been at. But the best professional I signed was Denis Irwin. He was coming to the end, at 36, yet he never missed a day's training. As a professional he was up there with the very best.

What he did at Wolverhampton was calm everything down. When we got promoted to the Premier League they were all dancing around, but not Denis, he just had a quiet drink. He'd seen all that with Manchester United; league champions, Champions League, FA and League Cups. Promotion to the Premier League was a walk in the park for him. As a professional you could not have found anyone better.

The other one who was like that is the boy who died [in March 2020], Peter Whittingham at Cardiff. Steve McPhail at Cardiff was another. Paul Butler at Wolves also. They were good for me.

With Denis Irwin, what it was, the year before we were promoted we faltered at the death. We had a young team and we drew too many games and allowed West Brom to catch us and get promoted. Then we lost out in the play-offs. We were headed where we wanted to be and I'd missed out on

Paul Merson. He went from Aston Villa to Portsmouth. I always felt Paul Merson would be the final cog in the wheel to get us promoted, but because of his background and the troubles he's had, I think the club were not so sure about him and Harry Redknapp nipped in and got him down to Portsmouth. We missed out there and I always felt that was one of the reasons we never went up that season. We lacked the knowhow of someone who had done it.

Then Denis and Paul Ince were available on frees. It was their ages that Wolves were worried about. My argument with the chairman was Irwin and Ince are coming here for a reason, we are just bringing them to get us promoted.

When we got promoted and I wanted to change it, the chairman said to me, 'Why are you looking for a left-back and a midfield player when we've got Denis Irwin and Paul Ince?' I said they were 'flawed', because of their age. It happens to us all. They'd done their job. Irwin and Ince did well, don't get me wrong, but we needed to change it then.

But before all that, Irwin was excellent. He never missed a game and was a calm influence around the dressing room. Irwin and Paul Butler were my generals in the changing room. Irwin could play right- or left-back, he chipped in with his free kicks for goals and the younger players looked up to him for what he had achieved.

He'd come from the biggest club in the country to our club. It wasn't a hard sell, it was easy. I think he supported Wolves. Not a vast amount of money. He just wanted to play. Incey was a different kettle of fish. He was the 'Guv'nor'. I always remember Incey coming in and saying, 'I can only train a couple of days a week.' Fine, I said. But we've got a team of young bucks and they want the shirt. If they are training every day and doing the business then I'll play them. Incey never missed any training, never missed any games. It was just getting him into that mentality. The older you get, the harder you have got to work. And that was Denis.

THE ONE THAT GOT AWAY

Phillip Cocu: PSV Eindhoven to Southampton on a free transfer in 1997

We could have had him on a free when I was manager of Southampton. But he wanted the famous word in those days of 'netto'. It was a million a year he was looking for, tax-free. The chairman of Southampton, Rupert Lowe, decided not to do it. Much as I tried to tell him we would make an absolute fortune on this player, I couldn't persuade him.

He was only a young player and PSV weren't as big then as they are now, a mega club. PSV hadn't the money they've got now. Cocu was out of contract and we had a shout on him. I tried desperately but because it was 'netto' – he would only deal in netto – the chairman didn't want to know. His famous saying was, 'If we pay tax, they pay tax.' I was adamant that if we took Cocu we wouldn't keep him long, he was that good. He went to Barcelona eventually but we were in with a great shout of signing him. No fee, out of contract, blimey, what a signing it could have been.

I'd only been at Southampton a few months and I think Rupert Lowe was a bit worried about players that I would sign, just a bit wary of going for something big. But I sold Kevin Davies for £7.5m and got him back for nothing. That might have been when the chairman realised that I knew what I was talking about.

I've missed many players in my career, but for a player to go on and achieve what Cocu did, he's up there. I remember being on a private jet with four other managers, David Moyes being one of them. We were all going to watch the same player in France but we never spoke about the player. No one mentioned it, it was, 'Oh, we're watching someone else.'

Cocu was keen to come to us, his agent was keen to come to Southampton in the Premier League. I was building a team. When I went to Southampton my criteria was to dismantle an old team and develop a youngish team. And that's what I did with the likes of James Beattie.

I have contacts all over the world, people I've met over time and they always keep in contact. They knew I was after a winger, which Cocu was then. I put it about and the next thing a call came in, 'Would I fancy Cocu?'

I went to watch him a couple of times and then we sat down. No disrespect to Southampton, but he wanted to come to England, to the Premier League and then go on from Southampton.

I thought the chairman would have gone for it to be honest because there was no transfer fee. It was all on wages. When you consider what Cocu would have cost us, he wouldn't have been with us long, I'm sure of that, and I think we could have got £10m for him even in those days.

It was proven how good Cocu was when he joined Barcelona and what he won there. I never said anything to Rupert Lowe when that happened. To be honest I've never really looked at the ones we've missed, I've been more about the ones we got in.

JOE JORDAN

Managed: Bristol City (1988–1990 & 1994–
1997); Heart of Midlothian (1990–1993);
Stoke City (1993–1994); Portsmouth (caretaker
2005 & 2008)

MY BIG DEAL

Bob Taylor: Leeds United to Bristol City for £300,000, including the part-exchange of Carl Shutt, in 1989

I thought about my greatest signing and tried to put it into perspective, because you can go and buy a player with an enormous case of money and try to buy success that way but a good signing is not always as straightforward as that. Especially if you're at a club where finances are tight as was the case with me when I was early in my management career at Bristol City.

They were a club who had experienced some serious challenges both on and off the pitch. They had suffered three successive relegations in the early 1980s to go from the top flight to the old Fourth Division and were, I believe, declared bankrupt at the stage.

By the time I came in the ship had already been steadied and it was a very well-run club financially, which was good for me in a way as it meant whenever I wanted to buy a player I knew that player had to be right for us as money was so tight. They weren't prepared to gamble with transfers and they would only sign a player if they had the money in the club to afford him. So, I felt that responsibility in the transfer market.

I knew we needed a striker so when I brought Bob Taylor into Ashton Gate the pressure was on. We couldn't afford to get it wrong after the horrendous few years the club had already endured. The pressure was on Bob to score goals because we had spent what was a lot of money for us. The pressure was on me for signing him after the club had put a lot of faith in my judgment, but I had done my homework and felt he was a natural goalscorer.

There was even more pressure because Carl Shutt, who had gone the other way as part of the deal, was quite popular with our fans so this had to work. There was even more pressure after Shutt went to Leeds to be reunited with Howard Wilkinson, who had him at Sheffield Wednesday, and scored a hat-trick on his debut at Elland Road!

Fortunately, though, Bob was also on form for us and he netted a hat-trick in his first month with us. Bob was a huge success and scored 34 goals in his first full season with us in 1989/90, the season we were promoted to the old Second Division. If he hadn't missed half a dozen games through a hamstring injury I'm sure he'd have scored 40 goals as he was such a natural goalscorer. It felt like I could rely on him every game to score and get us the win or grab a draw. He was later sold to West Brom and was a big success there also.

THE ONE THAT GOT AWAY

Kevin Campbell: Arsenal to Bristol City on loan in 1988

This is a difficult one to gauge because you show a lot of interest in a lot of players as a manager and you don't always know how close you are to signing him, if indeed you go that far with your interest.

I do remember, though, I went from player to player-manager at Bristol City and I had the job for about three months at the end of the 1987/88 season. We finished fifth and lost to Walsall in a play-off final replay. But if we rewind a couple of months before then I tried to bring in a young Kevin Campbell on loan from Arsenal before the March transfer deadline. I thought if we can just get him in on loan we'll go from there.

He was just a kid in the Arsenal reserves at the time but I saw him and felt he had a presence about him that would have been good for us. But Arsenal didn't want to let him go, even on loan. I don't know their reasons for that, it's a long time ago, but you'd need to speak to ask George Graham why he didn't allow him to join us.

It was a little frustrating when he went out on loan to Leyton Orient the following season and scored a few goals [9 in 16] but that's football. There would have been a few more of these near misses but this is the one that has stuck in my memory more than the others.

KEVIN KEEGAN

Managed: Newcastle United (1992–1997 & 2008);
Fulham (1998–1999); England (1999–2000);
Manchester City (2001–2005)

MY BIG DEAL

Ali Benarbia: Free transfer to Manchester City in 2001

It's an appropriate choice because he didn't cost us a penny, he was a free agent [having left Paris Saint-Germain]. The best way I can sum up just how good a player Ali Benarbia was is to say he was the best player for City, to that point, since Colin Bell – and they had a lot of good players over the years.

The transfer happened by freak really. The agent Willie McKay called me up to say he was taking this player to Sunderland and could they stop off for a break on the drive up and grab some lunch. I didn't have a problem with that but wanted to ensure they ate separately to my players because I had a rule that agents didn't mix with players at the training ground. Anyway, they came in for their stop-off and after training Arthur Cox came in to see me. He said, 'You know that player sat out there with Willie McKay – well, he's the guy who destroyed Newcastle United in the quarter-finals of the UEFA Cup for Monaco just after you left. Newcastle couldn't handle him. He's an unbelievable player.'

I didn't know him but found out later that Arthur was right, Ali was a 'number ten' and had in fact scored twice against Newcastle that night and ran the show in a Monaco team that included Thierry Henry, Emmanuel Petit, Fabien Barthez and John Collins. On hearing this, I went over and shook hands with the player and Willie and I found out that he had a trial match lined up. Reidy [Peter Reid] wanted to have a look at him. I told him if he wanted to train on the way back, he was welcome to have a session with us. I was warming to him not only because of what Arthur had told me but I noticed our French players like Nicolas Anelka and Sylvain Distin were going up to him and showing him great respect.

He went up and played his trial match with Sunderland and I heard Reidy wasn't there to see him and he didn't end up signing for them. He trained with us the next day and I saw all I needed to see. I phoned Willie up and said, 'You'd better come in and see me.' I wanted to sign him there and then. We got him registered, his wage demands were very reasonable, there was no fee due to any club, so he went back home to get his boots and belongings and he made his debut for me that same week at Maine Road against Birmingham City in what is now the Championship. We were 3-0 up at half-time and won the game comfortably. Very early on, even when he'd take a corner, the whole crowd stood up for him. Everyone could see straight away just how good he was.

I signed many big-name players for bigger transfer fees like Alan Shearer, Andy Cole, Rob Lee, Peter Beardsley, David Batty but Ali Benarbia was the biggest surprise to me in football in terms of how successful he was for me purely because I had no expectations. I have him as the most technically gifted player I ever coached, and I worked with a lot of gifted footballers like Beardsley and [David] Ginola. If you ask Thierry Henry who was the best player he ever played with I would be amazed if Ali was not in his top five. He was on another level to everyone we had and we had some very good players.

Ali was like an experienced Jack Grealish, maybe not as fast as Grealish but had amazing knowledge and awareness of his ability and the players around him. Ali was like another coach for me on the field. The way he used to speak with Shaun Wright-Phillips was incredible, he gave Shaun so much confidence and guidance. Those leaders in a team are a like gold-dust for a manager.

The sad part was that he only had two seasons with us. But he was getting on when he signed, he was about 32. He helped us win promotion to the Premier League in his first season and I gave him a two-year deal, but he only served a year. Ali was great but pace wasn't his biggest strength and I sometimes found the Premier League was a bit too quick for him, so I made him sub for a few games.

He came in to see me quite soon and asked if I was going to keep making him sub. He made it clear if I was, he would rather leave and play for another club. I reminded him he was due for a nice signing-on fee of something like 120 grand on the completion of his contract – so why would he want to jeopardise that. He said he wasn't bothered about the money and was more interested in playing football because he was nearing his mid-30s. I admired the fact he wanted to play and didn't stand in his way so I asked the board if they would pay up his contract even though he was leaving early, and they did.

Other notable signings I would mention would be Rob Lee from Charlton – he'd be a close second to Benarbia, Alan Shearer obviously, Andy Cole and someone who was probably my best signing at Fulham was Steve Finnan, before he was later sold to Liverpool. He was great for me at Fulham.

THE ONE THAT GOT AWAY

Zinedine Zidane: Bordeaux to Newcastle United for £1.2m in 1996

This is a story that the agent Barry Silkman came out with in the media, that I rejected Zidane, but I'm not entirely sure how accurate it is. I certainly don't remember it but that's not to say it definitely never happened because when you are manager at a big club like I was at Newcastle, you are sent lots of player names every day by agents with a view to taking a look at them for transfer.

Maybe, just maybe, Zidane was on a list that crossed my desk when he was starting out, but I don't recall turning him down. Generally, I don't have much memory of any players we missed who we really wanted through my managerial career.

I always tried to be very honest with players I was looking to sign and show the passion of why we wanted them. Take Alan Shearer for example. Most people know he had the chance to sign for Manchester United, but he wanted to talk to us to see how much we wanted him – and we certainly showed him.

JÜRGEN KLOPP

Managed: Mainz 05 (2001–2008); Borussia
Dortmund (2008–2015); Liverpool (2015–)

MY BIG DEALS

Dennis Weiland: VfL Osnabrück to Mainz 05 on a free transfer in 2001

Niclas Weiland: Tennis Borussia Berlin to Mainz 05 on a free transfer in 2001

This is difficult. There have been quite a few. It's not that I don't want to pick my best signing, it's that I haven't had the chance to do that with some [as they flourished much later after being signed earlier on]. I couldn't buy Robert Lewandowski when he's scored already 30 goals a season, that was never possible. So, finding Lewandowski [for €4.5m for Dortmund), so finding Shinji Kagawa [for €350,000 from Japan], finding Neven Subotić, Łukasz Piszczek [free transfer], finding İlkay Gündoğan [€4m for Dortmund) – all these guys in the moment when they cost three or four million euros, they were all terrific signings for me.

The difficult thing is whoever you sign nowadays is influenced by the public perception. I'm not, but the outside world, it is massively so. It means they really *have* to fit in immediately. That's why people say, 'Why did you make a signing if he doesn't play?' All these kinds of things. No one believes in process, in patience. No one wants to hear about that, but that's obviously very necessary. That's one thing.

The other thing is you see the potential, but you know they have to learn a lot until they become the player they can be. It's a risky situation because as much as you know about them as a player, and after a few talks about them as a person as well, no one can be *really* sure. You have to pretty much think ahead, to think in the future.

People might say Virgil van Dijk [has to be the best] for £75m, but the problem I had was not so much worrying about the people you sign, you will always find somebody, but my problem at Mainz and Dortmund was the best players always got sold.

So, you have these players at the point you want them, after all the time you have worked together with them, and somebody else gets the benefit. That rips a real hole in your team because the next player, he needs time again. So, I always would have preferred to keep teams longer together.

Signings are exciting and at times very necessary. In our case at Liverpool, it was very necessary for Van Dijk and Alisson. Without them we couldn't talk [about the subsequent success], we would not have had the same history.

I have signed so many players and pretty much all of them were good and all of them had an impact. It depends on the situation how big the impact is. Very often they fulfilled exactly what I thought they would. It worked out very often.

Gündoğan came from FC Nürnberg and was a number ten. But I bought him as a number eight. That's not a massive transformation but it was an important one.

I signed Łukasz Piszczek from Hertha Berlin. He was an average right-winger and he ended up as a world-class right-back. I remember his face when I told him, 'Yes we are going to sign you, but as a right-back.' He didn't know he could play there.

That's the interesting thing about making signings, why you scout that long, that's why you watch them for so long. And you *have* to talk to them as well. I always say, you can have two players, a world-class player and a top player. But the world-class player is an arsehole, the top player is a great guy. I take the top player because an arsehole in the group can cause you much more problems than you can solve. The top player, he can easily become a world-class player.

I was a manager for only three months and we had a really good team at Mainz 05. We didn't just stay in the league by one point or things like this, we avoided relegation from the second division with a game to spare. I was really confident with the team and made only two signings – and those two signings were brothers. They were my first signings as a manager.

They were from different clubs, but Dennis Weiland and Niclas Weiland were both brilliant footballers as young kids. Dennis played very early for Borussia Dortmund; the other [Niclas] was at Hannover and was a super talent as well. But their careers didn't go that well at that moment and that was the way we signed players at that time at Mainz. So, we brought them in.

It was their second chance and they took it. They helped us become a top team in the division, helped get us promoted to the Bundesliga at the third try [Mainz just missed promotion in 2002 and 2003 and succeeded in playing in Germany's top league for the first time in the club's history in 2004]. Dennis and Niclas became Bundesliga players and studied sports science after their careers and both still work in football. So, it's really nice.

But it was difficult making your first signing. I was 33 and suddenly I was realising you had to make decisions and you are not doing things for yourself like I was as a player for Mainz. These were decisions that affect everyone.

I watched videos, VCRs then, like crazy. It was a coincidence that they were brothers because what we were looking for, we hadn't got wingers and both these two, they were wingers, right and left. They were versatile, too. They could play centrally. One had the speed. Niclas was a right-winger and a striker too, and the younger one, Dennis, was a left-winger and a number ten. They gave us the opportunity immediately to change systems. The brothers were crucial to that and it was very exciting.

I watched about 50, 60 VCRs, wow! Yes. This was at home or in the office of the sporting director, who was also still working at that time as the manager of a car sales house. We were everything, we did everything, we were the scouts, we did the negotiations, all these kinds of things.

Back then I wasn't watching clips of players, not like we get now, I was watching full games and trying to find the situations where the player you are interested in is playing. That's how it was then, it was 'rewind, forward' all the time to find the situations and the right things you wanted to see. It took three or four days. And then it was, 'Can we get them?' It was a really long process.

It was no money, free transfers, but then it's what the boys want to earn. Mainz was a club where you couldn't get rich. Today it is like this also. Mainz was a club for second chances, for players who didn't make it in the first place. But we saw potential. To find the real player again without all the difficulties, you lose confidence in yourself, other people lose confidence in you. We were confident from our side and that helped the players a lot.

The younger one, Dennis, I knew because I'd played against him in that season I signed him and he turned me inside out pretty much. So, I was a big fan of his and then became his manager.

Those two signings, they gave me a lot of confidence. There were a few things I knew, but as a young coach, to make these kinds of decisions, it was good for me, it taught me. We didn't have a lot of money at Mainz, we couldn't sign a lot of players, so we had to make sure that these two really improved us. And it worked out brilliantly.

THE ONES THAT GOT AWAY

Son Heung-min: Hamburg to Borussia Dortmund for £10m in 2013

Sadio Mané: Red Bull Salzburg to Borussia Dortmund for £11.8m in 2014

It was my fault.

Son was at Hamburg and went to Bayer Leverkusen instead of us. The problem is that I made the same mistake twice. Pretty big mistakes. It was Son and then Sadio Mané.

The problem at Dortmund was the same problem pretty much that I had at Mainz – so much as our transfers, they had to work. So, it means you *have* to be *really* sure. That's why in the talk with the boys – they were very young – it just didn't feel right.

They are brilliant guys today. Son, my God! That guy and Sadio, how much I love him. That's all true. But on the day, when I spoke to each of them, I just didn't get that feeling [about needing to sign them].

On top of that I have to say, it was the price. It wasn't a free transfer. It was that combination in signing Son, my feeling and the price. It must work now, straight away, immediately. That was the difficulty.

It was in the office of the sporting director where I met Son. Where I met them both, actually. And in the end, we didn't do it. Of course, these were massive mistakes. *Massive* mistakes.

I worked closely with the sporting director at Dortmund. For most of the talks you are there together, it is a common decision. But the final decision, that was mine.

Once we have agreed on a price there is only one question: Do you want him? Or not? And that was twice, 'No.'

There is a picture of Son and me hugging after the Liverpool Champions League Final with Tottenham. Is there a mutual respect there? From my side for sure, I don't know exactly about his side.

I am happy that I could sign Sadio [for £34m from Southampton] later. I really regret I didn't do it at Dortmund, that's for sure.

Another signing that didn't work out was Kevin De Bruyne. We had agreed on everything pretty much but then José Mourinho said, 'No, you will stay here, you will make it here.' Then De Bruyne went from Chelsea to Wolfsburg [for £18m]. We had already made a new signing by then.

That was a tough one to take – when a signing doesn't work out and you are *that* close.

PAUL LAMBERT

Managed: Livingston (2005–2006); Wycombe
Wanderers (2006–2008); Colchester United
(2008–2009); Norwich City (2009–2012); Aston
Villa (2012–2015); Blackburn Rovers (2015–
2016); Wolverhampton Wanderers (2016–2017);
Stoke City (2018); Ipswich Town (2018–2021)

MY BIG DEAL

Christian Benteke: Genk to Aston Villa for €5m in 2012

The one who probably made the biggest impact – in his first year in England as well – was Benteke. He was a phenomenon in that first season, before he got that bad achilles injury prior to the 2014 World Cup.

There have been many that I have really enjoyed working with after signing them. Wes Hoolahan was really good – I signed him for Livingston from Shelbourne and then worked with him again at Norwich; David Fox was great for me at Colchester and Norwich; and Ashley Westwood did great for me at Villa and is now flourishing as a top midfielder. Westy was still very young at Villa. What he has gone on to do with Burnley shows that youngsters need that time to fully develop. He's a such a good passer of the ball. But my pick has to be Benteke.

It was a case of scouring the markets for a striker who we could afford and I knew the foreign markets reasonably well. We needed a striker at Villa and there were so many strikers being put in front of us [by agents]. Eventually, I sent my old assistant manager from Dortmund over to watch Christian play for Belgium. I asked him what he thought and he said he's an interesting option and was very powerful even though he was just 21 at the time.

So, I took my interest on a stage further and I phoned the Belgium manager Marc Wilmots, who I played against when he was with Schalke and I was at Dortmund. He asked me what price we were looking to get him at and I told him, about €5m. Marc said, 'He's raw but at that price he's a gift, you have to take him.' We didn't waste much time after that. He could still have been the biggest flop ever but I spoke to people whose opinion I trusted and their advice was proved right. We weren't paying for the finished article, he was still very raw.

It would have been a dream move for Christian at the time, for a young guy playing at Genk. He was exactly what we needed at that time and he came off the bench and scored on his debut against Swansea. He was incredible after that, scoring 19 league goals in his first season. What he did at Villa got him his big move to Liverpool, even after that bad injury. He was always going to go for big money. There were loads of teams in for him and he could even have gone a year earlier, but the offers weren't good enough at the time and he signed a new contract.

There was no way we could have replaced Christian Benteke at that time with the money Villa were spending on players, as Randy [Lerner] was trying to sell the club around then. When he did eventually go, I don't know why it didn't work out for him at Liverpool but I do know that in the time he spent with me at Villa he was sensational. I could tell straight away from his presence and power in training that he could be anything he wanted to be.

After he got his move to Liverpool he sent me a text message thanking me for giving him the opportunity, so that was nice to read as a manger.

THE ONE THAT GOT AWAY

Pierre-Emerick Aubameyang: Saint-Étienne to Aston Villa for £10m in 2012

When I came into Villa it was clear the loan market was going to be a requirement for us if we wanted to bring quality in. Therefore, prior to signing Christian Benteke I spoke to [Romelu] Lukaku, and we also looked at signing [Kevin] De Bruyne – when they were both kids at Chelsea. They would have been on loan. Look at De Bruyne now – he's one of the best in the world. I also looked at [Wilfried] Bony before he went to Swansea. That's what happens in football, you get so many you pursue but who slip through the grass for whatever reason. There are some really good players but there you have it.

The Aubameyang deal, though, felt like it was getting close and went back and forth between ourselves, St Étienne and the agent quite a lot of times but it never transpired. I was actually looking at emails recently that are still on my phone about this one, but unfortunately Aston Villa were on a different path then. Saint-Étienne wanted around €12m for him but I couldn't get close.

I tried every avenue to make it work, first trying to sign him permanently and then on loan but Saint-Étienne weren't prepared to loan him out. He was too good a player for that. He was only a kid when I tried to sign him so we were buying potential and obviously with a lot of sell-on value. But it wasn't to be and he eventually moved to Dortmund, where he really made his name on the global stage.

It was frustrating for a manager at a club like Aston Villa, with how big it is and with the expectation there, to identify these players and then not be able to bring them in. These are players who you think you could get and then, all of a sudden, they're not there because of the difference in the numbers.

This was a time when the owner was not willing to spend the kind of money that he had previously. I thought to myself, 'Something's not quite right here.' That was the way Aston Villa were operating then. It became difficult.

LENNIE LAWRENCE

Managed: Plymouth Argyle (caretaker 1978);
Charlton Athletic (1982–1991); Middlesbrough
(1991–1994); Bradford City (1994–1995); Luton
Town (1995–2000); Grimsby Town (2000–2001);
Cardiff City (2002–2005); Crystal Palace (joint
caretaker 2012)

MY BIG DEAL

Peter Shirtliff: Sheffield Wednesday to Charlton Athletic for £125,000 in 1986

We are going back to the 1980s when I was at Charlton for my best signing. Remember Peter Shirtliff? I signed him from Sheffield Wednesday when we were in the First Division. He became our captain, was an outstanding fella and was a very good player. At his best he wasn't far short of getting an England cap. Shirtliff, for some reason, was out of favour at Hillsborough. I didn't know the ins and outs of it but, as far as I was concerned, I got him for a good price, which turned out to be a bargain. Us not having our own ground didn't bother him, he was just looking forward to moving away and having a fresh start. He just wanted to play.

We had some good players then but the one thing I wasn't able to do in my managerial career was to get to a real big club and deal with the top players. But Peter was an excellent centre-half. When I had him, we were in the old First Division. We finished the season fourth from bottom and played Leeds, who were fourth in the Second Division, over two legs to see who would be in the First Division the next season.

It was 1-1 after the two legs and the deciding game was at St Andrew's, Birmingham. It was 0-0 after 90 minutes.

179

Then John Sheridan scored for Leeds in extra time and Shirtliff came up with goals in the 113th and 117th minutes to keep us in the First Division.

He hadn't kicked a ball for three weeks before that game, he'd been injured, but Shirtliff was instrumental in keeping Charlton in the First Division. That summed up the kind of character he was. After three years with me at Charlton, I sold Peter back to Sheffield Wednesday when Ron Atkinson was manager – for three times the money I paid!

Other good signings? Well, if you remember we hadn't got a ground back then, we were playing at Selhurst Park for four years, Crystal Palace's place. Charlton had gone bust in 1984, the new people bought it and we got a couple of years to get things sorted out. Then in the summer of 1985, I got some money and spent it on half a dozen players and then we got promoted to the old First Division.

One of those players was John Humphrey, who would be close to Shirtliff as my best. He was a right-back who I signed from Wolves for £68,000. He played well for me and then went on to Crystal Palace for many years.

THE ONE THAT GOT AWAY

Robert Lee: Charlton Athletic to Middlesbrough £500,000 in 1992

There were a couple, but Robert Lee was a player I knew well as he had been at Charlton for eight years when I left to go to Middlesbrough as manager.

When we got promotion at Middlesbrough in 1991/92 and became inaugural members of the first Premier League I thought, 'Right, I've got the money now, I'll try and get Robert Lee.' Charlton were short of money. I had some, not much, but I had some. And it was my fault I missed him because I tried to get him too cheaply. I fannied about too much.

West Ham wanted him, and Lee wanted to go to West Ham because that was his club. But they never had the money and so I thought I was on my own, with the money, and was looking for a good deal. Then, because of my slowness, Newcastle jumped in and the rest his history.

Lee became a legend at Newcastle. I remember he said to me, 'I can't come to Middlesbrough, it's too far.' I said, 'Hang on, Newcastle's 40 miles up the road from Middlesbrough!' To be fair to him he made absolutely the right decision but if I added him to that Middlesbrough team it might have been enough to keep us up [Middlesbrough were relegated in 1992/93].

If he hadn't have gone to Newcastle though, Lee would not have gone on to that fantastic international career he had [winning 21 England caps].

There were a few more I missed, actually. I tried to sign Gavin Peacock. And when I was at Charlton I also tried to put together Garth Crooks and Mark Falco, who had both played up front together with some success at Spurs. I was excited about that partnership and they still weren't that old then.

I got Crooks and he helped us stay up in 1987 and Falco was at Glasgow Rangers. I rang the Rangers manager, Graeme Souness, got permission to speak to Falco, agreed to pay the same money they had paid to Watford for him, which was £300,000, and got the number of the hotel where he was staying. But Falco wouldn't pick the bloody phone up! I must have rung his hotel room about 28 times and he wouldn't pick up. He obviously didn't fancy us, so that one got away.

But in terms of the impact he could have had, it has to be Rob Lee. I think I was paying £500,000 and he went for £700,000 but I might not have got him anyway. I didn't think I had any competition because I knew West

Ham didn't have any money. But then the Kevin Keegan bandwagon started at Newcastle and that was always going to be a massive pull, so I'm not beating myself up too much about it.

GORDON LEE

Managed: Port Vale (1968–1974), Blackburn
Rovers (1974–1975), Newcastle United (1975–
1977), Everton (1977–1981), Preston North
End (1981–1983), KR Reykjavík (1985–1987),
Leicester City (caretaker 1991)

MY BIG DEAL

Graeme Sharp: Dumbarton to Everton for
£120,000 in 1980

I drove up to Scotland to watch Dumbarton with our chief
scout Harry Cook and Graeme impressed us. It was clear
to us that he had all the attributes to be a top striker at the
highest level; he just needed an opportunity and we were
happy to give him that. He had presence, power and an eye
for goal and he was an exciting prospect at that time aged 19.

It is just a shame that his best years at Goodison came
after I had left the club, but I watched him from afar score
all those goals – over 100 in fact, not to mention all those
medals he won. It says a lot about what good business
his signing was that Everton were still able to recoup as
much as £500,000 from Oldham more than a decade after
I signed him.

Other signings I am proud of include Dave Thomas
from Queens Park Rangers after he had played for England,
Sammy Morgan while I was Port Vale manager and Alan
Gowling when I was manager at Newcastle. Morgan was an
intriguing one because he was a real unknown when I was
tipped off about him when he was playing as an amateur
for Gorleston Town in Norfolk. I was happy to have a look
at him at Vale and when he first joined us he was still part-
time, working as a teacher, but he soon showed us that

he was worth a professional deal and we signed him. The fact Sammy went on to join Aston Villa for about £30,000 and subsequently become a regular Northern Ireland international makes for quite a fairytale story considering how we plucked him from obscurity in the non-league.

Gowling's background was much different as he had started at Manchester United, though I bought him from Huddersfield, where he had scored a lot of goals. He was a very intelligent player who did a great job for me at Newcastle. He scored our goal in the 1976 League Cup Final before we lost to a famous Dennis Tueart overhead kick. He scored 15 goals for me also in the 1976/77 season when we came fifth in the First Division, which was the club's highest finish in the top flight for 25 years.

THE ONE THAT GOT AWAY

Ian Rush: Chester City to Everton

I went into the Everton boardroom with a double request in 1980. I told them I had spotted two strikers who I really wanted to pair together up front. Their names were Ian Rush and Graeme Sharp. The board's response was they could only afford one of them so the numbers tell their own story. Rush was interesting a few clubs and ended up going to Liverpool for £300,000. The fact there was less interest in Sharp allowed us to pick him up for less than half the price and that was of course a major factor in why we opted for Sharp and not Rush. But what a pair those two would have made!

I was also hoping to bring in Peter Withe before he left Newcastle, but he opted for Aston Villa instead for a whopping £500,000. A few months beforehand, Villa had sold Andy Gray to Wolves for just shy of £1.5m and John Gidman to me at Everton for £650,000 so they had cash to spend and we couldn't compete with them at that time. I liked Withe as a commanding target man but in hindsight, if I had signed him in that summer of 1980, I wouldn't then have opted for Sharp so it all worked out well in the end!

Neil Webb was another I was looking to bring to Everton, from Reading, but I lost my job before I was able to bring him in. I was pleased that the lad went on to play for Manchester United and England after spells at Portsmouth and Nottingham Forest. It's nice to think you know a player when someone you rated highly goes on to fulfil his potential.

NEIL LENNON

Managed: Celtic (2010–2014 & 2019–2021);
Bolton Wanderers (2014–2016); Hibernian (2016–
2019); Omonoia Nicosia (2022–)

MY BIG DEAL

Virgil van Dijk: Groningen to Celtic for £2.6m in 2013

We made some good signings at Celtic, there's no question about that, but the way Van Dijk has gone on, he is now peerless in that position in the world, so I have to say, for what he has gone on to achieve, he is comfortably my best signing.

I looked at some footage of Van Dijk that the scouting team had set up and I thought, 'Wow.' But you always worry, watching a player on video, you know. But he had good attributes, he comes out with the ball, reads the game well, good in the air, a little bit complacent at times defensively, but for where he was at his age and what he could bring to us, I thought this guy could be a good signing.

So, for a couple of games we watched him. Johan Mjällby, who was my assistant at the time, he's like a straight-talking Swede, doesn't muck about, doesn't mince his words, he came back and said, 'Yes, we should sign him. But he needs a bit of work.' I watched him for Groningen against Ajax, they lost 2-0 and Mjällby felt Van Dijk was at fault for one of the goals but said we should definitely sign him.

I don't get involved in the negotiations for players at Celtic but I think it was pretty smooth, pretty seamless when Van Dijk came to us. He and his agent had a plan, go to Celtic, play Champions League, get yourself in the shop window and it worked out very well for him. Sometimes these plans go awry, but in this case, they've followed it through to the letter.

So, we got Van Dijk into the club and my first day assumption was he was ticking all the boxes. I felt to myself that he will not be here long with us at Celtic. What you see now in Van Dijk is what we had a younger version of coming through the door. So physically imposing, technically perfect almost, amazing in the air in both boxes, a great range of passing and a turn of pace when he really wanted to turn it on. He didn't turn it on unless he needed to, he could read situations brilliantly.

I asked him one day if he would play as a number six-type holding midfielder. But he said, 'No gaffer. I'm quite happy at centre-half doing this.' There was no arrogance about Van Dijk, though, he wasn't a problem. He's intelligent. He was young then, only about 22, but he had Scott Brown around him and he and Scott were, and still are, very good friends.

After six or seven months I had scouts ringing me, that quickly, but they were a little bit reluctant and we didn't want to sell Van Dijk anyway. I said if you want to put a bid in, put a bid in, but you don't want to miss out on this guy because he's going to be something else. As we also felt about [Victor] Wanyama at the time, who went off to Southampton and Spurs.

Virgil had a graceful way about him. Never went to ground. It's said he makes it look easy. Well, yes, but it's not easy. That in itself is a skill. What he's doing now is not a surprise to me, not at all. What surprised me was he went from Celtic to Southampton [for £13m] rather than go to a top-four club directly from us. Then Liverpool made a big investment [£75m] and it certainly paid off.

Since they got him in and the goalkeeper, Alisson, Liverpool have gone through the stratosphere. Van Dijk is one of Liverpool's best signings in the last 25 years and he is in good company there. He's outstanding and you always feel he's got another gear. He makes it look quite easy. The word 'imperious' covers it. And, he's a specimen physically.

Van Dijk is like a modern-day Alan Hansen in the way he plays, never flustered and fancies himself against anybody. What you've got there is a complete centre-half. I thought he should have got the Ballon d'Or when Liverpool won the Champions League. I'd love to see him win that – he is that good. You always compare people. It will be interesting to see at the end of his career where Van Dijk is rated, how it pans out, but he reminds me so much of how Paolo Maldini played, just that effortless style. Class.

THE ONE THAT GOT AWAY

Jimmy Bullard: Hull City to Celtic on loan

It's a difficult one. Not many have gone on to bite me in the backside, if you know what I mean. But I tried to sign Jimmy Bullard in my first season at Celtic, on loan with an option to buy. We don't go out to get big-priced players at Celtic, we are normally quite diligent. But the Jimmy one is interesting because I met him in Portugal, we were out there, he came around to my house and had a good chat.

The clubs were discussing about a loan and then it was set up for him to come to Glasgow. While we were in Portugal, Hull were talking about going to supplement a percentage of the wages.

I had a chat with him, the chat went well, but then Jimmy says I've got to speak to the missus. You know that old chestnut? That's a get-out for a lot of players.

So, anyway we got him to Glasgow, showed him round the stadium and the training ground and then, because we knew Jimmy was a good golfer – he's a scratch golfer – the Scottish Open was on at Loch Lomond and we took him there.

The weather was brilliant, just perfect, Loch Lomond is beautiful, we've got him there on the first day, so you're thinking, 'This will sell it, the old Scottish Open.' So, I say, 'What you thinking?' And Jimmy says, 'Oh, I just need to go and speak to the missus.' He used that line again! Right, OK.

On the Sunday me and my assistant, Johan, were in hospitality at the golf and the next thing I get a call and it's Jimmy's dad, Jimmy Sr., and I say, 'Jimmy, we got a deal here?'

'No, we are still a little bit short.'

I said, 'What do you mean, short?'

'Just on the wages.'

And I said, 'How much short are we?'

He mentioned this figure and I said, 'Jimmy, no chance. But ring the chief executive and see what he says.'

I didn't say this to Jimmy Sr., but I thought the chief executive will have a heart attack when he hears that.

It was too much, so the deal fell over there and then. But he would have been good because Jimmy was a character and a good footballer. I think in the end he went to Ipswich. I've bumped into Jimmy a few times since and he's said, 'I made a big mistake not going to Celtic.'

And he was right.

BRIAN LITTLE

Managed: Wolverhampton Wanderers (1986);
Darlington (1989–1991); Leicester City (1991–
1994); Aston Villa (1994–1998); Stoke City (1998–
1999); West Bromwich Albion (1999–2000); Hull
City (2000–2002); Tranmere Rovers (2003–
2006); Wrexham (2007–2008); Gainsborough
Trinity (2009–2011); Jersey (2016)

MY BIG DEAL

Gareth Southgate: Crystal Palace to Aston Villa for
£2.5m in 1995

Gareth was something special as signings go. In the games
I saw him play for Crystal Palace initially, he was either
playing at right-back or as a holding midfield player. I don't
recall seeing him as a central defender, which is where he
obviously made his name eventually for Villa and then
England. Gareth was a natural at the back but like I say he
wasn't used to that role early on.

In one of my early games as Villa manager we got
hammered 4-1 at Palace in the League Cup and Gareth
scored twice as a holding midfielder. That was the first time
I really noticed him and I was very impressed and started to
think he would be the perfect player to bring in to eventually
replace Andy Townsend, not only as a deep-lying midfielder
but also as my captain. I saw those leadership qualities in
him. But as things panned out Andy was incredible and his
performances didn't drop so that was when Gareth moved
to the back instead. My original plan was to replace Andy
with Gareth and also sign Chris Coleman to take over from
Shaun Teale. But, for a variety of reasons, it didn't work out
that way.

I remember in pre-season we tried playing with a back three and asked Gareth to play in there with Ugo Ehiogu and Paul McGrath and it worked out brilliantly. Andy was immense also, so we realised we didn't need Chris Coleman. Around the same time, Shaun Teale received a three-year contract offer from Tranmere, when I was prepared to offer him a one-year deal. I was honest with Shaun and told him I was bringing someone else in, so he probably felt he was better off leaving and I've spoken to him since in more recent times and Shaun told me it was the best move for him at that time financially and in terms of his football. So, Gareth's move worked out in a number of ways.

The business side of the deal was pretty straightforward. I sat in on a phone conversation between Doug Ellis and the Palace chairman Ron Noades and it was like listening to old car salesmen. 'If you give me this, I'll give you that' kind of thing. Everyone was happy with the deal and Gareth was called into the England squad within three months of moving to Aston Villa so hopefully the move helped his international career somewhat, too. I liked to sign players who had the potential to play international football but who were not there yet so I was buying that hunger to improve and achieve more. That same thinking was the case when I signed Gary Charles, Mark Draper, Alan Wright, Tommy Johnson and so on.

The other signing at Villa I would highlight would be that of [Savo] Milošević. It was a brave decision to break up the Dean Saunders-Dalian Atkinson partnership but I just wanted a bit more youthfulness and I guess it was my vote of confidence in Dwight Yorke to give him the opportunity to lead the line with Savo. They were fantastic together, well balanced and linked up really nicely.

I'd also like to mention Mick Tait, who was brilliant for me at Darlington after playing around 300 games for

Portsmouth in the 1980s. I signed him for nothing and a couple of hundred quid a week [in 1990] and his experience was tremendous for Darlington and helped us win the old Fourth Division as champions in his first season. He was a Geordie lad so I think he enjoyed being back up in the north-east for a year or two.

THE ONES THAT GOT AWAY

Phillip Cocu: PSV Eindhoven to Aston Villa

Les Ferdinand: Queens Park Rangers to Aston Villa

I had a scout in Holland called Dougie George who I knew from when I was in the Villa youth team. He did all my scouting in Holland and he kept saying to me you've got to come out and have a look at Jaap Stam, Philip Cocu and Jon Dahl Tomasson. So, I went to Holland to watch a couple of games, including Heerenveen, who Tomasson played for, and PSV Eindhoven where the other two were. I loved Phillip Cocu so much. I was like, 'Wow, this guy can really play,' and I went back to Doug and was jumping up and down about Cocu but it quickly transpired through a few conversations that he was going to Barcelona so that was over before it had started and it was the same with Stam. As regards to Tomasson, I liked him as a striker but I just didn't feel the balance would be right with him as it was with Yorke and Milošević so I didn't pursue that avenue. He ended up going to Newcastle [where he scored three goals in 23 league games].

When I was after a striker I initially had the idea of playing Andy Cole with Dwight Yorke up front and I even spoke to Cole's agent to see if we could do anything but he told me straight away we had no chance because he was going to Manchester United. How ironic that he should end up being so successful with Dwight but at Man United and not Aston Villa. But with Ferdinand we did have a good old go at that deal and I think we were prepared to pay around £6m, but we always felt Newcastle were favourites.

We spoke to him and were always there nibbling away but I don't feel we were rejected at any time, by Les or anyone else. It was usually more a matter of the timing not being right at that particular moment. So that was about the time we ended up signing Stan Collymore from Liverpool instead. To be fair to my chairman Doug Ellis, though, he was always prepared to back me. Even when I approached him about signing Milošević – having had a good recommendation from Terry Venables – Doug said, 'I don't know him but let's jump on a flight to Belgrade and go and watch him.' And we did.

We also looked into Gazza, with Doug Ellis going as far as flying to Italy to speak to Paul [Gascoigne] because he said he knew him. But Gazza told him pretty quickly that he was going to Rangers so that was a no-go as well.

LOU MACARI

Managed: Swindon Town (1984–1989); West
Ham United (1989–1990); Birmingham City
(1991); Stoke City (1991–1993 & 1994–1997);
Celtic (1993–1994); Huddersfield Town
(2000–2002)

MY BIG DEAL

Neil Baldwin: 'Nello the Clown' as Stoke City's kit man in 1991

It is quite an easy choice actually, though I'm sure it will be very different to most of the selections in the book. If anyone has seen the film *Marvelous* they will know what I am talking about. That film won a BAFTA, it's all true and will make things become a lot clearer once people watch it. It started from when I was announced as the Stoke City manager. There were lots of supporters who turned up to welcome me outside the club, singing songs and all that. I was leaving about six hours later when it was dark and pissing down with rain and I saw that Neil [who had been diagnosed with learning difficulties as a child] was the only one still there.

I had a conversation with him and asked him why he was still there. He said he just wanted to welcome me as the new manager. I told him that was nice of him and asked him what he did for a living. He said, 'Oh, I'm a circus clown.' But he had lost his job after he'd been working up in Scotland and the ringmaster didn't pay him enough, they argued and he got the sack. Straight away I liked the idea of a circus clown in the dressing room, laughing and joking, so I asked him if he wanted a job working with me. He said he was Stoke City-mad and would love it. Come Monday morning, I went to a costume shop in the city and hired him a chicken outfit. Neil put it on and I introduced him to the players: 'Lads, I'd like you to meet Neil, our new kit man.' You can imagine the reaction.

The lads really took to him as an individual and he was great for banter and created lots of fun in the dressing room. Whenever we'd travel he'd have a funny outfit on. He was great and became a household name at the club. He was so infamous that I received a call a few years later from a filmmaker who wanted to make a film about the whole story and we did it, the public liked it and we got the BAFTA. It is one of those films that makes you laugh and cry.

There was one scene in the film that made everyone laugh and it really happened. We had a striker we took from Villa called Martin Carruthers and he was boasting about these designer label silk pants he'd spent £80 on in Manchester. So, when the lads went on to the pitch to warm up at Tranmere, I said to Neil, 'Get those pants on. In fact, put everyone's pants on, but make sure Carruthers' are on first!' He did just that, and when Carruthers couldn't find his pants after his shower, he was getting a fair bit of stick and then Neil came in and showed all the lads what he was wearing down below. It was hilarious. That was Neil for you.

People might say it was a nice gesture giving him the job and ask would any of my old managers have done the same like Tommy Docherty or Ron Atkinson. But it's quite simple for me. He was just like another signing. When you look for a new player, you're looking for that something extra you can get out of your team and that's what Neil gave me. He was fantastic for team morale and everyone loved him.

In terms of more conventional player signings, I'd single out Mark Stein, who was brilliant for us after we signed him from Oxford. And Mike Sheron was also very good from Norwich City. But no one comes close to Neil!

THE ONE THAT GOT AWAY

Peter Schmeichel: Brøndby to West Ham United

I was at West Ham and I had Phil Parkes in goal and he had been a terrific keeper for the club but he was getting on a bit and I knew I desperately needed a new goalkeeper. I flew out to Denmark to watch Peter at Brøndby. I went out there unannounced, paid for a ticket and sat in the crowd with the fans because I thought if he's any good I don't want to alert any other clubs that we're in for him and hopefully it will leave the field open for ourselves. Normally, though, if you're going to watch any game you'd have your club arrange a free ticket for you to collect, but I didn't want to do that on this occasion.

The first thing that struck me about him was his presence, the size of him. He could kick the ball almost the length of the pitch, which was unbelievable. I was so impressed and said to myself, 'I'm going to have him in my team.' So, I got back to West Ham with the intention of securing the backing from the board to go back to Brøndby with a bid so I could sign Peter.

But I was to find out pretty quickly that there was virtually no money available for transfers and that was the end of it, which was a great shame. West Ham was not in a good state financially then because they had apparently burned some money on a few transfers in the seasons before this one and it meant there was not much around for me to bring in who I wanted so it meant I missed out on signing Peter, unfortunately.

Peter ended up going to Manchester United for about half a million pounds and I signed the Czechoslovakian goalkeeper Ludo Miklosko, who became a brilliant servant for West Ham, playing over 300 games. Ludo was probably another of my best signings, given what I paid for him, which was about £300,000 with add-ons.

DON MACKAY

Managed: Nørresundby (1978–1980); Dundee (1980–1984); Coventry City (1984–1986); Blackburn Rovers (1987–1991); Fulham (1991–1994); Airdrieonians (2001)

MY BIG DEAL

Colin Hendry: Dundee to Blackburn Rovers for £28,000 in 1987

I first signed Colin as an apprentice in 1983 when I was at Dundee and then again for Blackburn for just shy of £30,000 so for him to go on and play over 50 times for Scotland suggests the clubs I signed him to had reasonable value out of him. That time I had with him at Dundee allowed me to find out more about his background. I always wonder how much research clubs do on players they are buying to get to know their character and I didn't have to do any research with Colin as I already knew him. From the first time I dealt with him at Dundee his attitude was top-notch, he would not lie down and thought he could win everything – every header, every tackle, every game.

In his early days he thought of himself as a striker and he did know where the goal was to be fair to him, as he scored the winning goal at Wembley when Blackburn won the Full Members' Cup in 1987. He had the ability to be a reasonable striker but once he moved to Blackburn we felt he could be a better central defender so we tried him there to see how he got on. The good thing was even after we converted him to a defender he never lost his eye for goal [scoring 12 league goals in his second season at Blackburn].

He did so well at centre-half that Manchester City became interested in him, at a time when Blackburn didn't have much money and so were helpless in letting him go. He went for £700,000, which was a great profit for Blackburn, who needed the money then. They signed him back after I lost my job for the same money, when he became Kenny Dalglish's first signing. I think the service Colin gave them offered a healthy return on their investment.

Steve Archibald was an exciting signing for us at Blackburn when he joined us for nothing on loan halfway through the 1987/88 season; we did well to do that deal. Just Steve's presence alone soon doubled our gate to about 15,000. I believe this was the start of Blackburn's rise because we also signed Ossie Ardiles in 1988 for five games and the local public recognised what we were trying to do and bought into it.

Brian Borrows was another of my best signings as we took him to Coventry from Bolton for next to nothing [£80,000] in 1985 and he never left Highfield Road until 1997. Another full-back, Greg Downs, was an equally shrewd investment for Coventry after we signed him from Norwich for not very much.

THE ONES THAT GOT AWAY

Gary Lineker: Tottenham to Blackburn

Teddy Sheringham: Millwall to Blackburn

Just after Jack Walker's money started to filter into the football club, I tried to sign both Gary Lineker from Tottenham and Teddy Sheringham from Millwall and they were close. At the start of the 1991/92 campaign, my intention was to play Gary Lineker up front with David Speedie and with Sheringham playing off the front two. I managed to bring in Speedie from Liverpool but we didn't manage to capture the other two, unfortunately. The formation that everyone raves on about in the modern day is 4-3-3, which is what I had planned and there would have been no better front three in England than these guys playing together.

Teddy was known more as a striker but I always saw him as a supplier or a creator of chances as he ended up being later in his career. I was on holiday in the West Country and I flew from Plymouth to London to meet with Teddy in a London hotel. We were looking to pay £750,000 for him but two things did not help our case in this regard. One was the fact we were still in the Second Division, and the second was that our rivals for his signature were Nottingham Forest and while they were in the First Division, they also had a manager who players didn't say no to – Brian Clough of course.

If I am honest Brian Clough had a far greater influence on Teddy than I or Blackburn Rovers would have so it was the right deal for him at that time. It wasn't the first time I had lost out to Cloughy. When I was at Coventry I sold Stuart Pearce to Forest when I didn't really have a choice. Although Stuart apparently said he would have stayed if Coventry had offered him more money, I don't believe it as he was desperate to move to Forest and work with Brian Clough.

As for the Lineker deal, in hindsight we at Blackburn were so naive about the way in which we went about it as we were not aware of the financial implications that Tottenham had at the time. Chairman Bill Fox sat down with Irving Scholar and a fee of £1m was agreed for him to join Blackburn Rovers. We offered £750,000 initially, which Tottenham rejected and insisted it had to be one million. Then Jack Walker got involved and said, 'If the manager wants him, let's get him!' There was nothing underhanded going on, it was all agreed properly, prior to us speaking to the player, which we never got round to doing.

What we didn't reckon on was Mr Alan Sugar coming on the scene and buying Tottenham Hotspur. This takeover resulted in our missing out on Gary Lineker, but what was doubly frustrating was the fact they allowed Lineker to leave at the end of the 1991/92 season for something like £500,000 to the Japanese club Grampus Eight. Ironically, after I had been replaced at Blackburn by Kenny Dalglish, they ended up with a great striker in Alan Shearer but only because Southampton wanted David Speedie so that all contributed to that deal getting done.

MALCOLM MACDONALD

Managed: Fulham (1980–1984); Huddersfield Town (1987–1988)

MY BIG DEAL

Ray Houghton: West Ham United to Fulham on a free transfer in 1982

When I was eight years old I used to wait at a bus stop near Craven Cottage with my autograph book as the players would often get off the bus and walk to the ground from there. One day Bobby Robson got off. I asked him for his autograph, he gave me his bag and took my autograph book, but not only did he sign in my book, he spoke to me all the way down Finlay Street.

I told him I was left-footed and when he heard that he said there was always a place in the game for quality left-footed players because they made the pitch bigger. What he meant by that was right-footed players playing on the left always cut inside. Bobby's comment always stuck with me.

It was that advice that led me to sign Peter O'Sullivan from Brighton, a left-footer on the left. In the summer of 1982, though, I knew I needed to replace him as he was in his early 30s. Anyway, before we flew off for a tour of Trinidad, a little birdie told me that Ray Houghton had been given a free by John Lyall at West Ham. I checked with my coaches Ray Harford and Terry Mancini whether they agreed he would be a good signing and they both said, 'Get him!'

I called John to check this information was accurate and he said it was and was also surprised I knew because the free transfer list wasn't due to be announced for a couple of days. Thank heavens for little birdies! So, I had a tight window to sign Ray.

I explained to John I was due to fly to the West Indies in a couple of days and didn't have time to wait for the list to be released officially and asked him if he would put a word in for me. John said the way Fulham played would be perfect for Ray and he would speak with him. He called me back a few minutes later and said, 'Ray is in his car and driving to you now.'

An hour later Ray met with me, we offered him a huge increase on what he had been earning at West Ham and put a contract in front of him. I said, 'If you sign that now you'll be off to Trinidad & Tobago with us in two days.' His eyes lit up and, after asking a couple of football questions, he signed there and then. We went off to the Caribbean for about three weeks and Ray got to know everyone.

That season I played him on the left and he was absolutely brilliant. Ray had a lovely way of dragging the ball away from the defender and circumventing the tackle. Apart from being a bloody good player, he was a lovely lad and I was pleased to see him going on to have a fantastic career.

To go back to that comment from Bobby Robson, although Ray favoured his right foot he had a wonderful ability to stay wide and would sometimes take the ball to the corner flag before he would cut in and cross with his right foot. He didn't come inside all the time like many right-footed players do. I had it in my head to bring a few younger players through like Paul Parker and Jeff Hopkins and Ray added to that mix wonderfully well, alongside some more experienced players like Gordon Davies. We missed out on promotion by one point and one place, coming fourth.

I was appalled that Fulham ended up selling Ray for just £150,000 to Oxford after I had left. I thought, 'Oh no, what is going on here.' I always said to him while I was his manager, if there is one club you will end up at, it's

Liverpool. But I certainly never expected him to play at Oxford in between!

THE ONE THAT GOT AWAY

Ian Allinson: Colchester United to Fulham for £100,000 in 1983

He was about to sign for me at Fulham after scoring 22 goals in 46 league games for Colchester. He looked at the contract and said, 'There's a problem with this contract.' He was referring to this error where the typewriter had struck the paper but there was no ink visible, so we had this blank. I said, 'No problem, I will get the whole thing re-typed.'

I met him in the East End of London, so I then had to return to Fulham in west London and get back to meet him in the east once again. I managed to do all that in a couple of hours. But by the time I got back to him, he was already talking to people from Arsenal. They nipped in and signed him there and then; I just missed out.

If it wasn't for that missing print on the contract, he would have signed for Fulham. It wasn't to be. He ended up being a good signing for Arsenal – so good luck to him. I wasn't one to kick buckets over or get angry. I knew there was nothing I could have done.

MICK McCARTHY

*Managed: Millwall (1992–1996); Republic of
Ireland (1996–2002 & 2018–2020); Sunderland
(2002–2006); Wolverhampton Wanderers (2006–
2012); Ipswich Town (2012–2018); APOEL
(2020–2021); Cardiff City (2021)*

MY BIG DEAL

Sylvan Ebanks-Blake: Plymouth Argyle to
Wolverhampton Wanderers for £1.5m in 2008

I never spent massive amounts of money, but the best
one was Sylvan Ebanks-Blake for Wolves. We were just
always a little bit short. We pushed for the play-offs in
my first season and got beat by West Brom in the semis.
Then we just missed the play-offs in the second season
and then it was the January of the next season and Sylvan
was playing for Plymouth. Ollie [Ian Holloway] was there
and I remember ringing him about Sylvan. He said, 'You
should sign him.'

But if you've seen Sylvan, he doesn't look the most
athletic, he's a big lad and there was always that question
mark. But we did it and it was one and a half million we
paid for him. It was a lot for us because we had not spent
anything. Steve Morgan had come in as owner and he gave
us a bit of money, so we signed Christophe Berra and Sylvan.

It wasn't hard to get Sylvan to come to us because he'd
been playing well for Plymouth. We'd seen him and he'd had
his time at Plymouth, he wanted to go to a bigger club. There
were others in for him but Wolves in the Championship were
a huge club. It went down to negotiations, but he wanted
to come. It lifted Sylvan, being at Wolves, he thrived on it,
loved it.

Sylvan had scored 11 Championship goals for Plymouth and then got another 12 for us. In a season and a half in the Championship for Wolves, Sylvan scored 37 goals in 61 games which, that one signing, gave us the edge. They say you can't buy goals, but you can and it got us into the Premier League. He came in and he lit the place up.

He could infuriate you though. He infuriated me because he didn't particularly want to be running around. There'd be times when I'm looking at him and I'm turning round, looking at the bench because Sylvan is not having a good game, and my assistant manager, Taffy [Ian] Evans, comes up behind me and says, 'Don't even think about it. You are thinking about making a sub aren't you?' I said, 'Yes,' then Taffy says, 'You've got the best team out on the pitch.' I knew I had but I'd still be looking round to see if I've got anything different. I left the team as it was on this occasion and we won 1-0 and guess who scored? Ebanks-Blake. He'd hardly had a kick.

He wasn't one of them who held things up, he wasn't particularly willing to run in the channel, it was sometimes hard work with Sylvan to get him to do that, but bloody hell, could he score goals. He'd scored 12 for Plymouth before us and he scored 25 for us in that season, 2008/09. In the two years he scored 50 goals in 93 games, for Plymouth and then for Wolves. Out of all of the players I had, and there were some very good ones, his goals were the reason we got promoted to the Premier League.

But he was a test. I remember one game at Watford, I think we beat them down there 3-2 and Chris Iwelumo was playing up front with Sylvan. We used to play 4-4-2 and one would drop in to midfield so we'd play 4-5-1 without the ball. Chris Iwelumo would do it and he'd also scored a goal into the bargain in this game. Sylvan had not bothered his backside and I'm screaming at him. Of course, every time

I scream at him to drop in he'd cock me a deaf 'un. Chris Iewlumo says to me, 'Gaffer, I'll do it.' I said, 'I know you will, but you'll be dead, I'll have to take you off.' That was just Sylvan. He was a challenge.

He could come in and he'd be as grumpy as hell if you'd made him run too far. Then he'd go out and he'd have the biggest smile for these fans who'd waited outside and me and TC [assistant manager Terry Connor] used to laugh at him. For three hours he'd been a grumpy sod. He goes out there and Sylvan is lovely all of a sudden, he's just fabulous.

We also signed Michael Kightly for 25 grand and he had a huge impact and we signed Matt Jarvis on the other wing who had a huge impact. Christophe Berra was a real solid performer, but it's goals that get you promoted.

THE ONES THAT GOT AWAY

Steve Sidwell: Aston Villa to Wolverhampton Wanderers

Rio Ferdinand: Schoolboy to Millwall

When I was at Millwall, I went to see Rio Ferdinand. He was 16 and only lived an hour from the ground so I went to see him with his mum, Janice. I wouldn't know what would have happened if he'd joined us. It wouldn't have changed history would it, because Rio had such a wonderful career. He obviously went on to West Ham. Even if he had signed for Millwall I don't think he'd have been there that long, he'd have been out of there. I was out of there anyway and went to the Republic of Ireland.

I sat in with Billy Sharp, I tried to sign him. He might have had an impact in the side. He went on to sign for Sheffield United and has been there ever since. James McCarthy is another I spoke to as the Wolves manager when he was in Scotland and we thought we'd got a deal, but he went to Wigan and signed for them. But the one that stands out for me is Steve Sidwell.

He was at Villa and he'd been left out the team. I couldn't understand why he wasn't playing, something had gone on, there'd been a fall-out. We were in our second season in the Premier League. So, we got him up to Molineux. He came up with his agent Eric Walters and sat down, we chatted to him, that was all good, everything was sorted out financially.

We were looking for a midfielder of Steve Sidwell's ilk and I'd have been delighted to get him. We got him to the physio for a fitness test, we'd got Steve on the running machine and Eric Walters is on the phone a hell of a lot. Whenever I look he's on the phone and I started to get a little bit suspicious. I'm thinking, 'There's something going on here.' Steve Sidwell's still doing his running. I go and see him: 'Steve, you all right?' 'Yes, no problem.' Then Eric comes in and I go, 'What's the story?' He says, 'Mick, Fulham have come in and they're offering him a three-year deal. We're going to have to do it.' That's football!

I said, 'You'd better get out of here quick because I'm gonna fuckin' punch the pair of you!' I've had a right growl at both of them. They are both looking sheepish. Steve's still sweating away on the running machine so I tell him, 'Steve, come on, you'd better go.' But I did fully understand. We were only taking his contract until the end of the season and, in all honesty, I said, I'd do it myself, I can't knock you for it. But I was fuming at first as it got to the point of being so close.

It was Mark Hughes who signed him for Fulham. Steve did all right there at Craven Cottage. He was someone I really wanted to sign. It's an absolute cert that he'd have made us a better team. That was the real one that got away.

STEVE McCLAREN

Managed: Middlesbrough (2001–2006); England
(2006–2007); FC Twente (2008–2010 & 2012–
2013); VfL Wolfsburg (2010–2011); Nottingham
Forest (2011); Derby County (2013–2015 &
2016–2017, technical director 2020–2021);
Newcastle United (2015–2016); Queens Park
Rangers (2018–2019)

MY BIG DEAL

Gareth Southgate: Aston Villa to Middlesbrough for
£6.5m in 2001

Without a doubt, my best signing was Gareth Southgate.
Middlesbrough was my first job and I wanted a captain in
the dressing room who kind of epitomised what we wanted,
what we believed in, who could police the dressing room and
play on the field as a leader.

I can't really remember the fee – but I know it nearly
never went through. I said to the chairman, Steve Gibson,
that we had a window of opportunity. We had got Gareth
and his agent in the office and I said to Steve, 'This is it.
Don't let him leave the office until he signs!'

But Steve ended up having an argument with Gareth's
agent and the agent and Gareth walked out. Can you believe
it? I think they were half an hour down the A1 and there's
me trying to persuade Steve to phone them up, get them
back and get the deal done.

It took me a while but eventually Steve picked up the
phone, told them to turn around and come back and said,
'Let's get it done.' So, I nearly lost it, but gentle persuasion
as they say, and it turned out right.

Gareth was perfect, plus the added bonus was that we had Ugo Ehiogu and they had played together at Villa for many years and formed a great partnership. Putting that combination back together and having someone in the dressing room who bought into what we wanted to do and could get the messages across to the players, that's how we wanted to be, off the field and on the field. Gareth was with us for five years and he was a perfect example for that.

As captain he led the club to its first trophy [League Cup in 2004], into Europe and the UEFA Cup Final in 2006 [lost to Sevilla]. Gareth was a quiet leader, shouted when he had to, but he was the glue in the team; he would talk to everybody, from the young boys, to the seniors, to the foreign players, he treated everybody the same. We had a lot of foreign players and he was the catalyst in bringing everybody together.

So, without doubt, he was my first signing as a manager – and he was 'the one'.

THE ONE THAT GOT AWAY

Diego Forlán: Independiente to Middlesbrough for £6.9m in 2002

It's not one I regret but is quite a funny one. We were looking for a second striker and we had spotted him. We watched some clips of him, and he was available. He'd had a good World Cup and he was perfect for what we wanted at Middlesbrough.

So, we got in touch with agents and everything and pretty much had the deal done. I knew there was a lot of interest from other clubs all around Europe. We sent the club chief executive and my agent to Uruguay to collect Forlán personally.

I said, 'Do not let him go, do not let him out of your sight. We can do this quickly and quietly and get him in the bag before anybody else can do something.' So, they went over, all seemed good. They met the player, met the agent. Still, all was good. Everything fine? 'Yes.'

They travelled back, no problem. 'Got on the flight?' 'Great.' I said again, 'Don't let him out your sight until he's up in Teesside.'

Then all of a sudden, I get a phone call from the chief executive. They've landed at Heathrow, they were sat down, they were between departure gates, waiting for the flight to Teesside. Forlán went to the toilet – and disappeared!

The chief exec called me and said, 'He's disappeared! We don't know where he's gone.' So, I said, 'You'd better find him. Search that airport and find him!'

Anyway, all of a sudden it came up on Sky Sports News, there's the pictures, cameras, live from Manchester Airport. Guess who's coming out? Diego Forlán. Manchester United had nicked him from under our nose. The transfer had got talked about and United must have heard about it, wanted him, got in touch with him, probably spoke to the agent and promised more money, and the agent has said get yourself away from those two and get a flight up to Manchester, as they want to sign you straight away. Which they did.

So instead of flying to Teesside he went to Manchester. What a day that was.

ROY McFARLAND

Managed: Bradford City (1981–1982); Derby
County (caretaker 1984 & 1993–1995);
Bolton Wanderers (co-manager 1995–1996);
Cambridge United (1996–2001); Torquay
United (2001–2002); Chesterfield (2003–
2007); Burton Albion (2009)

MY BIG DEAL

Martin Butler: Walsall to Cambridge United for
£22,000 in 1997

Martin was without doubt my best-ever signing. The fee
of £22,000 was a lot of money then to Cambridge. If I am
being fair my assistant manager David Preece spotted him
first and he talked about him to me and I only needed to go
and watch him in one match – that was enough. He struck
me as someone who would chase a piece of paper his work
rate was so good. In the modern game I would liken him
to Jamie Vardy.

He did a tremendous job for us and I convinced him to
stay when a lot of clubs were looking at him. I explained his
importance to the club and reassured him that there would
always be clubs wanting to sign him and, thankfully, we
managed to earn a promotion with him from the old Fourth
Division to the Third in 1998/99.

We eventually sold him for a huge profit to Reading
for £750,000. I was only given a fraction of that fee to
reinvest in the team but to be fair clubs like Cambridge
need the money to pay the bills. They sold Trevor Benjamin
to Leicester for £1.3m a few months later anyway so they
were then in good health as a club. It would have been
very exciting for us to keep Martin and progress as a

football club but I knew how the chairman and the others directors felt. In fact, because of the importance for the football club to survive, they would probably have sold him for anything over £100,000 as that would still have represented a healthy profit. And I knew that would be the situation when I took on the job.

I knew the challenge was to identify players who are capable of playing at a higher standard but who hadn't been spotted yet – like Martin – so I took the job in the knowledge we would always be a feeder club to bigger clubs. That's the way it works at that level and I enjoyed the job and the relationship I had with the club, the players and the fans. When I signed a player I always told them straight away I would never stand in their way if they had the chance of a move to a bigger club, as Cambridge was then a stepping stone for good players like Martin Butler.

My fear now is that there are still many like Martin in the lower leagues but more will go unnoticed by the bigger clubs because they are shopping more and more outside of this country for foreign players who are cheaper. English players in the lower leagues and non-league now are seen as more of a gamble. At least Jamie Vardy's story shows those players are still there!

THE ONE THAT GOT AWAY

Sammy Clingan: Wolverhampton Wanderers to Chesterfield

Sammy was with me on loan at Chesterfield and he did a real good job. He was an excellent passer and he kept possession very well and we offered Wolves £80,000, which they didn't accept. Unfortunately for us, Nottingham Forest bid £100,000 and he went there instead. We were not in a position to compete for money with Forest and simply could not have afforded that extra £20,000. I was grateful to the board for finding £80,000, which was a lot of money for us then.

Jamal Campbell-Ryce was another I missed about the same time, which was equally disappointing. He was one of those electrifying wingers who could run the length of the football field and win us corners and free kicks and just give us breathing space. We wouldn't have had to have paid as much for Jamal as we would for Sammy but I'm confident the club would have found it. The agent told me, though, that Jamal was homesick and wanted to return to London where his parent club was, Charlton Athletic. The next thing I heard was he had signed for Rotherham, which is even more northerly than we were.

That was very disappointing and subsequently I fell out with the agent who I had known for a long time. It was a great shame as both players would have a made a real difference to the team and subsequently we struggled after that.

MARK McGHEE

Managed: Reading (1991–1994); Leicester City (1994–1995); Wolverhampton Wanderers (1995–1998); Millwall (2000–2003); Brighton & Hove Albion (2003–2006); Motherwell (2007–2009 & 2015–2017); Aberdeen (2009–2010); Bristol Rovers (2012); Barnet (2017–2018); Eastbourne Borough (2019); Dundee (2022–)

MY BIG DEAL

Shaka Hislop: Howard University, Washington DC, to Reading on a free transfer in 1992

Someone said to me early on the first job you get you really need to make something of it to earn your next job, particularly if it's a lower-league club. My first club was Reading – I knew my recruitment had to be good. I was player-manager at the start, but I didn't want to play. I played because they wanted me to. I'd played against Reading for Newcastle the season before and on a couple of occasions we had battered them and I'd scored goals. So, Reading had this idea I'd be player-manager, but I wanted to stop playing and concentrate on managing. I busked it for a while and then gave it up.

I got the team fit, got them playing some really great football and people were saying we played well, but we would draw, or we'd miss chances, let in a couple of goals and lose. So, although we were playing a good style of football we were not winning enough games. Things had to change.

Then I had a couple of phone calls that totally changed things for me and the club. One was from a chap I knew, but not that well, in America. He used to live in Aberdeen. He phoned me one day in the summer and said there was a lad

215

over there, a goalie, I might be interested in. He told me he'd got a British passport and gone over there for university. He said he was worth a look and asked if I'd like to have him over for a trial. I said, 'OK, send him over.' He said his name was Neil Hislop. I knew absolutely nothing more about the boy than his name and he arrived one Sunday morning. A pal of mine, a driver, was good enough to go to Gatwick and pick him up. And Neil Shaka Hislop turned up at my door, all 6ft 5in of him. I didn't even know what colour he was. Of course, it didn't matter, but there weren't a lot of black goalkeepers around in those days.

He turned out to be brilliant. After I'd seen him in one training session I was running back to Elm Park to tell them to get a contract saying, 'Get this boy signed quick!' And we did. By God he looked the part straight away. He could be a bit too excited at first and throw the ball out too quickly, but he was a cut above, you could see that. Absolutely fantastic. He'd taken a degree in mechanical engineering and wanted to come back and play football. What a phone call that was, eh!

Soon after that, Bobby Williams, who was one of my part-time scouts, phoned me. Bobby was a salesman and travelled around the country and he was down at Bournemouth one day. He phones me and says, 'I'm down at Bournemouth and I've just heard they are going to let Jimmy Quinn go and will sell him for around 35 grand.' We had not spent any money at that time so I went in and said we need a centre-forward and this boy would do us. John Madejski, the chairman, said 'OK' so we spent 32 grand to get Jimmy Quinn.

Within a very short space of time I'd added Shaka Hislop at one end and Jimmy Quinn at the other. Those two signings transformed all the good football we were playing into winning football. Shaka was outstanding and kept the ball out the net and Quinny put it in the net up the other end. What a goalscorer he was. He gave us the end product we had been lacking.

I would have to say those two together were the most important signings I made in my career because they set me off. I'm not claiming I discovered them, because one guy phoned me up from America and another just happened to be in Bournemouth when he heard something. Call it fate!

THE ONE THAT GOT AWAY

Peter Crouch: Portsmouth to Millwall

I've been lucky in that I've had some brilliant chairmen, but Theo Paphitis at Millwall probably edged them all in terms of being an influence on me. He was a great chairman. We had a close relationship and he was very involved in what I did. I remember Theo came to me one day, around the time Richard Sadlier was injured. He was going to be an unbelievable player.

I reckon he'd have been the best player I'd ever worked with had he not got injured. A centre-forward, 6ft 5in, the season he got injured at Christmas he'd scored something like 14 goals. We were offered £7m for Sadlier by two clubs, but they didn't know he was already injured. So, we needed someone to fill his boots. We ended up taking Dion Dublin on loan from Aston Villa, but the person that Theo came up with was Peter Crouch.

I just didn't see it. I was a bit of a purist. I like footballers that look like footballers and I suppose in a sense I cut off my nose to spite my face. I was kind of reluctant to be excited about Crouchy. He was at Portsmouth and I said no. With hindsight he'd have been really decent for us. We had wingers, people who could get the ball in the box, and with that hindsight now, Crouch would have been a good signing for us. I don't even know if we could have afforded him but I should have explored it.

Because of the type of player Crouch was – he wasn't mobile enough for me – I wanted someone to hold up the ball. When people started to use Peter Crouch to his strengths and not expecting other things off him, that's when he started scoring goals. He would be the one that got away for me – I do regret not trying to sign him. It was the opinion I had at the time, but he's done well and he's proven me wrong.

At some other times you can want to sign a player but you're too late. For instance, when I was at Wolves I went to watch Ole Gunnar Solskjaer. I was at the game over in Norway and someone pointed out to me that the Man United scout was there and it was stitched up that he was going to United!

When I was at Millwall as well, the season we got promoted, we had Michael Tonge and Phil Jagielka at Sheffield United lined up. We offered a million quid, they wanted one and a half and we were going to pay that. But it was the time when ITV Digital collapsed. It meant we lost £2m at Millwall and, subsequently, we couldn't then bring in Tonge and Jagielka. If I had added those two to the squad I already had we would have been better than decent.

JOHN McGOVERN

Managed: Bolton Wanderers (1982–1985); Chorley
(1990–1991); Rotherham United (1994–1996);
Woking (1997–1998); Ilkeston Town (2000–2003)

MY BIG DEAL

Brian Borrows: Everton to Bolton Wanderers for
£5,000 in 1983

There is so much more pressure to management than playing
the game, and signing the right players is all part of it. We
were relegated at Bolton in my first season and the place was
like a morgue. I enjoyed it more at Bolton when they took
away most of my first-team squad because the club couldn't
afford to pay them. I therefore played with five 18-year-
olds in the side and we were topping the league at one stage
until we burned out and finished tenth. The youngsters died
mentally and physically from the added stress of first-team
football. But their success to that point goes to show that
hunger mixed with talent can take you a long way sometimes
further than players on a lot of money.

On that very topic, I pinched a young and hungry Brian
Borrows from Everton for just five grand and I told Brian
that Howard Kendall would sort out his signing-on fee out
of the transfer. Howard was on the phone to me saying,
'How can I afford his signing-on fee? You've only flipping
paid me five grand!' Howard had Gary Stevens coming
through around that time, so I was able to nick Brian for
next to nothing.

When I went to see him play for Everton reserves with
my assistant manager Walter Joyce, I only watched him
for ten minutes and I said to Walter, 'Let's go, I've seen
enough.' He said, 'Why, isn't he any good?' I said, 'Quite

the opposite, he can play! If I can afford him I'll have him.' Walter had already told me his character was good and those few minutes showed me all I needed to know. In those ten minutes I could tell his quality and temperament as a footballer just from his work rate and the way he played the game. He was brilliant for me. He could defend, get forward and when he passed a 30-yard ball it would be right at the feet of where he was trying to pass. Brilliant.

I signed another very good player called Tony Caldwell from Horwich RMI for two grand and the chairman sold him to Bristol City for about 30 grand – after I had left the club, so the club did well out of him.

I went to watch Tony four times because he was scoring lots of goals in the non-league. But the first three occasions I watched him he never scored a goal. But in the last match I saw him go straight through the centre-half with his studs. I said, 'That'll do, we'll have him.' He was ideal for us and scored 70-odd goals for Bolton in the four seasons he was with them. Mark Came was another of my best signings after I took him from Winsford United for £250! He stayed at Bolton for about eight years – long after I had gone, so he was a good recruit for not very much money.

THE ONE THAT GOT AWAY

Micky Quinn: Stockport County to Bolton Wanderers

I pleaded with the Stockport manager Eric Webster to sell Micky to me. I wanted him bad. I said, 'Eric, pick any three of my players and you can have them all if you flog Quinny to us.' Eric said, 'I need money, John.' I told him that was one thing I couldn't help him with as I hadn't got any! Eric said, 'John, if you can come up with the money you can have him.' He only wanted about 30 grand – but even that was too much. Micky would have suited us down to the ground. If I could have put him up front with Caldwell, flipping heck they would have done some damage together with their collective goalscoring abilities. I also looked at Bobby Davison, who was at Halifax at the time, and went on to do well for Derby County.

One of the difficulties I thought I might have as a manager was spotting players and especially those from the lower and non-leagues because that's often the area we have to work due to budget constraints. But I actually found it quite easy and the one consolation I took from missing out on Micky was seeing how his career progressed. All those goals he scored showed me I must have been able to spot a player. Just a shame I couldn't afford him!

A lesson I learned from Peter Taylor at Derby and then Forest, before I became a manager, was the amount of time he used to spend finding out about the character of a player. The ability of a player is there for all to see. But knowing whether he will be right for the football club and whether he has the right personality is something different. I never minded drinkers because nearly every player liked a drink in those days. It was the moaners and the idiots who get drunk and crash their car that I didn't want.

SAMMY McILROY

Managed: Northwich Victoria (1992–1993);
Macclesfield Town (1993–2000); Northern Ireland
(2000–2003); Stockport County (2003–2004);
Morecambe (2005–2011)

MY BIG DEAL

Chris Byrne: Flixton to Macclesfield Town on a free transfer in 1996

We had a lot of success at Macclesfield with two promotions, we won the FA Trophy and the Conference League Cup. Two players were especially influential, who I find hard to separate – Steve Wood and Chris Byrne.

Byrne was playing for Flixton in amateur leagues around the Manchester area and I wanted him for almost a year before I signed him. His manager then, Dalton Steele, who was a friend of mine, wanted to hold on to him because they were going for promotion and they were also going well in the FA Vase. My assistant Gil Prescott knew the non-league scene inside and out and had a black book of files on every club and player in the land so he was a precious resource for me. He helped me so much and every time I'd mention a player, Gil would turn to his file with stars next to his name from the games he had scouted. I had a good idea myself of Byrne because I lived in the area and used to watch Flixton – so I got him.

He was the most important player for me in that promotion year of 1997 [to the Football League]. He scored goals from midfield, got an unbelievable hat-trick actually at Kettering. Clubs were always looking at him, like Peter Reid at Sunderland. In fact, he was playing for me without a contract at one time when clubs were sniffing and he could have been nicked for nothing. But we had a sit down and he looked me in the eye and said, 'Sammy, I'm staying with you for this season.' And he did.

Because he was honest with me I didn't even then put him on contract so we could make a fee from him. I wish I did because we could have made a right few quid out of him, but because he was straight with me I was happy for him to go at the end of the season and no doubt get a signing-on fee. When he did eventually move on to Sunderland, Peter Reid gave me a [pre-season] game so we made a few quid that way.

Steve Wood was with me longer after I took him from Stalybridge Celtic. He was a utility player and was so valuable for me. He could pass it, tackle, score goals, never moaned whatever position I played him in – just a fantastic lad who was great in the dressing room. He was brave and showed terrific character too. He broke his cheekbone once but never wanted to miss games and just said, 'Get me a mask!' You'd think the mask was there as a joke as he played as if the injury meant nothing to him. He was getting in there with his head and everything – he was so determined. At that level he was a Bryan Robson-type player.

THE ONE THAT GOT AWAY

Steve Morison: Stevenage Borough to Morecambe

He was averaging more than a goal every two games for Stevenage [68 in 127 league games], was scoring goals for fun, so he was of interest in a big way to me and I got to speak to him. I tried to get him but ultimately couldn't pull it off. But he was fair and told me straight, 'I'm a London lad and want to be around London,' which is why he ended up going to Millwall. So there was no time wasted on this one. It was a shame because he was a handful in the non-league scene when Stevenage were doing well. The club also wanted 100 grand for him so that was never going to happen.

I was also keen on Jason Beckford, the brother of Darren, when I was at Macclesfield. I didn't get him in the end because of tragic circumstances with my chairman, Arthur Jones, who took his own life. Beckford came down on a Tuesday night and had a look at us training. I spoke to my chairman and explained that I would really like this player because he has experience and can score goals. He asked me to see him on Thursday to talk it over, but he was dead by then. It really upset me. That was a shock to me and, though the news of losing a personal friend meant much more, one of the side issues was not signing Beckford.

Tottenham manager Keith Burkinshaw seals the audacious double signing of Argentine World Cup winners Ricky Villa (left) and Osvaldo Ardiles in 1978.

Southampton boss Lawrie McMenemy proudly stands with star signing Kevin Keegan (to his immediate right). Keegan scored 30 goals for the Saints in his second season.

Jurgen Klopp has proudly managed Senegal striker Sadio Mane at Anfield, but still regrets not signing him sooner when he had the chance as Borussia Dortmund manager.

Legendary Northern Ireland defender Mal Donaghy (centre) in action for Luton Town. David Pleat regards him the best signing he made in his career, when he joined the Hatters for just £5,000.

Manager Ron Atkinson and chairman Martin Edwards flank England midfielder Bryan Robson after his signing at Old Trafford became the British transfer record at £1.5m in October 1981.

Liverpool legend Emlyn Hughes playing for Wolves after he switched to Molineux, where he won the League Cup as skipper in 1980, the only major trophy he hadn't won at Anfield.

Ron Atkinson rued not being able to sign Gary Lineker (left) from Leicester City. He was a revelation at Everton instead. He did, though, bring Paul McGrath to Manchester United.

Ian Wright was nominated as the best signing of two manager's careers: Steve Coppell took him to Crystal Palace as a rookie; then Stan Ternent signed him for Burnley later in his career.

Three legends: Goalkeeper Nigel Martyn was plucked from the non-league by Gerry Francis on the tip-off of a tea-lady; Didier Drogba might have signed for Sheffield United for £100,000 had Neil Warnock listened to one of his overseas scouts; and Tim Cahill was nominated by David Moyes as his best ever signing.

France great Michel Platini was chased by both Arsenal and Wolverhampton Wanderers when playing for St Etienne, but eventually opted for Juventus.

Barry Fry (manager) sits alongside his greatest signing George Best, who was given special permission to play a fund-raiser for Dunstable Town by Manchester United boss Tommy Docherty.

Mark Hughes rates Belgium legend Vincent Kompany as his greatest signing. The defender remained an important member of the City team long after Hughes departed.

Three of the best: Gareth Southgate (left) was regarded as the best signing by Brian Little and Steve McClaren; ex-Leeds United manager Allan Clarke said David Seaman was his greatest recruit; while Dennis Bergkamp might have ended up at Chelsea had Glenn Hoddle got his way.

Alan Shearer was former Southampton boss Chris Nicholl's number one signing; while David Beckham might have ended up at Norwich City if Ken Brown had not overlooked his talents, before his Manchester United career flourished.

Marvellous: Neil 'Nello' Baldwin was Lou Macari's kitman and dressing room chief entertainer at Stoke City – and subsequently his best-ever signing.

ALEX McLEISH

Managed: Motherwell (1994–1998);
Hibernian (1998–2001); Rangers (2001–
2006); Scotland (2007 & 2018–2019);
Birmingham City (2007–2011); Aston Villa
(2011–2012); Nottingham Forest (2012–
2013); Genk (2014–2015); Zamalek (2016)

MY BIG DEAL

Dado Pršo: Monaco to Rangers on a free transfer in 2004

When you're managing a big club like Rangers, certainly in the time I was there, you naturally follow what is happening around the world and all the big strikers. Who is doing what and where. And Dado was always high up on the agenda in terms of players you'd want to bring to your club. Whether you could do the deal is another matter but he was certainly one player we were very aware of.

We went to watch him playing against Real Madrid in the quarter-finals of the Champions League and it was a real open game and Madrid won 4-2 but Monaco went through [2004, on away goals after the 5-5 aggregate score – Monaco lost to Porto in the final]. Big Dado ran the Madrid defence ragged and he was really impressive. He had already been on our radar in the January transfer window before this match. And we later got to find out when we did speak to him that he had always been keen on Rangers because of the amazing atmosphere he felt at Ibrox when playing there in an earlier Champions League match [in 2000].

My biggest fear actually was that because he was on a free transfer, could Rangers really compete for his signature? I half expected that he would end up in Paris or Turin or somewhere else in Europe as I know for a fact there were clubs from Spain, France and Italy all in for him but he was dogmatic from the start that he was coming to play for Rangers. He couldn't get the Monaco game out of his head from a few years before when the Ibrox atmosphere was electric. So it wasn't a difficult deal to do as it turned out because he was so driven about moving to Rangers. His transfer was a huge present to the fans.

He was a big, swashbuckling centre-forward with a nice touch who brought people into play and he was a goalscorer. He's the best striker I've ever worked with. Dado helped us reach the last 16 of the Champions League in my last season at Rangers and in the games against Porto he ran their defenders into submission. When you bring a player like that into the dressing room it inspires the rest of the team so everyone wants to play above themselves and raise their game by an extra two or three per cent and it gives the whole club a lift at the same time.

There was also big Franck Sauzée, a France international, and the Trinidad & Tobago legend Russell Latapy. They were two of the biggest players that Hibs have ever had so I was pleased with those signings. I signed Mikel Arteta at Rangers before he went on to be a huge success in the Premier League at Everton, and also Jean-Alain Boumsong who I brought to Rangers for nothing. He struggled in England when he went to Newcastle but I told him he was going too early. He should have had another season in Scotland first. Rangers sold him for £8m so the club did very well out of him.

THE ONES THAT GOT AWAY

Andrés Iniesta: Barcelona to Rangers on loan

Gareth Bale: Tottenham to Birmingham City on loan

Moussa Dembélé: AZ Alkmaar to Birmingham City

I rarely had the budget throughout my managerial career to go after the real big household names but you are on occasions presented with an opportunity to sign a player who has the *potential* to become a household name.

I had an opportunity to go for [Andrés] Iniesta when I was at Rangers. Jan Wouters was working with me as my assistant and he was friendly with the coaches inside of Barcelona at the time. Jan had obviously had a terrific career himself, winning the Euros in '88, so his network was pretty strong.

The Barcelona manager then was Frank Rijkaard and his assistant was Henk ten Cate. Jan got on well with Ten Cate and he picked the phone up to him and said, 'Have you got any boys who might be available for a loan, especially a midfielder who can go past a player or two?' Ten Cate told him there was one boy, Iniesta, who was about 18 or 19 at the time, and he explained he probably wasn't going to be ready for the first team for another couple of seasons so he was a possibility.

Jan said he might not thank him for sending the boy to Rangers as he would probably get battered in the Scottish League and return to the Camp Nou with no legs. But Ten Cate was adamant and said, 'Trust me, they won't get near this boy. He will have gone past them ten seconds before they try to bring him down!' So we started to get a bit excited about Iniesta, especially when we noticed with some surprise over that weekend that he had played for Barcelona's first team.

Jan got back on the phone on the Monday morning and Ten Cate said, 'Listen, we've got a problem with the loan. We had a few injuries and the manager threw him in and he came on as sub and was brilliant so he's now been brought into the first-team squad.' The rest is history. That's how close Rangers got to signing Andrés Iniesta!

And when I was at Birmingham City, we had finished ninth and were looking to push on to the next level. I then spoke to the Chinese owners about Moussa Dembélé. I had seen a fair bit of him in Holland and my good friend from Rangers, Arthur Numan, did a bit of scouting work for us over there and he was well aware of him also. I said to Arthur, 'What do you think about Moussa Dembélé? I think we can get him for around the £5m mark.' Arthur said I should take him blind at that price, meaning I didn't even need to watch him, he was such good value.

I didn't waste any time and I invited the player's agent over to St Andrew's to discuss a move. He was then in my car afterwards as I drove him to New Street station and he told me he was happy to take his player to Birmingham because he was not against the idea of using stepping stone clubs to get his players a bigger move and he told me he did the same thing with Ruud van Nistelrooy.

I was OK with that because I know how it works and ultimately if he did go on to a bigger club for ten million it would have meant the player has done a brilliant job for Birmingham and they'd end up doubling their money. Unfortunately, two days later I heard he had signed for Fulham. I don't really know why we lost him but it's probably fair to say that the Birmingham board were not exactly roasting hot on the deal. They didn't really go for it, which was a shame because ultimately they are left to run the club and it should be my business to pick and choose the players.

The other most notable near miss was Gareth Bale who had moved to Tottenham for a lot of money but was struggling a wee bit. He was playing at left-back then and he wasn't really pushing on. I called Harry [Redknapp] and asked him if there was any chance I could take Bale on loan, maybe even with the chance of a permanent move further down the line. He said he would give that some serious thought. But Harry went and played him in the UEFA Cup further forward up the pitch and he was a revelation. After that there was no way he was letting him go to Birmingham!

That's the fine line around transfers. I know from my own career as I heard years after from Terry Neill that he wanted to sign me for Arsenal from Aberdeen. It was probably around the time Willie Young had left Highbury. Terry told me he had a chat with a certain Alex Ferguson. 'Alex we need a defender. What about McLeish?' And Terry said, 'Do you know what Fergie said to me? "Fuck off!"'

LAWRIE McMENEMY

Managed: Bishop Auckland (1964–1967);
Doncaster Rovers (1968–1971); Grimsby Town
(1971–1973); Southampton (1973–1985);
Sunderland (1985–1987); England U21 (1990–
1993); Northern Ireland (1998–1999)

MY BIG DEAL

Kevin Keegan: Hamburg to Southampton for
£420,000 in 1980

I read in the paper that Kevin was linked to Real Madrid
and Barcelona and that's what got me thinking as I then
realised he may well be leaving Hamburg. Around that
early stage in proceedings I thought of an excuse to call
the Liverpool chief executive Peter Robinson and I said
casually in the conversation, 'I hear Kevin might be leaving
Hamburg. Would you have him back?' I only asked as
I'd heard Liverpool had first option on him and I needed
to know I wasn't wasting my time here. Peter said quite
definitively, 'No, we wouldn't.'

So that was the first potential obstacle overcome. I still
had the *small* matter of attracting the European Footballer of
the Year for the past two seasons to little old Southampton,
but I was up for the challenge. About this time I was
building my house and in a conversation with the architect
he happened to mention that I had a slight problem because
the only place I could get the type of light fitting we needed
to hang above my staircase was made in Germany. I said,
'Oh aye, Germany?' He said, 'Yes, Hamburg to be precise.'
Again, I said, 'Really, Hamburg? Interesting.' So that was
another twist of fate.

I found out about this company and used this as the perfect excuse to call Kevin after discreetly getting his number from someone. I'm not sure how well he knew of me then but anyway I called him and explained about my light fitting and asked if he wouldn't mind bringing it over with him the next time he returned for an England international. He said it wasn't a problem. I then followed that conversation with a succession of calls, each time about the light but gradually I brought in football talk and I asked him if it was true that he was leaving Germany. He kind of confirmed it. I mentioned that he was being linked with the big Spanish clubs and that given he's got a baby it might be prudent for him to move nearer home.

In another call after that I finally said, 'Kevin, how would feel about coming back to England?' If he would have said 'no way' that would have been the end of it, but he was very receptive. So I said, 'How about coming to Southampton? We're on the up, I've already got Bally and Mick Channon,' who he knew. 'Tell you what Kevin, you're coming back soon for the England match. How about we meet up and I'll take the light off you and we can talk football and Southampton?' So we made arrangements to meet.

I hadn't told anybody by this stage, not even my chairman. But as I'd arranged to meet Kevin on this Sunday before the England international, I needed to tell someone so I told our finance director who was also my neighbour and accountant. He couldn't believe it. I swore him to secrecy and told him to accompany me for the meeting and asked him to source a private meeting place, which he did in central London.

Kevin arrived on his own before he met up with England that evening. We spoke money and we found out that there was a fixed transfer clause if anyone wanted to buy him out of his contract at Hamburg, which was about £400,000.

That was unbelievably cheap when you think that nearly every club in the league had their best gate against us just because they wanted to see Keegan and in those days we were getting a share of the gate. And I seem to recall we doubled the price of season tickets as we hadn't put prices up for a while and the fans at The Dell were clamouring for season tickets when they heard about Keegan.

So we were exchanging small talk when I finally gave him the big sell that we play good football and we're ambitious. And he turned round and said, 'Have you got a contract?' Fortunately my finance director had a blank one in his brief case. Kevin signed it there and then, with no financial information or dates on it.

He trusted us to do the right thing by him, which we did. I said, 'Bloody hell Kevin, I can't believe that.' He said, 'Before you say anymore, I've got to tell you something – I forgot to bring your light!' I said, 'Stuff the light!' We had a chuckle and went our separate ways. Can you imagine how smug I was when he played for England three nights later when I sat in the stands and was probably the only one in the stadium apart from Kevin who knew he was coming to Southampton?

He went back to Germany and told Hamburg he was leaving and we eventually announced the news in England publicly, but it wasn't any old press conference. I arranged the media to come along to the Potters Heron Hotel and Restaurant in Romsey but I didn't tell them what it was all about. I just said, 'Make sure you're there as you will have some big news to report on.'

Nobody had a clue and when Kevin eventually walked in you could feel the collective gasp in the room. Somehow we had managed to pull off the transfer of the best player in Europe [with Keegan still in his prime aged 29] without anyone finding out. He was fabulous for me, scoring 30 goals in his second season, so he was comfortably my best signing by a mile.

Alan Ball was another one, after I took him off Arsenal. I made him captain and he helped get us promoted to the top flight in his second season. That League Cup Final against Forest in 1979 was his bonus as he honestly never expected another taste of a cup final when he signed. Yes, he was nearer the end of his career than the start, but he was still one of the best footballers I've ever worked with and anyone who met him couldn't help but love him.

Peter Osgood coming to us began the upward curve at Southampton, when I was able to start attracting the bigger names who gave us more quality and experience. Ossie had fallen out with Dave Sexton at Chelsea and therefore I was able to bring him in. He was such a good influence on the younger lads. And there were others like Peter Shilton, Dave Watson, Mick Mills, Russell Osman, Charlie George and more. They all made an impact at some point.

Shilts was a massive signing but I don't remember there being a big queue for him. In fact I'd agreed to sign his England team-mate Ray Clemence first. Clem looked like he was coming but he ended up going to Tottenham so I switched my attention to Shilton after Cloughy asked me if I wanted him. He was totally focused. After an away game on the team bus, the lads would be at the back playing cards but Shilts would often be up front with me talking about the game and where we could improve. He was great in the five years we had him. I only went for a new keeper after a conversation with John Lyall, who told me that Phil Parkes was worth 15 points a season to him. I then thought, 'Right, fair comment, I need a top keeper!'

David Armstrong, too, wasn't a big name but one of the best left-sided players around and was a terrific signing from Middlesbrough.

THE ONES THAT GOT AWAY

Trevor Francis: Manchester City to Southampton

Colin Todd: Everton to Southampton

Man City's manager at the time was John Bond, who was an old pal of mine. In my head I was thinking we could win the title and Trevor was going to be the last cog in the wheel. I had the deal done and he was coming but at the last minute John called me to say, 'Sorry but the chairman is stopping it.' That was it.

I reflected on it afterwards and I felt John, bless him, didn't want me to win the league for whatever reason. Chairmen very rarely stop a transfer because they want the money and I believe Man City were not in great financial health at that time so they would have been happy to get Trevor off their wage bill. It was a huge blow because, off memory, Kevin was still with us and Francis would have been the icing on the cake. But as it happened, Trevor ended up going to Sampdoria in Italy and we lost Kevin around that time, too, to Newcastle.

Trevor was the biggest name I missed out on on but Colin Todd would be equal to him. He wasn't the typical big, strapping defender I had with Chris Nicholl and later with Dave Watson, who were both fantastic defenders, of course, but Colin played in a different way. Toddy came down to Southampton with his family and we met at a local hotel I think it was. I explained why I wanted to sign him and where he would fit in and he looked very keen. But I remember his missus saying, 'It's a long way down here isn't it?' As soon as she said that I knew I was struggling.

I explained to her how lovely it is and once anyone moves here their family and friends always want to visit and they'd want to stay here after their career. But I lost him and he ended up going to Birmingham City. That's when I turned to big Dave Watson as he was keen to leave Germany.

Ray Clemence was another near miss, as I mentioned, but I didn't lose too many though. It looked like I was going to lose Mick Mills when he was on the motorway driving up to sign for Sunderland from Ipswich, but I managed to persuade the police to turn him around and head to Southampton, to sign!

GARY MEGSON

Managed: Norwich City (1995–1996); Blackpool (1996–1997); Stockport County (1997–1999); Stoke City (1999); West Bromwich Albion (2000– 2004 & 2017); Nottingham Forest (2005–2006); Leicester City (2007); Bolton Wanderers (2007– 2009); Sheffield Wednesday (2011–2012)

MY BIG DEAL

Gary Cahill: Aston Villa to Bolton for £5m in 2008

The best would have been Gary Cahill. We took him from Aston Villa reserves, but he wasn't just a reserve player. He'd played 20-odd games for the first team and he'd been on loan at one or two clubs. But we wanted to buy him at Bolton. I had an idea of what I thought we'd have to pay and I was thinking a couple of million. Then the price started to go up, as he got England under-21 caps. He wasn't established and he wasn't the complete player yet but he was proceeding as a player and eventually the price was set at £5m.

You've got to back your own judgement, and the chairman, Phil Gartside, said do you want to do it or not? I thought Cahill was decent, but five million quid was a lot of money at the time. But it was a case of if we don't sign Gary Cahill who are we going to sign? It'd be the same thing, a young player to progress and who is going to sell for a few quid. So, I said go on, let's do it. Thankfully we did do it and Cahill did really well for me and did really well for Bolton and then moved down to Chelsea and had a great career.

When you are at that level and buying players you always think you paid too much. It's afterwards you realise it's a decent deal. Especially when you are going for younger players, you always think, 'Crikey, we've had to pay too much.' Then it's down to how well they do whether it's too much or not. It wasn't just the money, he was a real good player, he's a good lad as well, one of those you're pleased he's done well and you wanted him to. A good pro.

I don't think it was so much a surprise that Villa were letting Cahill go because they were a team doing well in the Premier League. Martin O'Neill was the manager and he would have his own ideas, I don't know, but all the time you make the decision for the team and your club and I'm guessing Gary wouldn't have been included in the team at that time. Our selling point at Bolton was obviously we are nowhere near as big a club as Villa but we could guarantee him first-team football. That was the difference.

If you put yourself in Martin's shoes you're thinking it's five million that we bring in, if we turn it down we are going to have a player who might want to be playing first-team football and we can't guarantee him that. Cahill still wasn't easy to persuade, though. It was Bolton after all and his agent, quite rightly, is telling him he needs to look at other things, the other clubs interested. He didn't sign straight away, he took a day to think it over but I'm guessing we must have done a decent job on him.

He probably saw us as a stepping stone. Looking at it from his point of view, what I'd have thought if I'd been in his shoes, would be, 'I'm an England under-21 international and I've not had a great opportunity anywhere yet,' even though Bolton was a much smaller club than Aston Villa to move to. The opportunity was there. He came in and we managed to stay up and we pushed it on a little bit. Then Gary left for Chelsea a few years after I left.

But once he did sign for Bolton there was none of that 'I'm a big fish in a small pond' attitude, he really got stuck into it, did everything well and was popular with the supporters and his team-mates. He was obviously a top player, too. He was quick, decent on the ball, good in the air. I used to say to him at the time, 'The only difference between you and John Terry is that he's louder than you. He commands performances from his team-mates.' I told him he needed to add that to his game. He did eventually do that. But Gary was never brash, he was never loud. The big thing that we were really pleased with was that he started becoming a big threat in terms of goals scored. For a centre-half he got quite a few goals.

Bolton later got their five million pounds' worth without a doubt. They stayed up and he became the main man. Arsenal watched every single game he played after we'd stayed up. In the end Arsenal didn't take him, but Chelsea did [for £7m].

THE ONE THAT GOT AWAY

Tim Sherwood: Portsmouth to West Bromwich Albion on a free transfer

There weren't that many actually. I'd like to think I was pretty pragmatic, we wouldn't go for people you just had no chance of signing. But the one I was most disappointed in was at West Brom. I'd got Tim Sherwood. I'd spoken to him on the phone, got him to come to the ground for talks. It was a training day so I met him at nine o'clock. He came with his agent, Eric Hall, who is a lad himself. Good bloke, really funny.

The two of them turned up at half past nine at The Hawthorns. We'd spoken and Tim wanted to come. We put him and Eric in one of the boxes overlooking the pitch. I never got involved with the finances or the talks or anything like that, I just had the players and spoke to them in terms of football. I thought Tim Sherwood would be a good fit for the club. Anyway, I left him at half past nine in one of those glass boxes and went back at half past 12 after training.

I went into the box to see how it had gone and the chairman, Jeremy Peace, never turned up. He just left them. Didn't talk to them. He knew Tim Sherwood was there. He didn't want to sign him, obviously. So, it never got done. It just showed us in a really bad light because it was rude and ignorant. And it showed the manager wanting to do one thing, with the chairman not doing it. Not only that, rather than discussing it, it was taken out on the player.

In the end I went in, embarrassed. They were still there, three hours on, waiting. I don't think they'd been given a cup of tea or anything. Eric was fuming. Not with me, but he was fuming as you would expect and I said to him I can only apologise. I said I can only be honest, if I was you I wouldn't come because obviously they don't want you to. It was a really strange situation. It was a bad thing because the club had a lot of positives and Tim would have been a good signing for us, but to treat somebody of that ilk like that was really poor.

It's not even a 'one that got away', as we pushed him away, which was ridiculous. Tim had been around for the best part of 20 years and must have thought he'd seen it all. If I was him, though, I don't think I'd have stayed there for three hours! In the end, I said to Tim, 'If I was you I'd go to another club.' That episode stuck in my throat for a while.

GORDON MILNE

*Managed: Wigan Athletic (1970–1972); England
U18 (1972–1974); Coventry City (1972–1981);
Leicester City (1982–1986); Beşiktaş (1987–1994);
Grampus Eight (1994); Bursaspor (1996–1997);
Trabzonspor (1998–1999)*

MY BIG DEAL

Mark Hateley: Youth to professional at Coventry
City in 1978

It's hard to single players out as, throughout my time at
Coventry, I made quite a few influential signings because
we never had any money to spend and were therefore always
looking for kids to join us who could develop into top players.
That lack of money helped in a way because it meant I never
had the chance to waste money and we had to be prudent
with whatever funds we did have.

Mark Hateley, Garry Thompson and Ian Wallace were
three of my best, though, and were strikers who all scored
goals for me. Hateley's subsequent achievements abroad would
place him as my top recruit given what he did with Milan and
Monaco, not discounting his international career [33 caps].
And he also had a fine swansong at Rangers. Thompson was
a handful and Wallace was prolific but neither went on to do
what Mark did. Mark was good in the air but not as strong as
Garry Thompson or as good aerially as Mick Ferguson but
he was quick for a big lad and was athletic.

It was interesting how I managed to recruit him. My
number two at the time was Ron Wylie, who had played
with Mark's dad, Tony, at Aston Villa and Tony respected
Ron. Liverpool were in for Mark big time and was obviously
a bigger stage than Coventry but Tony recognised that his

lad would be given a better opportunity to impress with us than at Anfield when they had such fine players then in the late 1970s. Ron and Tony used to talk a lot so Tony knew his boy would be well looked after with us than get caught up in a big club like Liverpool and not get the care he needed. Mark was a quiet lad and we were happy to put an arm around his shoulder.

There was another link in the chain also as, when I left Liverpool, Tony was on his way to Anfield and he bought my house. I still remember when he came round to take a look at the house, he brought Mark with him and he was running all over the garden and the bloody flowerbeds, but it did mean we struck up a rapport from there, which helped when we came in for Mark years later.

Strikers always get the limelight but I was also proud to bring in Danny Thomas, Gary Gillespie from Falkirk and I also signed Gary McAllister as a kid at Leicester from Motherwell and he combined superbly with Alan Smith and Gary Lineker. It's one thing signing a top player but unless you have others to complement that player you will never get the best out of him. So I always tried to add enough quality to help the good players I already had.

THE ONE THAT GOT AWAY

Trevor Francis: Birmingham City to Coventry City

Trevor was easily the biggest one that got away from me. The Birmingham manager at the time was Jim Smith and Jim was a big pal of mine and I came to know that Trevor was going to go and the price would be £1m, which was a huge amount of money in those days. There were no agents then and deals were always done through discussions between manager to manager; even chairmen didn't get involved that much but our chairman Jimmy Hill also knew Jim Smith. We were going to push the boat out after Jimmy Hill had got the Coventry City board to agree the fee.

People may ask how could little Coventry afford that kind of fee – good question! We didn't have the money but we would have raised it as there was always interest in players like Wallace, Ferguson and the rest. But it wasn't to be anyway, when Cloughy [Brian Clough] came in at the death and Nottingham Forest appealed more to Trevor than Coventry – and rightly so. But that deal was very close to being done. Jimmy was a great persuader and he had convinced Trevor that Coventry was a good move for him and another stepping stone towards him going higher in his career. Curiously Jimmy took Trevor to Detroit Express not long after so his recruitment efforts were not totally in vain!

DAVID MOYES

Managed: Preston North End (1998–2002);
Everton (2002–2013); Manchester United
(2013–2014); Real Sociedad (2014–2015);
Sunderland (2016–2017); West Ham United
(2017–2018 & 2019–)

MY BIG DEAL

Tim Cahill: Millwall to Everton for £1.5m in 2004

After long deliberation, I selected Tim Cahill. It's for lots of reasons. I'd been a Championship manager before I got the job at Everton and I had seen Cahill play quite a lot for Millwall.

I took the Everton chairman, Bill Kenwright, with me to Millwall to watch Tim play. Millwall at that time had several good players, a bundle of them. We drove to Millwall in the chairman's Jag and the car was getting thumped by the supporters.

But we got there and what I saw in Cahill was his great attitude to football, his effort, all the things you need in a good player. He wanted to improve, to climb the ladder and he had a lot that he could develop.

Later on, we got Tim to come to Bill's office. I liked Cahill as a player but I didn't know how good he was going to become. Bill was a good judge of character and he loved Tim's charisma, his personality, which Cahill has gone on to show at every club and everywhere he's been.

Coming from Millwall to Everton he had a big jump to make, he had to prove he could become a Premier League player and he went on to do that. Tim was a real tough boy as well. He got better and better for us at Everton and became a key player, a key member of the dressing room, very much involved with the improvement Everton were showing at that time. We relied on him because he was so hard-working. He would pop up with the goals, always a regular goalscorer for us.

Tim was great to work with, a very hard worker. Over the years at Everton, he scored goals in most of the big games. He made his debut for us away to Manchester United in about the fourth game of the 2004/05 season and played well in a 0-0 draw.

In his next game Cahill scored his first goal for Everton, a header from Tony Hibbert's cross, away to Manchester City. He took his top off in celebration and got sent off by referee Steve Bennett within a minute!

Cahill was a big help in where we were going at Everton. He made a huge impact when we were trying to change a lot of things, change the age of the group, for instance, bring in different types of personalities.

Tim coming from the Championship and being such a success, that led to the door opening to other people like Phil Jagielka, Leighton Baines and Joleon Lescott thinking they could do it too. It was a period of growth, not just for the club but for those players as individuals going on to become internationals.

It's a difficult choice when you have signed a lot of players to just pick out one, but I just think Cahill's impact, the price, one and a half million, where we got him from, his longevity at Everton [2004–2012, 226 games, 58 goals] – that's the reason I selected him.

I don't know if there were that many clubs chasing Cahill at the time. He wasn't that well-known. But he was a terrific header of the ball, he was great in both boxes.

It was a little bit between whether he was a midfield player or was he an attacker? It was a difficult one to work out. He was probably a little bit of a number ten really.

If asked he could play as a nine as well. He did that for Australia at different times.

Tim is the sort of lad who would fly with Australia, play on a Wednesday night in a game for them, and be back with us and want to play on a Saturday. He was that way and it never looked as if it had any effect on him at all.

That takes some doing. We'd let him get some sleep quickly and then see if Tim could play on the Saturday, which he nearly always did.

I could easily have said goalkeeper Nigel Martyn, he could easily have been my best signing from Leeds United to Everton because we got him for no money. Louis Saha was magnificent for me at Everton for five years.

But I pick Tim because he had a great career for his country and scored goals in World Cups and played on nearly all the continents.

He's a highly acclaimed young man and was a really good footballer for me.

THE ONE THAT GOT AWAY

Toni Kroos: Bayern Munich to Manchester United for £25m in 2014

I think he *would* have been my best-ever signing.

I had agreed to sign Toni Kroos for Man United from Bayern Munich before I lost my job at United in the April, just before the end of the 2013/14 season. He would have joined us in the summer. But when I left, he then chose to go to Real Madrid. He was my biggest miss as a manager. I would have loved to have worked with him.

I saw Kroos in a Paul Scholes mould. Scholes had been such an unbelievable passer of the ball for Manchester United and I saw Kroos, such an incredible passer himself, coming in and being the equivalent of Scholes. Kroos would have been terrific.

I met him and his wife at their house in Germany, with my wife Pamela. We spent some time there with them and had a cup of tea as we talked. Kroos was leaving Bayern Munich and, as far as I was concerned, he was joining Manchester United.

I'd watched him at Wembley playing for Germany against England and I felt he was the best midfield player on show and certainly the best passer. I had known about him before and watched him quite a lot, but that game, that sort of triggered it for me to try and get him.

When I left, I think it changed Toni's view on where he was going to go. Real Madrid were quoted as then paying €30m for him.

Carlo Ancelotti signed him for Real on a six-year deal and look what he's won there, two La Liga titles and the Champions League three times. Plus winning the World Cup with Germany of course in 2014.

There are loads of players that got away, many others that I could mention. It's a difficult question for managers because we all have a bundle of 'nearly signings' – the ones that we think we had, but then didn't.

But that Kroos one, that would have been a great fit for Manchester United.

ALAN MULLERY

Managed: Brighton & Hove Albion (1976–
1981 & 1986–1987); Charlton Athletic (1981–
1982); Crystal Palace (1982–1984); Queens
Park Rangers (1984); ATM FA (1990–1993);
Barnet (1996–1997)

MY BIG DEAL

Mark Lawrenson: Preston North End to Brighton & Hove Albion for £100,000 in 1977

I am very proud of the squad we assembled at Brighton. The fact we achieved promotion to the top flight for the first time in the club's history says it all. And when they were relegated after I had left, they never returned until 35 years later. I had some fine players but the best of the lot was Mark Lawrenson.

I only saw him play a couple of times before I signed him. He marked Peter Ward against us and, although Peter scored in a 1-1 draw, apart from that he never had a kick courtesy of Lawrenson's marking and pace. Soon after that I got on the phone to Nobby Stiles who was coaching there, while Harry Catterick was manager. I told him I wanted to buy Lawrenson. 'You're too late mate, Liverpool are going to sign him,' Nobby said.

I told my chairman that it was off but, refusing to give up on it, he said maybe it wasn't and we could still have a go until the ink was dry on a contract with Liverpool. So the next morning in the chairman's office we got on the phone to Harry Catterick and bid £50,000. That wasn't enough as Liverpool were paying £75,000. We increased our offer to £100,000 with £50,000 up front. Preston went back to

Liverpool and they refused to pay any more so he was our player. Yet it still nearly didn't happen!

Mark came down to our place for his medical and, after two or three hours, our medic came to me and said, 'You can't sign him, he's got sugar diabetes.' He said he never drank apart from the odd Guinness. But after some investigation I found that he was quite partial to Ribena and had just sunk a load of the stuff, undiluted. So there was the logical explanation and we signed him.

He had four good years with us and was wonderful among a strong Brighton team with guys like Brian Horton, Gordon Smith, Steve Foster, Andy Ritchie, Michael Robinson, John Gregory and others. But while Mark was the best signing I ever made, he was also the reason I left Brighton.

I knew we were not going to be able to hang on to a player of his quality long-term. It was almost a weekly ritual to receive three or four phone calls every Friday from managers who wanted to sign Mark Lawrenson. So when Ron Atkinson came in with an offer of £1m to take him to West Bromwich Albion I knew it was a great deal for the club and a step up for the player as West Brom had a top side in those days.

At the time I looked after the wages, signing-on fees, sales, everything connected to the team, my fingerprints were all over it and that's how I liked it. But that suddenly changed when I told the chairman I had agreed a fee of £1m with Ron for Lawrenson. He said, 'He's not going to West Brom because he's going to Liverpool.' Even though I told him he could have the £400,000 in the bank that he wanted as long as I had £600,000 to spend on the team, it still didn't make any difference. He thought he was going to get more, obviously, but it backfired as he went to Liverpool for £900,000.

THE ONE THAT GOT AWAY
No one (because I had a little trick that always worked)

Every player I tried to get, I got. I used to play a little trick that never failed. If I was meeting a player with a view to signing him, I would always ensure he brought his family down, or just the wife. So often it is the player's other half who has the real influence on whether they move to another club or not so I wanted to make sure the wife was always taken care of.

We had this limousine at Brighton that would take me to games for scouting and such like. So when a player and his wife would arrive for transfer talks, I would ask the driver to take the player's wife out shopping for a couple of hours and make sure he showed her all the nice houses in the area. I'd say, 'Don't come back for at least three hours.' I remember when I signed Eric Potts from Sheffield Wednesday, he was keen to join us but delayed signing until he spoke to his wife. Then as soon as she arrived back at the ground and was told it wasn't yet done, she said, 'Where do we sign!'

PHIL NEAL

Managed: Bolton Wanderers (1985–1992);
Coventry City (1992–1995); Cardiff City (1996);
Manchester City (1996)

MY BIG DEALS

Alan Stubbs: Free to Bolton Wanderers in 1990

Jason McAteer: Marine to Bolton Wanderers for £500 in 1992

I find it impossible to choose who was my better signing out of Alan Stubbs and Jason McAteer. They were two terrific footballers whose respective transfers to Celtic and Liverpool ended up netting Bolton around £8.5m so I like to think it shows I know a thing or two about spotting a player. That money significantly helped fund the new ground when they went to the Reebok. It was just unfortunate, for me, that I never got to see Stubbsy or Jason blossom at Bolton as that happened once I had left, though I did manage Stubbsy longer than Jason. It was no surprise to me when they each continued to have magnificent careers.

In terms of the specifics of both signings, I used to gather a group of lads who had missed the scouting net for whatever reason at Liverpool and Everton and give them a run out in a trial match. We would take them over to our old ground at Burnden Park and have a look at them. That was how we came across Stubbsy. He thought he was a centre-forward at that time but I converted him into a centre-back. He had great feet and while he considered himself a striker I just saw a player in the mould of Alan Hansen who, like Stubbs, was a reluctant defender and capable of going on a sortie but was a good defender at the same time with good pace.

Jason was different in that he was at Marine, the Northern Premier League club in Liverpool, but was only playing in their reserves at the time, though he was still quite young at about 20. I spotted him first when their reserves played against Bolton's A team. I used to like to watch those games as I felt it was a good way of spotting talent. He had totally missed the scouting net but I just saw something in him that I liked, especially his energy. I wanted a right midfielder with good legs in front of our right-back Phil Brown, who was a good, experienced pro, and Jason fitted the bill perfectly.

When it got round to doing the deal, I invited the long-serving Marine manager Roly Howard out to lunch at a restaurant on the Formby bypass. As all good non-league managers would do, Roly quickly tried to get Jason to sign a contract so that Marine could command a decent fee off us. But I was one step ahead of him and had already spoken to Jason's mum and I had asked her to ensure that her boy did not sign any contracts before he agreed a deal with Bolton. Thankfully, Jason must have listened to her!

Although Jason was a non-contract player and we had every right to sign him for nothing, I did not wish to be a total minge-bag so I told Roly that we could provide Marine with £500 of goalposts, footballs, bibs and such like. We kitted out their club so they at least had something to show for losing Jason to us. We also paid Jason a £600 signing-on fee.

The other one I was pleased to get hold of was Dion Dublin after I somehow persuaded Fergie that Dion was too good to be surplus to requirements at Old Trafford and that he should sell him to us at Coventry City. We picked him up for £2m but the club more than doubled their money on him when they sold him to Villa later on [for £5.75m]. He was great for me. He had this leadership quality about him and it was a no-brainer that I made him my captain as soon as he walked through the door. He was comfortable with it and conducted himself perfectly like a great captain and leader of a football team should do.

THE ONE THAT GOT AWAY
No one

I can't think of one that I missed out on. I always scouted players many times before I signed someone and I usually got the players I wanted. I used to talk to the former head scout at Liverpool, Geoff Twentyman, who spotted me and was instrumental in me signing for Liverpool. He told me that he watched me 23 times and that 22 of those occasions were away games because you only find out about a player's character when he is away from home. So with that advice in my head, when I became a manager I generally had a clear idea of who I wanted and usually got my targets. There might have been the odd exception, though!

JOHN NEWMAN

Managed: Exeter City (1969–1976); Grimsby
Town (1976–1979); Derby County (1982);
Hereford United (1983–1987)

MY BIG DEAL

Tony Ford: Youth to professional at Grimsby Town

Tony came to Grimsby as a 16-year-old and was actually one of the first black players in the English game. He had already made his debut at the club when I came in from Exeter but he was only on a short-term contract and I think it's fair to say there were a few doubts about him as he was a rookie and some people at the club were not too sure about him.

But I could tell straight away that the kid really had something and I had no hesitation in securing his future and tying him to the club on a more long-term basis. Tony came through at the same time as some other good players like Terry Donovan, who I sold to Aston Villa, Kevin Drinkell, who went on to become a legend at Norwich and also played at Rangers, and Kevin Moore, who played at Grimsby for ten years. But for me, Tony was the pick of them all.

He had pace to burn, his skill levels were more natural and better than most, he knew where the goal was and he just got people out of their seats, which is an asset you don't see much of nowadays. Tony could play right wing or striker but I liked him as a striker. The fact he went on to play in over 1,000 games shows you how fit he was and he would have had his fair share of kicks over the years but he was too quick for most defenders! He was on the better side of brilliant and went on to have a good career at bigger clubs like West Brom and Stoke. He might have been unlucky not to have achieved more in terms of playing for even bigger clubs and winning trophies. As a character you couldn't meet a nicer lad in your life.

I was also pleased to have played a major part in the signing of Kevin Wilson, from non-league club Banbury to Derby County. I spotted him during a testimonial game. He stood out a mile and I recommended him to the manager Colin Addison. He said, 'Would you sign him if you were me?' I said, 'I'd sign him now.' We brought him over for a trial and he scored a hat-trick for our reserves against the first team and that was his deal done, for £20,000. Kevin had a terrific touch and was a great finisher as his goals per game ratio would demonstrate.

THE ONE THAT GOT AWAY

Bobby Davison: Halifax Town to Derby County

He was at Halifax Town when I went there as Derby manager and he really stood out. He impressed me so much that I spoke to their manager after the game, Mickey Bullock, and made an offer right away [£80,000], which was accepted.

Unfortunately, I was sacked by the club not long after, before he actually joined us. Therefore, while he ended up being a huge success for Derby, scoring over 100 goals before he moved to Leeds for a much bigger fee [£350,000], to me he will always feel like the one that got away because I spotted him yet never actually got to work with him, which was a shame because I rated him highly.

TERRY NEILL

*Managed: Hull City (1970–1974); Northern
Ireland (1971–1975 part-time); Tottenham
Hotspur (1974–1976); Arsenal (1976–1983)*

MY BIG DEAL

Pat Jennings: Tottenham to Arsenal for £40,000 in 1977

It is difficult to single out one player but the one who I
should have been locked up for signing is Pat Jennings. I
played with Pat for Northern Ireland for years and also
managed him at Tottenham. Pat was only 32 when I signed
him but in those days you were considered over the hill if
you were past 30. Tottenham were also excited about Barry
Daines coming through so I went and took Pat. You always
remember key events and this signing was a key event. I
signed Pat for 40 grand at 9.30 on a Wednesday morning
and sold Jimmy Rimmer to Aston Villa for 95 grand at 12.30
the same day.

I gave Pat a four-year contract and there was a fair bit
of nudge-nudge, wink-wink going on as people thought it
was a deal borne out of an old pals' act. But Pat was still in
the first team eight years later! So much for the old pals'
act! Bob Wilson was our goalkeeping coach. Out of respect
for him I went round to his house the night before of the
announcement to let him know about Pat's arrival. Bob said,
'What do you expect me to do with him?' I said, 'Just keep
him happy.' Bob knew there was little he could teach him.
It was a no-brainer of a deal.

Alan Sunderland was another of my best signings. I was
scouting him playing for Wolves and he was being played
at right-back. I knew he was never a full-back. I felt he
was a forward with pace, sharpness, a great touch and good

passing ability, so I signed him without any competition. He did great for me.

I also have to give a special mention to Don Howe, who wasn't a player signing for me but was a fantastic first-team coach. Don was a team-mate and a room-mate of mine when we were at Arsenal in the 1960s, but after our playing careers finished we were temporarily separated. I became manager of Hull and then Tottenham, while Don took over at West Brom before a few other jobs.

I brought Don back to Arsenal after I became manager. People called him my number two but I never thought of him like that. We were joined at the hip. We had the same positive outlook on football and thought along the same lines so to me it was a partnership. Don wasn't at his happiest when dealing with all the other things managers have to do like the media side, liaising with the board or sorting out players' contracts. I didn't mind those things so we dovetailed very well and it allowed Don to concentrate on what he did best, which was to be out on the training ground coaching players.

I did my fair share of coaching and when Don was away with England I took all the sessions and we knew we were preaching the same message as we lived out of each other's pockets. We were a great combination and had absolute trust in each other, bouncing ideas off one another about tactics and players.

Don was a great coach, very innovative with his tactics at Arsenal when I was still a player and back with me again in the 1970s and 1980s, and also in his role with Bobby Robson and the England team. I used to get very angry when Don was called a defensive coach because 80 per cent of everything we did was geared towards attacking football. I would invite all the media to attend our training sessions. We had nothing to hide and if journalists were prepared to leave their warm offices and come out and watch us train or have lunch with us and talk about our philosophies they would have known Don was anything but a defensive coach. Of course defending is still a vital part of the game and, yes, we worked on defensive routines but that wasn't our main focus.

THE ONES THAT GOT AWAY

Michel Platini: Saint-Étienne to Arsenal

Diego Maradona: Boca Juniors to Arsenal

Hugo Sánchez: UNAM to Arsenal

Zbigniew Boniek: Widzew Łódź to Arsenal

Frank Arnesen: Ajax to Arsenal

Johan Cruyff: Ajax to Tottenham

How can I single one of these guys out?

I think every manager has a few of these stories. I had to start rebuilding having lost Liam [Brady, to Juventus in 1980] and then Frank Stapleton [to Manchester United in 1981] and I was intent on signing the best quality in the world. They all happened between 1980 and 1982 when we were going through a mini transition. I could have pushed the boat out and signed two of these players and we tried our damnedest, but they just didn't get over the line. That's how good Liam was, that we were looking at these types of players to replace him. The two who came closest to signing were Hugo Sánchez and Frank Arnesen.

Don and I went to see Michel Platini over in France and tried to talk him into joining us from Saint-Étienne. I think his wife had a big say and he chose in the end to go to Juventus, ironically to replace Liam Brady, who had moved on to Sampdoria.

I was also in very serious talks with Maradona. I knew I had to replace Liam Brady, which was nigh-on impossible but I never stopped trying. We did our best to keep Liam and offered to make him the best-paid player in the Football League but he wanted to test himself in Europe, which I understood. We had first option to buy him back if things didn't go well for him but I knew that would never be the case, as it proved. So two years after Liam left us, I tried to bring Maradona to the Arsenal – but he ended up at Barcelona.

Another who would have been superb for us after I lost Liam was Frank Arnesen after he left Ajax. He scored a lot of goals from midfield for Ajax and would have fitted in perfectly at Arsenal. He was a great leader, his football philosophy was the same as mine and after Ken Friar and I went to Copenhagen to spend a day with him and his agent I thought it was a done deal. But he ended up going to Valencia.

It's interesting that his family have more Arsenal stuff than the Arsenal club shop and when I see him now he says to me, 'Why didn't you sign me?' Well, we tried bloody hard, but couldn't match what Valencia were prepared to pay him. It was a shame as he would have been a driving force for us in midfield and, who knows, maybe even helped us win the league. But you lose some and you win some.

The Hugo Sánchez deal was also close to getting done in 1981. He was an established Mexican international by then, in the early '80s. I went down to Mexico and spent a couple of weeks with him and one of his coaches over there. He was a smashing lad, but he signed for Atlético Madrid in the end and then sometime after I left Arsenal he moved on to Real Madrid and was a sensation there [scoring 164 goals 207 league games], so that was another hard luck story.

I was chasing Boniek as well and spent many hours in the Polish Embassy in London trying to see if they could influence a move on our behalf. Again, we lost him to Juventus at the same time that we lost Platini to Juve. Italy had won the World Cup that year, in 1982, so Italy was the country for the best players to be and we couldn't compete.

Wages were more even in those days but we still had to box clever and we tried to fund some of these kinds of deals through sponsorships. In fact, when I was at Tottenham I went to Amsterdam to spend a day with Johan Cruyff. We had just escaped relegation in my first season and I never wanted to be in that position again. But despite our best efforts we couldn't tempt Cruyff to White Hart Lane and a year after I left he went to Barcelona, who I think had probably long been in his ear. People talk about players going for money now but it was no different in those days either. It's a short career so why not? I understand why players should want to do the best for themselves.

CHRIS NICHOLL

Managed: Southampton (1985–1991); Walsall
(1994–1997)

MY BIG DEAL

Alan Shearer: Youth to professional at Southampton in 1987

It's funny how you can make signings for big money, or at least relative to the years we are talking about, yet my best signing was a kid who cost us nothing. I signed Alan Shearer as a 16-year-old schoolboy before he came through the ranks at Southampton. Lawrie McMenemy was instrumental in setting up satellite academies around the country and we were then able to handpick the best talent they attracted and Shearer was such an example. To sign him ahead of Newcastle United when he was brought up in Newcastle and was a Newcastle fan was a surprise but we managed to get him, which was a bit of a coup. I don't know why he chose Southampton over Newcastle – maybe he saw us as a better route to first-team football and getting noticed?

His ability was clear to me. I know my assistant Ray Graydon wasn't so sure about Shearer at first when he saw him in the reserves but I just spotted something. We used to have this huge gym at The Dell with goals marked up in there and we'd bring the young kids in on the afternoons after the first team had left. I always tried to watch the young lads if the first team wasn't preparing for an away game. I saw youth development and bringing the kids through as much a part of my job as looking after the first team.

We used to practise finishing skills in that gym and I could see from the age of 16 that Shearer had something special about him. So it should not then have come as any shock when I gave him his full first-team debut against

Arsenal at The Dell and he scored a hat-trick. From there on, we all knew what we had. He was driven, had tremendous mental strength and would not accept being second to anyone. Those were the qualities that put him ahead of Matt Le Tissier. Shearer just got better and it was a shame we lost him after three years but we were a selling club and couldn't say no to Blackburn, who were spending a lot of money at that time.

Shearer was the best of the lot, but Le Tissier was technically better. He came over after his older brother had been with us already. His brother was actually a better player but, because Guernsey is 20 years behind, he couldn't handle the way everything was. So by the time Matt came over he handled what was expected of him much better because his brother told him what it was all about, though I know he trialled with Oxford before us. Matt was a terrific player who could do everything with the ball. He could be lazy and didn't like to train too much but he was a wonderful talent.

Tim Flowers was another of my better signings as I took him from Wolves reserves for £60,000 and sold him to Blackburn for £2.4m. I brought my old mate from Villa, John Burridge, in to show Flowers the ropes. Budgie was a nutter but he knew the game, was an enthusiastic trainer and was a good influence on Tim.

THE ONE THAT GOT AWAY

No one

No one! I was often on the phone to other managers and I am sure there would have been players I was interested in but who were not available for whatever reason but once a door shuts on a player I tended to move on pretty quickly and not spend any time worrying about it.

I must say, though, I thought Russell Osman would have gone in this section but somehow we managed to sign him from Ipswich, even after he had become an England international. It was a deal I never expected us to pull off so I was pleased to bring in Russell's experience as I seem to recall there were a few clubs in for him. He slotted in nicely to replace Mark Wright, who subsequently moved on to Derby and then Liverpool.

DAVID O'LEARY

Managed: Leeds United (1998–2002); Aston Villa (2003–2006); Al Ahli (2010–2011)

MY BIG DEAL

Rio Ferdinand: West Ham United to Leeds United for £18m in 2000

The gist of the Rio thing was I was coach at Leeds and we had this lad who was great on the field and great off it called Lucas Radebe. He had a degenerative knee injury, like Paul McGrath, that was getting worse and he was going to pack the game in. It wasn't a case that we were replacing Radebe because of his ability. It was sad he was coming to the end with a knee injury that, because he was such a brilliant lad, he had probably played on a couple of years more than he should have. That was his fighting spirit.

So, the club came to me and said we want you to nominate three players of different variety and what you think price-wise. I gave them the low end, the middle end and the Rolls-Royce. They said give a valuation and I thought there's no way Leeds will pay it – about £10m, but I added I don't know if you would get Rio Ferdinand out of West Ham.

Then they asked me a couple of questions – they must have been hearing this from other people. They said they had heard he is very casual on the ball and he's this, that and the other. I said, yes, he could be that way but it would be up to me to knock that out of him, which I think will be very easy because the bottom line is Rio Ferdinand is top-class.

I just left it with them. Seven, eight, maybe nine months went by and, in the end, I couldn't believe that we got him.

They went for the top end more than the in between end. If it had come down to me paying as much as £12m for Rio Ferdinand I probably wouldn't. But I wasn't involved with the fee or the negotiations. My input was to recommend the player and then that was me out of it.

I kind of thought they might have to pay about £10m. But they paid £18m so it wasn't as if we were getting a snippet. But I thought to myself, being a centre-half and all, that Rio would go on to bigger things as he did with [Manchester] United. I sold Rio on.

We worked well together. I was a centre-half – I thought I was a good one – and I told him I thought he could learn from me. I said we were a team going places and it could be another stepping stone in his career to launch him somewhere else, a massive club coming in for him down the road.

Rio was as good to work with as I thought he would be. I thought he was a lovely boy who was mad on football, he wanted to talk football, loved playing football, loved even after dinner sitting there just talking about football. And he wanted to get better.

I knew that Rio would develop and go on further from Leeds and we would get an unbelievable bid in from somewhere and we wouldn't be able to hold him because he'd want to go to the next level, like Real Madrid or something like that and he'd be outstanding.

And I knew, if anybody asked me, that you can buy individuals who look good at other clubs but you've got to watch them and make sure you are buying the mentality as well, of a fella who can cope with the pressure of a big place. The demands of every game. I saw loads come to Arsenal who had great ability at a smaller club, but they came to Arsenal and couldn't cope with the demands of playing there, the demands on them every game to do well.

Rio had that mentality and the more I worked with him, the more he wanted to learn. He was quality.

THE ONE THAT GOT AWAY

Nemanja Vidić: Spartak Moscow to Aston Villa for £5 million in 2005

God bless him, we'll reminisce about [former Aston Villa chairman] Doug Ellis on this one. I flew to Belgrade and then I met Vidić in Moscow, went to a game, tried to beg Doug to give me £5m to buy Vidić. I said, 'He'll be a steal, Chairman, we'll make loads of money. We get him in and another Premier League club will buy him for lots more.'

I thought I had Vidić over the line after I got back from Moscow. But Doug just wouldn't do it. He had Liam Ridgewell and Gary Cahill he was telling me. No disrespect to Ridge, who was a very nice lad, and Cahill, who had a good career, but Vidić was a steal. I just couldn't believe that nobody was watching him, no other club.

But I had plenty of calls once word got out that Doug wasn't giving me the money for him. I won't name the Premier League managers who asked me after, all of a sudden, they'd heard I'd been in Belgrade and Moscow. Had I seen this fella? I just said it was a no-brainer, he's made for the Premier League.

I even met Vidić; he was a very nice lad. He wanted to come. He was telling me he loved Aston Villa and everything else, but I think he felt that Aston Villa was a Premier League launchpad for him, which was fine to me.

The day I went to Moscow, Vidić was playing in wintry, absolutely freezing weather. I absolutely nearly broke my neck on the ice at the ground. Then I looked at the pitch – how it was playable I do not know. All of the players came out with hats on, gloves, tights, the whole lot. Vidić, though, came out in short sleeves. In that weather. He was diving around on an ice pitch and that convinced me even more how hardy he was as a lad.

I had a breakfast-come-lunch with Vidić the following day in Moscow and he was dead keen that the Premier League was the place to come and play. He was made for it, with his physicality. That was proven when he went to Manchester United and what he won there [United paid £7m and Vidić won five Premier League titles, League Cups and the Champions League in eight years and 300 games].

I might not know much, but it's like what I said about Rio Ferdinand, being a centre-half, I do know about centre-halves and both Ferdinand and Vidić were certainties.

But Doug wouldn't budge! I think Doug asked me, honestly, about the Moscow trip more, like did I fly Aeroflot? He was more concerned because if I'd had gone BA it was more expensive. He asked me more about how I got there and where I stayed to watch the game. That was how he worked in that way. And we never got Vidić because of it.

MARTIN O'NEILL

Managed: Grantham Town (1987–1989);
Shepshed Charterhouse (1989); Wycombe Wanderers
(1990–1995); Norwich City (1995); Leicester City
(1995–2000); Celtic (2000–2005); Aston Villa
(2006–2010); Sunderland (2011–2013); Republic
of Ireland (2013–2018); Nottingham Forest (2019)

MY BIG DEAL

Neil Lennon: Crewe Alexandra to Leicester City for
£750,000 in 1996

I've said Lennie here because the editor is insistent I have
to give one name to keep the continuity with all the other
selections by managers. The truth is I have found it near
impossible to nominate just one player out of so many. But
I've gone for Neil Lennon because there's a bit of a story with
him that might raise a smile.

He had initially come over from Northern Ireland to
Manchester City as a young kid. He was out of the game
for about a year, though, because he'd got a massive problem
with his back and he had to get it fused. He was immobile
for a long time. Anyway, when I was at Wycombe Wanderers
we played Crewe. They had a really fine side and Lennon
was part of that. So fast forward to when I was managing
Leicester City. We were in a bit of trouble, not winning
many games early on, the crowd was getting agitated, all that
kind of stuff. And I had this opportunity to see Neil Lennon
and remarkably was able to see him in three consecutive
games: Southampton were playing Crewe in the FA Cup,
they drew and played the replay.

There was a game as well against Bradford City. This
would be the January and February of 1996. So, I saw

Lennon three times in quick succession and wanted to sign him. There were a few others in also, the likes of Mark McGhee at Wolves.

We made our minds up we would take Lennon if we could. I phoned up his manager Dario Gradi and we thought the price might be half a million. As it turned out they wanted a bit more – £750,000, because that's what Crewe claimed they'd agreed with Premier League club Coventry City. Remember, we were in the First Division at the time, the second tier as it was then. Big Ron [Atkinson] was managing Coventry. I know that Dario, for whatever reason, wanted Lennon to go to Coventry so we thought, 'Listen, we've got a bit of work to do.'

John Robertson, my assistant manager, and I went up to Neil Lennon's house. He was living in Stockport – it was a friend's house. I must admit, we went into the house that evening and whatever Lennon and the friend did, I don't think washing-up liquid existed in their mind. It was an absolute hovel of a place. Anyway, we talked to Lennon, told him it would be great if he came to us, that we still felt we could make the play-offs and get into the big league. I think Big Ron was just going on some recommendation, he'd not seen Lennon play. In fact, we were told Ron had even asked Neil a question: could he head the ball? So, me and Robbo were all over that. And Robbo and me are going, 'Hold on. He's asking if you can head the ball because he doesn't know what you can do. We've watched you three consecutive times, we know everything about you, we know what you can do.'

Although Lennie always looked a bit heavy, no one, and I mean no one, could get away from him over ten yards and I just said, 'Coventry? You might be a bit-part player there for some time, though I'm sure you'll get in at some stage but it won't be immediately. With us you'll be straight in – and you can take us up.' John and I remembered that our old mentors, Brian Clough and Peter Taylor, had once decided when they were signing Archie Gemmill that they were not leaving Gemmill's house that evening until he had signed.

We didn't leave Lennie's house until three in the morning! Even then, it wasn't absolutely guaranteed until the next morning when Neil kept his word, phoned and said he was coming. We hung in there, but it was a hovel. I think even the mice were turning up their noses at the cheese. But we got there.

Then there was Steve Claridge who we signed for £1.2m because we had money in from Julian Joachim going to Aston Villa [£1.5m]. Muzzy Izzet on a £50,000 loan from Chelsea and eventually costing £800,000. I knew all about him because I used to see him every second down at Kingstonian playing for Chelsea reserves when I was manager of Wycombe. There's Robbie Savage for £400,000, but those three signings of Claridge, Lennon and Izzet were massive; not just getting us promotion via the play-offs, but winning the League Cups and all the rest of it.

There was James Milner at Aston Villa. We were signing him for £4m from Newcastle and on transfer deadline day of 2006 he was two miles away from our training ground and he got a call from Newcastle saying they now couldn't afford to let him go and he turned around and went back. We eventually got Milner the following year, though his price had gone up to £12m, but we got £24m for him when he went to Manchester City. Big John Carew was such a good deal for Aston Villa, too, when we swapped him for Milan Baroš.

Going back to Wycombe with Terry Evans, Jason Cousins and Keith Ryan, they were good players and I can hear all of them I managed saying, 'Wait one wee minute there. In the dressing room you told me I was the best player you ever had.' And they'd be right!

THE ONE THAT GOT AWAY

Rivaldo: Milan to Celtic

I knew Henrik Larsson was leaving and we had Ľubomír Moravčík retiring so we needed someone to come in and give us a lift to get the Celtic crowd going again. I knew Rivaldo's contract at Milan was up and he had been on loan with Cruzeiro back in Brazil. He'd won the Champions League with Milan only a year earlier and he was only 32.

People thought he was starting to go over the hill a little bit, but he would have been terrific for us, we could offer him Champions League football, which he wanted, and he would have lifted the fans, everything seemed right. We were in strong negotiations, he wanted to come. There was a very real chance of it happening but then the personal terms got out of hand, too much for us, and he went to Olympiakos.

We took Juninho instead who, at his best, just ghosted past people. We hoped to get a semblance of that and started fine, but all those things he did when he was one of the best midfielders in Europe were on the wane and Juninho left us for Palmeiras. I don't regret Juninho, but Rivaldo would have been a real interesting one to play for us for a year.

In my last days at Villa when James Milner was leaving and Randy Lerner was keeping the money, my chief scout, Ian Storey-Moore, asked me to watch a player in the Dutch league playing for AZ Alkmaar. He wanted to come to us, we could get him at a snip for £2.5m, it was all sorted but we couldn't do the deal because we had no money. It was Moussa Dembélé.

DAVID PLEAT

Managed: Nuneaton Borough (1971–1977); Luton
Town (1978–1986 & 1991–1995); Tottenham
Hotspur (1986–1987 & caretaker 1998, 2001,
2003–2004); Leicester City (1987–1991); Sheffield
Wednesday (1995–1997)

MY BIG DEAL

Mal Donaghy: Larne to Luton Town for £20,000 in 1978

I signed many players over the years and there are a select
few I would single out like David Moss from Swindon,
Brian Horton, a very good captain for me who I bought
from Brighton, I got Ricky Hill from school for nothing
and he went on to play for England, and I took Brian Stein
from Edgware Town in the non-league. I always tried to
sign players from a lower standard as, although Luton was
a little club with a ramshackle ground, it was like coming
to Wembley for most of the guys I was signing considering
where they had come from. And that was the case with my
best signing of the lot, Mal Donaghy.

I went over to Dublin to watch the Northern Ireland
under-21s play the Republic at a time when all the political
unrest was still very prevalent. I also watched him play for
Larne. The standout memory I have of him from those
days, which impressed me most, was his courage. He got
absolutely poleaxed by a tough challenge that would have
seen many players substituted. But he got up, didn't make a
fuss and played the rest of the game.

The game came easy to him; he was a Rolls-Royce of
a defender. He was quick and therefore could catch a pacy
striker or winger in his stride and most of the time you
hardly noticed him because he rarely made a mistake and

271

was unflappable as a character. Players come and go and indeed Mal did play with a few central-defensive partners like Mick Saxby, who I bought from Mansfield, a young Paul Elliott before he went to the Villa, and then Steve Foster. So as my defensive combinations changed it was always reassuring to have the reliability of a Mal Donaghy in the centre of your defence.

He played nearly 500 games for Luton and even after his ten years at Kenilworth Road he wasn't done there and had another five seasons at Manchester United playing for his boyhood heroes and then finished his career with another couple of seasons at Chelsea. I remember Sir Alex calling to ask my opinion of Mal. I was no longer at Luton by then but I was of course more than happy to recommend the lad and told Sir Alex that he couldn't go wrong and Donaghy wouldn't let him down. And I don't believe he did, either.

THE ONE THAT GOT AWAY

Gary Mabbutt: Bristol Rovers to Luton Town

I met Gary at a hotel in Reading while he was still at Bristol Rovers, after I had spotted him playing for England youth when John Cartwright was coach. As manager of little Luton Town I was always looking for talented, younger players or players who were in the reserves at bigger clubs; those who weren't in the Liverpool or Aston Villa first team, for example, and were not making their mark for whatever reason.

That's how I signed Mick Harford – he was in the Birmingham City reserves when I saw him play. Paul Elliott and Paul Walsh were kids at Charlton Athletic, Jake Findlay and Steve Foster were both in Villa's reserves, at different times, obviously. I picked up David Preece from Walsall. Those were the types of deals we had to do at Luton.

So the Mabbutt deal was as good as agreed but he wanted a little something extra, which my chief executive John Smith wasn't prepared to do. I believe he wanted a flat to be provided and paid for by the club, as he wasn't married at the time. So the transfer collapsed over something as petty as that. Then just a few months later Tottenham signed him. I was so disappointed at the time to miss out on such a potentially good player through what was plain meanness really.

Of course managers identify players but what many outside of football probably do not realise is that the chief executive or the chairman can stop that deal going through, which was the case here. Those occasions are probably few but it does show how a manager can do his job right and identify talent yet still not manage to recruit that player for reasons beyond his control.

At that moment in time Mabbutt was just aged about 20 or 21 so that particular transfer would not have cost Luton too much money. He ended up moving to Tottenham for around the £100,000 mark so it was especially frustrating not to get him after I had scouted him and met with him. He was ready to come, but these things can crop up.

I guess it was ironic that Gary and I ended up working together when I became Tottenham manager in 1986. He developed into the strong, powerful defender that I thought he would become and was also a wonderful leader. Luton's loss was certainly Tottenham's gain as he ended up having a long and distinguished career at White Hart Lane.

TONY PULIS

Managed: Bournemouth (1992–1994); Gillingham (1995–1999); Bristol City (1999–2000); Portsmouth (2000); Stoke City (2002–2005 & 2006–2013); Plymouth Argyle (2005–2006); Crystal Palace (2013–2014); West Bromwich Albion (2015–2017); Middlesbrough (2017–2019)

MY BIG DEAL

Ricardo Fuller: Southampton to Stoke City for £200,000 in 2006

He got us promoted at Stoke to the Premier League and was our talisman for that and for the first couple of years in the Premier League. On his day he was just unplayable. He was frustrating too, like they all are. The best players can be up and down, but on his day, some of the goals he scored and what he did for us was just terrific.

We paid £200,000 for him and when you think of what we got from Ricardo that was a good deal. I'd watched him play at Preston and in Scotland as well with Hearts and he'd done exceptionally well. Then he was with Portsmouth and Southampton. When Ricardo was at Pompey Harry Redknapp was manager before he went onwards and upwards, so I just rang 'H' one day and asked him about Ricardo. Harry told me that Ricardo was a 'maverick' but he'd got all the tools and ability.

Ricardo, though, had a very, very bad knee and we used to have to manage that, give him a couple of days off during the week to rest it, get him ready to play on the park rather than training. He was just an exceptional player. Ricardo was frustrating for a manager and frustrating for the players he played with, but the fella could just do stuff in games others couldn't, either create opportunities or score goals for us. In the end that brought respect from the players, they all bought into him.

With all my teams through my career, I've always preferred to have a 'team' rather than a group of individuals. But the players at Stoke accepted Ricardo missing days, or some days, when he didn't have a run in him and wasn't performing. You'd be looking at him and thinking, 'I've got to get him off.' The number of times David Kemp, my assistant, would say, 'Nah, keep him on.' And by keeping him on we had that edge. Ricardo would have been looking absolutely knackered, then all of a sudden he'd do something for five minutes and, goodness me, it's, 'Where has he got that energy from?' And he'd score.

He scored one of the best goals I've ever seen and didn't get the credit he deserved, early on, at the Britannia, against Aston Villa I think it was. The ball came into him, facing away from goal and he touched the ball around the player, spun it with his right foot, Ricardo turned and ran on to it and drove in his shot. Unbelievable.

THE ONE THAT GOT AWAY

Marcos Alonso: Bolton Wanderers to Stoke City for £1m in 2013

The Spanish lad is doing brilliantly at Chelsea now, at left-back. He's a big, tall lad who has played for Spain, got a few caps and I honestly thought I'd got him in my second stint at Stoke, not long before I left the club. Alonso's grandfather, Marcos, played for Real Madrid for eight years and was a defender in that Real side that won all those European Cups on the bounce in the 1950s. His father also played in Spain's top flight and both his grandad and dad played for Spain so his pedigree is incredible.

The lad was with Real Madrid, but he was struggling to break through. When I got involved he was doing well with Bolton and the fee we were looking at was about £1m, I think it was. We had him and his dad in for a couple of days at Stoke and we really thought we'd got him. But in the end, we just couldn't get it over the line and Alonso ended up going abroad to Fiorentina. The reason we lost him was financial; he went for more money.

It's interesting that he came back to this country again on loan with Sunderland but then he went back and really made it big in Italy and Chelsea ended up taking him for a fee in the region of £25m. I'm not surprised; the kid was class and he's gone on to show that with Chelsea hasn't he. He really was the one that got away from us.

CLAUDIO RANIERI

*Managed: Vigor Lamezia (1986–1987); Puteolana
(1987–1988 & 1988); Cagliari (1988–1991);
Napoli (1991–1992); Fiorentina (1993–1997);
Valencia (1997–1999 & 2004–2005); Atlético
Madrid (1999–2000); Chelsea (2000–2004);
Parma (2007); Juventus (2007–2009); Roma
(2009–2011); Inter Milan (2011–2012); Monaco
(2012–2014); Greece (2014); Leicester City (2015–
2017); Nantes (2017–2018); Fulham (2018–2019);
Roma (2019); Sampdoria (2019–2021); Watford
(2021–2022)*

MY BIG DEAL

Frank Lampard: West Ham United to Chelsea for
£11m in 2001

I think Frank Lampard has to be my best signing. I watched
him with West Ham during my first season with Chelsea and
I liked how he was playing. When I talked to Frank he came
to my house with his agent. It wasn't difficult to persuade him
to come to Chelsea because his uncle [Harry Redknapp] had
been sacked by West Ham, maybe a month before, and we
could then buy him. That made it easier to buy him.

So, when Frank came to my house that was the first
time I had met him. My wife was in our house too, but not
in the meeting, she wasn't involved in the talks – she was
in a different room! I don't know why we didn't go to the
club for the talks, Frank just came with me. My house was
very close to Stamford Bridge. We had some drinks, cups
of coffee or tea and we talked about Chelsea.

The cost, if I remember it well, was £11m. A lot of
people said, 'Oh, it is too much, too much.' But at the end

of Frank Lampard's career and what he achieved and did for Chelsea, it wasn't too much. It was very cheap.

Frank was very young when he signed, I think 22, 23. I said to him that in my opinion he was a fantastic player and he could go forward, that I wanted to improve him. That is why he should join me. What I said was correct because Frank became a legend for Chelsea, at the top of all the great players the club has had.

He was good to work with; he understood what I wanted from him. There are players who you have to repeat, repeat, repeat to them. With Frank once you said something he remembered; a very intelligent player.

After I left Chelsea, I watched Frank's career. He achieved the maximum. It wasn't a surprise to me. Chelsea have had fantastic teams and Frank was always an important player of many of those teams. I feel pride at taking Frank Lampard to Chelsea and what has happened.

In my opinion Frank can be a really good manager. Maybe needs a little more experience but for me he can achieve bigger things and be successful.

There was also Petr Čech and Arjen Robben. I bought them both for Chelsea without seeing them train once. I left Chelsea before I could even do that. They didn't go away, though, as it was me who was sent away [sacked]! But that's OK, that's life. I built a good team, but then it was goodbye.

THE ONE THAT GOT AWAY

Samuel Eto'o: Real Mallorca to Chelsea for £6m

There was Eto'o when I was with Chelsea. We wanted him and he only didn't come because there was a difficulty in that he was half and half with Real Madrid and Mallorca [on loan to Mallorca from Real Madrid]. And then he joined Mallorca as their player and after he went to Barcelona.

Chelsea, I think, was a much better move financially for Real Madrid, selling him to us rather than Mallorca, but that was it, it was what Eto'o wanted. It's football.

We were in talks with Madrid about Eto'o. I said to the Chelsea people I wanted Eto'o but it was impossible to buy because they didn't want to sell. But they sold only a few months afterwards.

Also, when I was at Chelsea I went to the owner [Roman] Abramovich and asked him if we could sign Didier Drogba. But then I was out and Drogba came! So, while I missed out on signing Didier, at least Chelsea did not. Abramovich took my advice at least!

KEVIN RATCLIFFE

Managed: Chester City (1995–1999); Shrewsbury Town (1999–2003)

MY BIG DEAL

Cyrille Regis: Wycombe Wanderers to Chester City on a free transfer in 1995

My biggest and best deal has to be my first-ever signing and that was Cyrille Regis. I had just taken over and I was determined that my first signing would make a statement that we meant business. When you sign players who are heading towards the end of their career it can sometimes backfire whether it be injury or if they've just suddenly lost their appetite for the game or for the challenge but that was far from it with Cyrille. Him coming in gave me the time to allow a good, young striker that we had at the club called John Murphy the chance to develop a bit more and John ended up a terrific striker for Chester.

Cyrille was surprised when I called him about joining us because he had literally walked out the door at Wycombe where Martin O'Neill had told him he wouldn't be required for the following season. But I had an agreement with Martin that I'd be the first one to know if he ever left. I asked Cyrille to come up and have a chat about joining us and he must have liked what he saw and heard because he signed. He was paid about five grand a year more than any of the other players but he was worth every penny with how he paid us back through his performances and professionalism.

It was ironic that my second-last game for Everton was against Aston Villa when Cyrille was playing for them and he scored at Goodison. He was always a handful to play against as a defender. He was a man-mountain but with quality; not just power, he had the skills and technique to make life difficult for defences also and of course was very strong in the air. He never gave you a free ball, he challenged for every ball, even if it was just a nudge here and there. You always knew he was around.

By the time he joined me at Chester he was more of a target man who brought team-mates into play. One thing he couldn't believe when he came up to Chester was after a game I'd say, 'See you on Monday, Cyrille, for a light training session and then I don't need to see you again until Thursday.' He couldn't understand it but I was keen to give him more of a break in midweek as I knew he would use his time wisely.

Cyrille was great for me, great for the club and great for the youngsters. We even signed him again for another season but, unfortunately, he injured his ankle and he never got to play a second season for us.

Luke Beckett would be a close second to Cyrille in terms of my best signings. He was a good striker and I only signed him because Barnsley were promoted and their manager Danny Wilson told me if they went up we could have him, as it turned out.

THE ONE THAT GOT AWAY

Gary Martindale: Bolton Wanderers to Chester City

Gary was one of those I was in for who I felt would have made us better. He was one of those strikers who always seemed to be on the end of crosses or chances in general. People sometimes say it's luck, but it can't be luck when strikers find themselves on the end of opportunities so often. It's a great skill to find the space to be able to create goalscoring opportunities as often as they do.

Gary was a striker in Bolton's reserves when I spotted him and my plan was to sign him and Neil Fisher. I managed to sign Neil but Gary got away from me and signed for Peterborough instead.

HARRY REDKNAPP

*Managed: Bournemouth (1983–1992); West Ham
United (1994–2001); Portsmouth (2002–2004
& 2005–2008); Southampton (2004–2005);
Tottenham Hotspur (2008-2012); Queens Park
Rangers (2012–2015); Jordan (2016); Birmingham
City (2017)*

MY BIG DEAL

Paul Merson: Aston Villa to Portsmouth on a free
transfer in 2002

Merse changed the club when I took him to Portsmouth
from Villa in my first season there in the Championship
[the First Division as it was named at the time]. They had
finished something like fourth from bottom the year before
and while I was trying to put a new team together I got a
phone call asking if I'd be interested in Merse because Villa
wanted him out after John Gregory thought it was time he
moved on.

I said, 'I'd love him, but I don't think I could afford him.'
The agent said Villa would pay nearly all his wages as they
just wanted to shift him. There was no fee and Villa paid
almost three-quarters of his wages in the end so I was able to
take him. I spoke to Merse and told him I'd be making him
captain and he really responded to that extra responsibility.
He scored goals, made goals; he was on another level to
anybody else in the league that year.

We were 33/1 to win the league at the start of the season
and he was the one who inspired us to win promotion to the
Premier League that season. The club had finished around
the bottom for eight of the last nine years beforehand so
Merse knew he was coming to a club that had done nothing

for a long time but he was up for the challenge. I remember a good friend ringing me and saying, 'Harry, I'm going to have a few quid on you this season.' I said, 'Don't waste your money, we've got no chance. I'll be well pleased if we're in the top half.' He rang me up at the end of the season and wasn't very happy with me!

But as soon as Merse walked into the dressing room everyone got a lift. Linvoy Primus had been around the lower leagues and he said to me one day, 'I never thought I'd get to play with Paul Merson.' That summed up his impact. Merse was a proper lad but I loved him and he knew the game as well. Underneath all of the bravado and the fun there is a real student of the game. I only kept him for a year but he was incredible for that one season.

Paolo Di Canio was a great signing for me at West Ham. I remember the chairman had his head in his hands when I told him I wanted Di Canio. He was like, 'Oh no, anyone but Di Canio!' I took him on the back of him pushing the referee Mr Paul Alcock over so no one wanted him. He wasn't flavour of the month then but he became a cult hero and ended up being one of the best players ever to play for the club I would think. People don't realise what a great professional Paolo was. He was in such fantastic shape. He would come in on his own on a Sunday with his own fitness coach and do two hours training. He was a serious footballer.

I took Rafael van der Vaart at Tottenham and he was very good for me, and I also signed Kyle Walker along with Kyle Naughton for about nine million quid from Sheffield United. I had Vedran Ćorluka, the Croatia right-back, and Alan Hutton at the time but I knew Walker would be one for the future. As it has turned out, he did go on to be a fantastic player.

When I was at Bournemouth I signed a boy called John Williams from Port Vale for 25 grand and he was fantastic for me at centre-half. As soon as I brought him in he changed everything in the team for the better, though not many people would know Willo now. He helped me get Bournemouth promoted into what is now the Championship, for the first time in their history – in over 100 years they had never been that high. Willo came in at Christmas, played about 27 games and was only on the losing team once. He was a big Scouser, a big influence in both boxes, a great character and was a real leader.

THE ONE THAT GOT AWAY

Eden Hazard: Lille to Tottenham Hotspur

Joe Cole, who was obviously with me at West Ham, called me from France and said this kid is the best player he's ever played with and suggested I took a look at him. I went to watch him three or four times and Joe was right. He was an amazing talent. The frustrating thing is we could have got him then. The fee they wanted was about £18m, which was a lot of money then, but nowadays he'd be more like £80m! He was the type who could have made a real difference to us and, who knows, may have pushed us on that extra mile into title contenders.

I met him in Paris in a hotel, spent a couple of hours with him and he was very keen to come to Tottenham at that point. Chelsea weren't in the picture then. We could have done that deal but it dragged on and dragged on and took too long to do. We were haggling over the fee and that's why it never happened.

He was my type of player, like with Merson. I like players who can do things on the ball and make something happen. I would always want one in my team if I can find one. When games are tight and you can't break anyone down, that's when you need someone who can do something clever, unlock a defence, score a goal, make a goal. There are not many of those players around, players who can dribble.

All these young coaches nowadays are obsessed with 'pass, pass, pass'. But I like to see a player dribble and make something happen, like Jimmy Johnstone at Celtic. What does Lionel Messi do? He's a dribbler. As soon as he gets some space, he goes on a run and scores goals. It's fantastic to see players beat people. We had Gareth Bale at Tottenham. How great would it have been to have had Hazard as well?

PETER REID

Managed: Manchester City (1990–1993);
Sunderland (1995–2002); England U21 (1999);
Leeds United (2003); Coventry City (2004–
2005); Thailand (2008–2009); Plymouth Argyle
(2010–2011); Mumbai City (2014)

MY BIG DEAL

Kevin Phillips: Watford to Sunderland for
£500,000 in 1997

Kevin Phillips was a massive signing at the time because of
the predicament and the situation at Sunderland where I was
always looking for a goalscorer. I saw him play for Watford.
I just had a little sneaking feeling about him. I think he
cost me about £500,000, £250,000 down, I don't know the
exact figures. But when you look at Phillips' record and the
career that he had, and where I bought him from, you don't
get many better bargains than that.

I look at Niall Quinn – a great buy, Gavin McCann,
Allan Johnston and people like that did brilliantly for me.
You are always looking for that player who can make a
difference for you. The goalkeeper Thomas Sørensen did
well for me, too. But you always have a look for the one
who sticks it in the net and the Sunderland fans nicknamed
Phillips 'Super Kev' so I think that speaks for itself.

He won the Premier League Golden Boot; that tells
you how good he was. That's not bad for the club either.
We'd just got promoted then so that even magnifies his
achievements. I think Ipswich were in for Phillips and
one or two more. He's a southern lad and I think he was
wary about coming so far up north, but I managed to
persuade him.

I said to Kev, 'You could be a superstar up here, son.' You use different things to get players. When Lee Clark was moving from Newcastle to Sunderland I persuaded him with about four bottles of champagne! So, it's different deals for different people. I learned that off Howard [Kendall]. I told Kevin he could be a superstar – and he was. He scored every sort of goal. He got a lot of headers, cute shots, little chips, he could pass it in, he could smash it in. Every conceivable goal. His movement in the box, you can't coach that, these lads who have got it have got a natural instinct.

Kev was easy to manage too. I just had one problem with him when he wanted to play in a League Cup game against Chester. I didn't want to play him, but he persuaded me. He scored and I was going to drag him off, but I didn't and then he did his metatarsal!

He's a bright and sparky lad. I think he got four away from home [twice, away to Rotherham in the FA Cup and away to Bury to secure promotion], but the game I remember is when we got beat by Chelsea when we first came up [in 1999], first game, lost 4-0, you know, when Gus Poyet did the scissor kick goal? The corresponding game at our place Kev got two, including one from about 30 yards. Marcel Desailly and Frank Leboeuf played. These are world-class players. Kev and Quinny on the day were just brilliant. All game Phillips was a threat, Super Kev was like a wasp, here there and everywhere.

THE ONE THAT GOT AWAY

Zlatan Ibrahimović: Ajax to Sunderland for £6m in 2002

I was in for Ibrahimović after Andy King had spotted him when he was young, playing for a small Swedish club and then he ended up going to Malmö.

I tried to get Ibrahimović for Sunderland when he was at Ajax. I remember flying over to Amsterdam and having a meeting. Leo Beenhakker was technical director there and I had a meeting with him about Ibrahimović.

We were offering £6m and they wanted a bit more and we couldn't do it. From when Andy King picked him up as a young lad and scouted Ibrahimović, I had him on file, watching where he went. That comes to mind now because of what Ibrahimović went on to do and became one of those iconic players.

Through a third party we had information that he would have fancied coming to Sunderland if we could have done it. It would have been unbelievable.

There was also another one from Sweden that I fancied – a lad called Henrik Larsson. He was a young player with Feyenoord in Holland in the early to mid-'90s. Bobby Saxton had scouted him and through Ian Greaves he knew a lad called Barry Hughes.

I'll always remember his name because he said the English league might be too physical for him and we sort of lost interest at that. The rest about Henrik Larsson, like Ibrahimović, is history. Larsson played for Celtic and Manchester United, didn't he? He's one you look back on and think what might have been, Larsson, along with Ibrahimović.

BRYAN ROBSON

Managed: Middlesbrough (player–manager 1994–1997, manager 1997–2001); Bradford City (2003–2004); West Bromwich Albion (2004– 2006); Sheffield United (2007–2008); Thailand (2009–2011)

MY BIG DEAL

Juninho: São Paolo to Middlesbrough for £4.75m in 1995

Juninho was the best signing I ever made – he was a top player. I first saw him when I was assistant manager to Terry [Venables] with the England team. There was a tournament in England a year before the 1996 European Championship called the Umbro Cup between us, Brazil, Japan and Sweden. I saw every Brazil match in that tournament and I thought Juninho had it all. I enjoyed everything about his game, especially his energy and quality on the ball.

It wasn't a difficult deal to do. He was with São Paolo as a 22-year-old and I found out that he had an Italian agent. I contacted this agent and told him I would like to sign Juninho if it was at all possible. I don't remember there being any other clubs interested in him at the time, so we never faced any opposition for his signature. We signed him for around £4m and sold him two years later for £13.25m so the club also made a great profit on him.

I would have loved to have kept him, but we were relegated so I couldn't stand in his way, especially as Atlético Madrid paid us good money, which was a sizeable fee back then. He had helped us reach two cup finals in 1997 so his contribution was huge.

He had a fantastic attitude to training and to doing things right in terms of being a dedicated professional. He really got the crowd going at Boro and they loved to watch him play; he was a real entertainer. Some people said the Premier League would be too tough for him. But one thing I know about Brazilian footballers is that they are very strong mentally and really tough physically, as it proved. Juninho was very tough and was able to look after himself.

Another signing I made who doesn't get enough of a mention is Mark Schwarzer. He was a great lad and a terrific goalkeeper – certainly one of my best signings.

THE ONES THAT GOT AWAY

Steven Gerrard: Liverpool to Middlesbrough in 1999

Roberto Carlos: Palmeiras to Middlesbrough in 1995

Stevie was about 17 or 18 when I first saw him play and he impressed me hugely. He was tall and slamming into tackles, never stopped running, he looked like he had it all.

I think it was a reserve game. I enquired afterwards about him as I'd seen enough to know I would be happy to take him, but Liverpool were not interested in selling. It was made quite clear to me that they saw this young lad playing a significant part in the club's future. In fact, I still remember Roy Evans's words. He said, 'Bryan, are you trying to get me sacked?' They all knew the talent that Stevie had and they weren't budging from that belief but it didn't stop me trying though.

Steven had great physicality for his age, was a terrific passer, he was quick, good on the ball – it was obvious he had a lot to offer. It was no surprise to me that Steven went on to have the career he did.

The other near miss worth mentioning – a deal I might have done if circumstances had been different – was Roberto Carlos. Ironically at the time of signing Juninho, I also enquired about Roberto.

I was told that a deal had already been agreed to take him to Inter Milan from his club in Brazil. But they also said if I had enquired a week earlier, I could have signed him – and I would have done as well. I would have happily signed Juninho AND Roberto Carlos!

BRENDAN RODGERS

Managed: Watford (2008–2009); Reading (2009);
Swansea City (2010–2012); Liverpool (2012–
2015); Celtic (2016–2019); Leicester City (2019–)

MY BIG DEAL

Philippe Coutinho: Inter Milan to Liverpool for
£8.5m in 2013

He was a young player I was aware of when I was at Chelsea
as youth coach. Unfortunately, we were unable to bring him
to Chelsea. He had already been bought by Inter Milan from
Vasco da Gama and was back at the Brazilian club after
being loaned back there from Inter. Then, when he became
available at Inter Milan – because they were struggling
financially and because he was a young player that maybe
wasn't going to play so much – we were able to bring him
into Liverpool as a 19-year-old for £8.5m.

I'd seen him play in high-level games with top players in
it, so I always felt that he could come to the Premier League
and do well. He has a wonderful personality and had great
technique. The way he developed was quite sensational and
he went on and made the club an awful lot of money [the
fee when Coutinho joined Barcelona from Liverpool in 2018
was an initial £105m, rising to £142m).

He is the player that immediately springs to my mind as
the one who stands out as my best signing. It wasn't hard to
persuade Coutinho to come to us, not at all. It was the status
of Liverpool. He was obviously at a great club in Inter Milan
but wasn't playing so much and I think the opportunity to
come to the Premier League was a big draw for him.

He was aware of how I worked from my time at Swansea,
he knew I knew of him from Chelsea, so, yes, he was very

keen to come. Of course, Liverpool really sells itself as a club, an historic club, and the chance to come in and be a part of our project was really appealing to him. Coutinho needed to play and, also, he needed to play in a certain style. I think the big question mark when he came in was, 'Will Coutinho be big enough or strong enough to play in the Premier League?'

For me it was about the talent. I knew that physically he was good, he needed to improve in certain aspects of his defending so he could be strong in the Premier League, but his talent was pretty clear and how he adapted to play in the Premier League was sensational, virtually from when he first came in. Each year he got better and better.

After I joined Liverpool in 2012, after the first six months we signed Coutinho and Daniel Sturridge for virtually £20m. When Coutinho came in, it gave a great boost to the team, just the sheer quality of his game and he then grew in personality, his confidence and he felt at home at Liverpool. Initially I'd converse with Coutinho in Spanish but then he learned English. He had a real love for football, wanted to train every day, play in all the games. With Philippe he needs to be loved, like a lot of players, but that creative player like him, they need to have that trust put in them, to let them go and play, to have that freedom to play, but always in the structure of the team.

We made a great environment at Liverpool of learning with a young squad and Coutinho just blossomed in that environment. He wasn't hard to manage, it was a breath of fresh air to see that quality and that enthusiasm and love of the game. It was funny because we did some images of him when he played futsal, 11, 12 years of age, and we showed this video to some of the young players in the academy. How Coutinho played futsal at 11, 12, in Rio was how he played football at Anfield. An amazing talent and as a guy a really special boy.

I've worked with some brilliant players, had the good fortune to bring in some really good players and coach players that already existed at clubs I went to. But Coutinho, in terms of who I have brought in, in terms of value, it would be safe to say that Coutinho was my best signing.

THE ONE THAT GOT AWAY

Alexis Sánchez: Barcelona to Liverpool for approximately £30m in 2014

There were a few who we thought we had at Liverpool. But the one that really gave us the biggest loss, simply to not have him anymore, was when we lost Luis Suárez [to Barcelona for £65m in 2014].

We wanted someone of similar profile of player to Luis, somebody that could come in and have that energy, have that tireless running and that wanting to score goals. The one we thought we had was Alexis Sánchez when he was coming out of Barcelona. I'm unsure what the fee for Sánchez would have been off the top of my head, but it was around £30m. We felt we were very close to getting him. We had contact with him and he was very keen to come and then Arsenal came in at the last minute, got ahead of us.

The one player who would probably have impacted our team and continued with our development at the time would have been Alexis Sánchez. That was a tough one for us. I believe that his family were keen on locating to London. We had dialogue over the course of that summer and it just fell through in the end.

It was a huge disappointment because when you lose someone of Luis's quality, personality and energy, then you want to replace that, that profile, with like-for-like and we saw that when Sánchez went to Arsenal, that energy and quality; he scored goals. And we missed that.

We had a style of play that had nearly won us the league at Liverpool, with the high energy I wanted in 2013/14. But when Suárez left us and we ended up not getting Sánchez, our football suffered because of that. We didn't have a high-profile player up front. We ended up bringing in Mario Balotelli and I finished up playing Raheem Sterling higher up the pitch.

Losing Luis showed that if we didn't have that type of player, the impact it had on the team [finishing sixth]. That was when we looked at signing Roberto Firmino. The following summer [2015] we signed Robbie. He was injured early on and I left, but he has become a fantastic player for Liverpool.

JOE ROYLE

Managed: Oldham Athletic (1982–1994 & 2009);
Everton (1994–1997); Manchester City (1998–
2001); Ipswich Town (2002–2006)

MY BIG DEAL

Denis Irwin: Leeds United to Oldham Athletic on a free transfer in 1986

It's hard for me to single out one player because I made a few good signings over the years, like Andy Ritchie at Oldham for £50,000 from Leeds United and bringing Andrei Kanchelskis and Gary Speed to Everton. But in terms of value for money I don't think anyone tops Denis. He was probably the best and most consistent full-back in Europe for ten years.

We got him out of Leeds on a free when they were having a bit of a clear-out. I couldn't believe it. He just got better and better. He had played over 50 games at Leeds and myself and my chief scout Jim Cassell were well aware of him as we strategically only scouted five teams: the two Manchester clubs, Liverpool and Everton and Leeds. Jim and I felt that we knew as much about their young players as they did. Then one day someone inside the Leeds setup who knew we rated Denis called me to say they were giving him a free and we were on it straight away as we knew we wanted him. He wasn't hard to deal with in terms of his wages – he just wanted to play football.

Denis played right-back for 99 per cent of his time at Oldham so the fact he joined Leeds as centre-half and, later, was so consistently good at left-back for Manchester United demonstrates how versatile he was too. Let's not forget how effective he was as a great taker of free kicks and penalties as well. He was a dream to manage, was a great trainer, was very seldom injured, just got on with his game and was never any trouble at all. He had a football brain and stood up and never committed himself unless he had to. He was quick over short spaces but most of all he read the game and knew where to be at all times. I always got the feeling that he would have made a good midfielder because of his reading of the game.

I never wanted to lose him but to be fair to Denis he couldn't turn Manchester United down and £750,000 was excellent money for Oldham given their financial frailties and especially as we never paid anything for him. Sir Alex Ferguson is on record as saying Denis was one of his greatest buys, which speaks volumes for his ability given the amount of quality that Alex brought to United. It was a shame Denis was gone by the time that we did finally get promoted to the top flight but he was certainly a big part of the DNA of what we had created at Oldham during those times along with a few other players like Ian Marshall and Andy Ritchie.

Kanchelskis was awesome for us at Everton in his one full season that he gave us, scoring 16 goals in 32 games from his position out wide. He was never a winger, though, more a wide striker who could hit the ball ferociously hard with either foot. Andrei was a nice lad as well and is rightly a legend at Everton for those two years he had with us.

Gary Speed was marvellous for us also and was a terrible tragedy [when he died in 2011]. Andy Ritchie was a great technician and was perfect for the plastic pitch at Oldham – when the ball came to his feet, it died. He became Mr Oldham and I would think many of the fans would regard Andy as their best-ever player.

We did well out of Leeds. Not only was there Irwin and Ritchie but we also took Andy Linighan from them for £40,000 and sold him for £450,000. Billy Bremner was a great footballer and a good man, bless him, but in hindsight they probably let too many leave at that time. All that stopped when Howard Wilkinson joined as manager.

THE ONE THAT GOT AWAY

Stan Collymore: Nottingham Forest to Everton

There weren't too many that got away but the one we nearly nicked at Everton was Stan Collymore when he was leaving Forest. Everyone had known for a long time that he was going to Liverpool, but I had this notion of pairing Stan with Duncan Ferguson. The deal was never close to being done and I knew he was bound for Liverpool, but we still entered the market late for him and had a cheeky stab at getting him, which I understand cost Liverpool a few more quid!

We had just won the FA Cup, had escaped relegation and all that nonsense and were on the up so this bid was a sign of our ambition. Everton was becoming a force and we were looking to build. Stan would have been a major capture for us but it wasn't to be.

Apparently, Stan acknowledged years later that our approach did cause him to waver at whether going to Anfield was the right move for him or not. But in the end he came down on the Liverpool side. If we had managed to bring Stan to Goodison and pair him with Duncan, they would have made an awesome partnership. I do wonder how those two would have got on together: Stan with his pace and Duncan with his power and leadership of the line.

Certainly those two together would have given defences a lot of headaches. I remember speaking to the Forest manager Frank Clark, after he advised that I was probably too late to stop Stan from going to Liverpool. Frank said, 'If you do manage to put those two together, that will be trouble!'

JOHN RUDGE

*Managed: Port Vale (1983–1999); Stoke City
(director of football 1999–2013)*

MY BIG DEALS

Ray Walker: Aston Villa to Port Vale for £15,000 in 1986

Dellice Rudge: My wife, Huddersfield to the Potteries
– priceless

Ray's probably my best player signing in terms of value for money and reasons I'll expand on, but I cannot leave my wife out of this as she's been so important to me over the years.

I was lucky that I was with Port Vale for 19 years in total and then I was at Stoke City for 14 years as director of football. When I was at Port Vale I'd be out three nights a week watching matches, watching players. It's all different now, as you are watching the computer. Massive changes, but I always wanted to go and watch players myself. That was a lot of work and time away from home.

At Port Vale we went from the old Fourth Division to what is now the Championship and I got one or two really good players. People ask me, 'Who was your best signing?' My answer to that is always, 'My best signing is my missus, Dellice Rudge.' I soon changed that to 'Dell'.

When I signed Andy Jones for £3,000 from Rhyl, that was down to Dell. We sold him on to Charlton for £350,000 and then took him back on loan when we got promotion to the Third Division in 1988/89. Jones wasn't in the team when I went to see him with Dell at Rhyl. He was on the bench with a strapping on his knee and I said to the missus, 'Let's go home.' But Dell said we should stay and when Andy Jones did come on I was so impressed I took him there and then. He got 50 goals in 107 games in his two spells for Vale.

I met Dell at my first [playing] club, Huddersfield. I lived in the house where Denis Law used to be in before he went to Manchester City. He left some slippers in a wardrobe and I gave them to my dad. He loved walking about in Denis Law's slippers!

I was very fortunate with the players I had at Port Vale, but I was more fortunate with Dell. We've been married 54 years and she has had to put up with so much with me being out the house so often. When I first started at the Vale we used to play on a Monday night, then Tuesday and Wednesday I was off watching matches, and she was great about it was Dell.

In terms of players, I never like to say 'he was the best signing' because they all did so well for me. But as I said, for value for money, I signed Ray Walker for £15,000 from Aston Villa when he was struggling to establish himself in their first team and he went on to play over 400 games for me. Ray wasn't one of those that I sold on [for big money], but he was a great value for the football club. He linked up really well with Robbie Earle in midfield.

Robbie went on to play in the Premier League with Wimbledon. If Ray had that opportunity, after having gained the experience that he did with us, he could also have been a big success. If he could have played with Robbie as a combination in the top flight, they would have been successful together, without a doubt.

There was also Darren Beckford, Mark Bright, Gareth Ainsworth, Steve Guppy, Robin van der Laan, Jon McCarthy, and Ian Taylor of course. I signed him for £15,000 from non-league [Moor Green] and sold him to Sheffield Wednesday for a million quid. He was an exceptionally good player and then went on to Aston Villa and did wonderfully well there. Throughout that time Port Vale sold £10m of players. Goodness knows what they'd be worth now!

So many did well for me. Getting them in, selling them on and then finding another one, it got more and more difficult having to replace them all the time. You are only as good as your players and the most important thing was finding them. I bought Ainsworth for £500,000 from Lincoln and sold him for two million to Wimbledon. I sold McCarthy to Birmingham for £1.5m after getting him for £450,000 from York. I spent £225,000 on Guppy when he was in the Newcastle United reserves and sold him to Leicester for £850.000.

But none of them trump the missus!

THE ONE THAT GOT AWAY

Steve Bull: West Bromwich Albion to Port Vale

I was desperate to get Steve Bull. He was at West Brom but he wasn't in the team. He was in the reserves and I was watching him. I tried to get him to the Vale, but Ron Jukes, who was the Wolves scout, was too quick for me. Ron was a friend as well but working for Wolves and he had the edge over me. Steve preferred to go to the Wolves rather than Port Vale. I did my best to get him for the Vale, I could see what he could do, but I didn't get to speak to Steve. I did speak to his father about it but, as I say, Ron was too quick for me.

Steve was a brilliant goalscorer and in the fullness of time we played plenty of games against Wolves at Port Vale and him and Mutchy [Andy Mutch] were brilliant together up front. If I had got Steve Bull to Port Vale it would have turned out to be a bit of a coup. But Ron was a well-known scout and he pipped me to that signing.

Wolves were a famous club, but they weren't riding so high at that time. They were going through a bad time on and off the pitch and Steve helped pull them round with his goals. I'm from Wolverhampton and supported Wolves as a kid so in the end I was pleased with what Bully did for the club.

BOBBY SAXTON

Managed: Exeter City (1977–1979); Plymouth
Argyle (1979–1981); Blackburn Rovers (1981–
1986); York City (1987–1988); Newcastle United
(caretaker 1991)

MY BIG DEAL

Jimmy Quinn: Swindon Town to Blackburn Rovers in 1984

I noticed him when he scored against us for Swindon in the FA Cup. I thought he was a good, strong centre-forward who led the line very well. I found out that his contract was ending in the summer of 1984 so we moved in and signed him. I heard that the new Swindon manager Lou Macari wasn't best pleased that we took him but that was the nature of the game. He was very good for me at Blackburn and he made his Northern Ireland debut while he was with us, which shows how moving up a couple of divisions helped him to develop.

He spent two-and-a-bit seasons at Ewood Park until Macari took him back to Swindon, just before I left the club.

Other signings I was pleased with would be Terry Gennoe, who was more or less the first player I signed at Blackburn. I brought him in from Southampton. There was Scott Sellars from Leeds when their manager Billy Bremner was selling off a lot of their talented younger players. Scott was very good on the ball. And Ian Miller, also from Swindon – he was a great crosser of the ball.

THE ONE THAT GOT AWAY

Mark Hughes: Manchester United to Blackburn Rovers

If he had not played so well for Manchester United when he was given a rare first-team opportunity away at Oxford

United in the League Cup, I am sure I would have signed him, probably on loan at first. I used to watch the reserve teams of the bigger clubs quite often, especially Man United, Man City and Bolton in the days when the reserve teams played on their own pitch.

I remember watching Man United's reserves at Old Trafford this one match and Hughesy caught my eye. I liked how when the ball was hit into him, it stuck. Once your centre-forward holds the ball up, you're in the final third and are on the attack, whether he plays through the middle or out wide, you're on the attack. He had tremendous body strength, which helped him no end.

I got on to Ron Atkinson after seeing this lad, as he'd have been just about 20 at the time was Hughesy. I asked Ron if he would let him come to Blackburn and he said he would think about it. Not long after that, Hughes played at the Manor Ground with all their stars – Bryan Robson, Ray Wilkins, Frank Stapleton, etc. and scored in a 1-1 draw. It was goodnight Eileen for us as far as signing Mark Hughes went after that! But what a great player he went on to become. At least I can take some comfort that I can spot a player when I see one!

JOHN SILLETT

Managed: Hereford United (1974–1978 & 1991–1992); Coventry City (1986–1990)

MY BIG DEAL

Richard 'Dixie' McNeil: Lincoln City to Hereford United for £25,000 in 1974

I had been coaching at Bristol City and as soon as I took over at Hereford I made a move for Dixie as I knew he was a prolific goalscorer at that level. In fact, when I finally got to work with him I thought he could have succeeded at a much higher level. Initially I recommended him to Bristol when I was there but they turned him down so when I became Hereford manager I got in touch with Lincoln about signing him. His manager at the time was Graham Taylor and I had a few problems with him in terms of them letting him go. We were hoping to get him for £15,000 but they wanted more. Our chairman ultimately said, 'Go on, give them what they want,' and we had to pay £24,000. It was a step up for him as we were in the [old] Third Division and Lincoln were a league lower. In his first season Dixie scored 31 goals in 44 league games and then 35 goals in 41 league games the season after, when he helped us win the league to go up to the Second Division. We went up by a record number of points when it was still two points for a win and one for a draw, so every penny we paid for him was money well spent.

Dixie carried on scoring in the Second Division, with 16 goals, but we were relegated straight away and the board started to become panicky about money and made noises about cashing in on Dixie. I said, 'If you sell him, I'm off.' They sold him and I left too. Hereford more than doubled their money by getting £60,000 for him but Wrexham also did well out of his goals. They went up to the Second Division as champions in his first season, while his 11 FA Cup goals that season helped steer them to the quarter-finals.

He was a phenomenal striker, could easily have played Premier League, or First Division as it was then. Bobby Charlton kept ringing me when he was manager of Preston and said, 'I want to buy your striker.' But I wasn't willing to sell and the board stuck with me on that one. He ended up settling in Wrexham, working for St John Ambulance. It's funny how things can work out. For instance, Ian Rush did well at Chester City in his early days and was able to get his move to Liverpool. I'm not saying Dixie would have done what Rushy did but I know he would have scored goals at that level. He was a lovely bloke as well. You'd have been delighted if your daughter brought him home and said, 'This is the bloke I'm going to marry.' He had a terrific temperament and if you'd give him a roasting in the dressing room he'd just smile back at you and promise to get the job done next time.

At Coventry, I bought David Speedie from Chelsea when there were quite a few clubs after him and Kevin Gallacher from Dundee United. I drove up to Scotland with my wife to watch Kevin and coming back I asked her, 'What did you think?' She said, 'I thought he was brilliant, I want him for Christmas!'

Dean Emerson from Rotherham was also another shrewd signing and may have become the best if he hadn't have injured his knee. Bobby Robson told me he was picking Emerson but he did his knee and the operation didn't go to plan. I signed Kevin Sheedy also on his first professional contract, at Hereford United. What a player he later became at Everton with a wonderful left foot!

THE ONE THAT GOT AWAY

Trevor Francis: Plymouth Argyle to Bristol City

I was doing dome coaching at the end of my playing career at a school in Plymouth and I saw these two boys who were very impressive. One was Trevor Francis. I then got a job working with Alan Dicks at Bristol City, as reserve and youth team coach. I said straight away there are a couple of boys I'd like to go and get from Plymouth and was given the green light to go and speak to the parents. I met with Trevor's dad and he said, 'We're professionals, he needs some money in his bank before we sign for anyone.'

I relayed this to Bristol and they said, 'We don't pay money for kids.' So what happened? He went to Birmingham City and later became a European Cup winner, scoring the goal in the final for Nottingham Forest, played 52 times for England and was a big success in Italy. I heard some years later that Bristol were then prepared to pay for kids! They learned their lesson.

Trevor's ability was clear to me from such an early age. He was a wonderful athlete, a good mover, had great pace, he had natural ball skills that you can't teach, he had appreciation of positioning and was always cool in front of goal which made him a great goalscorer. He had absolutely everything you would want to see in a youngster. Trevor was the best schoolboy footballer I ever saw, though Kevin Sheedy was a fine prospect also when we had him at Hereford, but Trevor had pace.

DEAN SMITH

Managed: Walsall (2011–2015); Brentford
(2015–2018); Aston Villa (2018–2021);
Norwich City (2021–)

MY BIG DEAL

Matt Gill: Norwich City to Walsall on loan in 2011

My best signing is somebody who probably not many people will know about. It's Matt Gill, who I signed on loan from Norwich. I'd just taken the job as caretaker manager at Walsall. We were nine points adrift at the bottom of the league and it was looking like we were going down to League Two. I think we had played four more games than anybody else. It was in January and I felt we needed more quality in the midfield area. So Matty came in and he was excellent from the start of his loan to the finish. We ended up safe, one point away from relegation to League Two. Unfortunately, though, Matty was doing that well for us at Walsall that Norwich called him back, so he missed the last couple of months of our season. But I understood why because he went on to get promoted to the Premier League with Norwich that season under Paul Lambert, though I'm not sure he featured too much after he returned.

I can honestly say, though, that even for such a short period Matt Gill is the most important signing I made because if he had not come in to help us at Walsall and hit the ground running as well as he did, I might never have got the Aston Villa manager's job, my boyhood club, or even any club in the top division.

It was my first job and when younger managers speak to me now I always tell them that survival in the job is the most important thing.

It's about getting those players to play for you and I brought in Matt Gill, who was a very good character and influenced the dressing room for me, so he is my most important one.

THE ONE THAT GOT AWAY

James Justin: Luton Town to Aston Villa

There are loads that get away. It's very hard to pinpoint just one. There are many that you go and speak to and you are hopeful that they are going to sign for you but then a bigger club with more money, ambition, all kinds of different things can occur.

I remember missing out on Lewis Grabban when I was at Walsall in League One. He ended up going to Rotherham for more money, which I can understand. He has gone on to have a good goalscoring career, ironically with Aston Villa on loan as one of his clubs.

James Justin was another that myself and Suso [Jesús García Pitarch, Aston Villa's former sporting director] really liked when we were in the Championship with Villa. Luton understandably wanted him to stay and help them get promoted to League One. He then ended up going to Leicester [for a reported £8m fee] and is having a very fruitful career at Leicester so far.

Those are just two names that came to me quickly, but there are loads that get away. I'm struggling to name just one as there would probably be 10 or 11 players I have missed like this! It's part and parcel of being a league manager.

DENIS SMITH

*Managed: York City (1982–1987); Sunderland
(1987–1991); Bristol City (1992–1993); Oxford
United (1993–1997 & 2000); West Bromwich
Albion (1997–1999); Wrexham (2001–2007)*

MY BIG DEAL

Andy Cole: Arsenal to Bristol City for £500,000 in 1992

I saw him scoring goals when I was up at Sunderland so
when I was given the Bristol job, he was was someone I
wanted to sign pretty quickly because I knew he and George
Graham didn't get along at Arsenal. Andy was a typical
young man who felt he should be in the side but wasn't
getting picked. Alan Smith and Ian Wright were Arsenal's
first-choice strikers at the time and Andy wasn't getting a
look-in.

He was a quiet lad, shy almost, but as a footballer he
had got pace, a good first touch and believed in himself
and I always liked players who believed in themselves. His
inner belief kept him going through those tough early days
at Arsenal. He liked to come short and get the ball deep. But
I told him I didn't want him to do that, I wanted him on the
shoulder of the last defender, poaching goals. He said, 'But
Gaffer, I can do more than that.' I said, 'I know you can, but
I don't want you to.' He was excellent with his pace and his
finishing was first-class. I was delighted with what he went
on to do in his career.

I am only sorry that we had him for such a short
period as he would have got us promoted. We signed him
in March 1992 and he was off to Newcastle a year later,
in March '93. The fact he scored 12 goals in his first 12
games after signing for Newcastle showed what a great

signing he was for them and equally what a huge loss he was for Bristol City.

Ironically it is partly due to Andy that I left the club. I was a realist and knew we were not going to be able to hang on to him because he was too good, he needed to be playing in the highest division and we were one league down. So I said to the board, if we sell Andy for this fee we can rebuild the side, bring in more quality in various positions and have a real go at promotion.

They said they didn't want to sell and I then left and the club sold him a month later, for £1.75m, which more than tripled our investment in him. When I was manager nearly every club in the land wanted to buy him and I know we could have got a fair bit more than the fee they took for him in the end.

I was also pleased to sign Matt Elliott from Scunthorpe for just £150,000 before he was eventually sold on to Leicester for £1.6m. He was a big lad but was a much better footballer than many gave him credit for. He was a lot better than just a stopper. Enzo Maresca was another I was proud of when I was West Brom manager. I signed him for nothing and they got £4m for him from Juventus after I had left.

THE ONE THAT GOT AWAY

Gary Penrice: Bristol Rovers to Bristol City

There aren't many I can say I missed out on that I was too disappointed about but if circumstances had turned out different I would certainly have brought Gary Penrice to Bristol City. That signing was dependent on Coley moving [from City] and freeing up some transfer funds for me but it didn't happen. Penrice wasn't as good as Coley but I knew he would have scored me goals.

My proposal to the Bristol City board was, 'Let's get £2m for Coley, you'll get your £500,000 back and more and then give me £500,000 to bring in three or four players,' and one of those I had in mind was Penrice. That transfer might have upset a few people because of the rivalry between the two Bristol clubs, but I'm sure most people would have accepted he was going up in the world considering where both clubs were at that time.

GRAEME SOUNESS

*Managed: Rangers (1986–1991); Liverpool (1991–
1994); Galatasaray (1995–1996); Southampton
(1996–1997); Torino (1997); Benfica (1997–1999);
Blackburn Rovers (2000–2004); Newcastle United
(2004–2006)*

MY BIG DEAL

Richard Gough: Tottenham Hotspur to Rangers for
£1.5m in 1987

The player who I have always regarded as my greatest
signing by a country mile was Richard Gough, as much for
the relatively low fee of £1.5m as anything else. He came
to us from Tottenham because he spent a year at White
Hart Lane after making his name at Dundee United but
Jim McLean wouldn't sell him to us so he played at Spurs
for a season first. He ended up giving more than a decade
of service to Glasgow Rangers so he became a huge signing
for the football club.

I knew him as a young man when he played for Scotland
with me, so I knew all about his character, and he didn't
disappoint. Wherever he played he was fabulous, was a
wonderful athlete with an excellent attitude. It wasn't easy
to sign him because David Pleat was manager of Tottenham
at the time and clubs like that never want to lose their best
players. Fortunately for me and my club he was determined
to play for Glasgow Rangers and he put himself out on a
limb to join us.

He had been brilliant for Tottenham as he'd been for
Dundee United beforehand and he was fabulous for us too,
given the fee we paid and the longevity we got from him
and the service he gave. I loved his attitude; he put his head

where many people wouldn't put their boot, was very brave, quick and intelligent. I was still joining in with the five-a-sides in those days and I always made sure I was on his side! He was all elbows and knees and I lost count of the times he was sat in the dressing room after a game with a cut on his head – but it never bothered him. Brave as a lion.

I should also mention Terry Butcher because he was an England captain and was one of the first I brought in at Rangers. He was significant to what we achieved at Ibrox. Once I signed him it was then easy to bring in more quality players at Rangers.

THE ONE THAT GOT AWAY

Eric Cantona: Nîmes to Liverpool in 1991

I was Liverpool manager at the time and we were playing Auxerre in a UEFA Cup second round game [second leg, on 6 October 1991]. We had lost the first leg 2-0 away but won the second leg 3-0 at home. Anyway, I was sitting in my office after the game when I had a knock at the door. The Anfield dressing room attendant told me that a Mr Michel Platini wanted to speak with me. I thought to myself, 'I wonder what he wants?' I invited him in and we cut to the chase pretty quickly when he recommended a player to me.

Platini was the France manager at the time and we obviously knew one another from our time as players in Italy in the 1980s. He said, 'I've got a fabulous player for you but he is controversial and has had his share of problems, but if you can get him playing he will be good for Liverpool.' He then said his name was Eric Cantona, which at that time meant nothing to me. Cantona was with Nîmes but was apparently seeking a move to England.

I explained to Platini that it was a difficult time for Liverpool and a difficult time for me personally as I had inherited an ageing squad and was rebuilding the team and that I didn't need any issues or any more problems than I had already. There were ageing players at Anfield that were coming to the end and I was trying to ease them out gently and some players don't accept that so it was tough. That was keeping me busy enough without the added problems that Eric Cantona may have brought.

Every manager can look back on his own career and think, 'God, I wish I had done that differently or I wish I had signed him,' but to be honest I don't regret that decision because nobody had heard of him. He had not made his mark by then; he was just a young, promising kid in France. Sheffield Wednesday also had the chance to sign him and had him on trial for a week when Trevor Francis was manager. There was snow on the ground so he had trained on the plastic and Trevor wanted to see him for a second week on grass. But Cantona said, 'No, I'm off!' He turned up at Leeds United not long after. The rest is history.

GORDON STRACHAN

Managed: Coventry City (1996–2001);
Southampton (2001–2004); Celtic (2005–
2009); Middlesbrough (2009–2010); Scotland
(2013–2017)

MY BIG DEAL

Shunsuke Nakamura: Reggina to Celtic for
£1.6m in 2005

There are two signings that I would highlight but the
best would be Nakamura at Celtic for £1.6m, which was
good value. He was still playing football [in 2020] with
Yokohama in the Japanese J-League while approaching his
42nd birthday!

Not only was he a fantastic footballer but he was a great
human being and a humble gentleman. For the four years
I had him, he was just magnificent for the club. He set
standards that brought the kids forward at Celtic by the
things he did. For instance, after any game at Celtic Park,
it didn't matter what the weather, he changed, put more
gear on, went up the stairs to the gym and worked out for
45 minutes. Nakamura was also in early in the morning.
He set the boys off like Aiden McGeady, Shaun Maloney,
Stephen McManus, Gary Caldwell, they all kind of saw
that and followed suit.

I was travelling the world looking at footballers and
I saw Nakamura playing for Reggina somewhere in Italy.
And when I took the job at Celtic I remembered that guy's
name. So, I got hold of tapes of him playing. I gave one to
my assistant Garry Pendrey, I took one, coach Jim Blyth
took one and I said, 'Go and watch this guy tonight and tell
me what you think in the morning.'

They all came back with, 'Ooh, he's a bit of a player.' We didn't know how good he was as a person at that point and how good he was as a professional. But that was the way we picked Nakamura. He wasn't hard to sign either. There was an eccentric chairman at the time at Reggina, so it was easy to pick up players there.

For value for money, the other guy I'd like to single out is Paul Telfer. I had him at Coventry, Southampton and Celtic. He was a guy who set standards at training that were unmatched by anybody. His biggest asset was being a great team-mate. I knew him well and he's a good friend now. His work rate, his ability to soak in information, he kept himself incredibly fit.

Everywhere we went, every club, everyone at Coventry, Southampton and Celtic thought he was fantastic.

Strange fella, though, as he loved to play golf more than he played football! He got his handicap down to four at one point. I played golf with him once in Spain and after 13 holes Paul had eight birdies. I was just literally holding the flag and he was playing. I should have had his name 'PAUL TELFER' across my jersey because I was like his caddie. He was somebody who, if you were picking a team to save your life, you'd have Paul Telfer. Those two are the ones I'm happy to single out. I apologise to anybody else that I signed and haven't mentioned. But I signed a few dodgy ones as well.

THE ONE THAT GOT AWAY

Emmanuel Adebayor: Metz to Southampton

There were a few we went to see and thought about and usually went, 'No, maybe, no, maybe aye, aye,' but the one in particular who was right on the doorstep who we went for was Emmanuel Adebayor. It was at Southampton and I went with my assistant Dennis Rofe after our European scout Terry Cooper had asked me to watch a left-back at Metz. We knew Wayne Bridge would be leaving. So after about half an hour I said to Terry, 'The left-back's not bad but have you noticed the big striker there?' And Terry went, 'Yes, he's not bad.' I went, 'I think he's better than not bad, this fella.'

I was keen to sign him and I left it with Rupert Lowe, the chairman. It was near the end of the season so I went on holiday and arranged it for Adebayor to come across and speak to Rupert and do a deal. I had the fee sorted. I phoned Rupert and said how did you get on with our man? 'I sent him away, Gordon,' says Rupert. 'I didn't like the cut of his jib.'

In a way, Rupert was right. Adebayor has not been the easiest of people to get on with, so I can understand Rupert, and he wanted what would have been one of the better wages at the club. Rupert wanted to offer him half that and instead Adebayor went to Monaco and then on to make his name with Arsenal.

If I'm honest with you I think I missed a bit of stress by not getting Adebayor. I think he has tested every manager he's ever played for, that fella. Full of ability, aye, but he seems to have tested every manager. I reckon I was more relaxed in my bed without signing him.

DAVE STRINGER

Managed: Norwich City (1987–1992)

MY BIG DEAL

Robert Fleck: Rangers to Norwich City for
£580,000 in 1987

Fleck has to be my number one signing because when I took
over, after Ken Brown had been sacked, we were around the
bottom of the First Division and were desperate for a lift. I
realised we needed to bring someone in who could lift the
club straight away. I had only seen Flecky on the television
a couple of times but he looked like a very busy type and a
real trier so I went after him and fortunately we got him as
he wasn't a regular in the Rangers team.

I spoke to the Rangers manager Graeme Souness and he
was quite happy to let Fleck leave as I don't think Flecky was
the easiest person to manage at that time. He was certainly
a 'Jack the lad' type when he came to Carrow Road also
but I didn't mind that and I liked his spirit. His intensity
in training sessions was such that the whole standard of
training improved because of him as other players wanted
to show what they could do as well.

Fleck was great for us. He always gave his all, was a
threat to defenders and had a goal in him. His spirit and
upbeat demeanour lifted the whole club and we were able to
pick up results from thereon and climb the table. We were
in the doldrums before he arrived, but things changed on
the back of his energy and goal threat. He helped us to push
on the following season when we finished fourth in the top
flight and reached the semi-finals of the FA Cup.

Flecky's goals-per-game ratio wasn't prolific overall
but he scored a lot of important goals and I can't overstate

his upbeat nature that was infectious in the dressing room and even on the field his livewire style seemed to make life difficult for opposition. He matured a lot as a person as well after coming to Norwich and it's interesting to know that he has now settled in the Norwich area post-retirement, which usually indicates a great deal about where a player was at his happiest.

I should also mention other signings I was very pleased with like Andy Linighan, who ended up leaving us for Oldham Athletic where Joe Royle was manager. He obviously moved to Arsenal from there. He was a rock in our defence and took some replacing. Andy Townsend, Tim Sherwood and Dion Dublin would be other notable signings but I allowed Dion to leave for Cambridge United before he made his name and from there he earned a move to Man United. But at least I can say I saw his talent otherwise I wouldn't have signed him in the first place!

THE ONE THAT GOT AWAY

Peter Schmeichel: Brøndby to Norwich City

I went out to Denmark to have a look at Henrik Mortensen, who had been recommended to us. He was playing for Aarhus then and the game I watched was against Brøndby, with the great Peter Schmeichel in goal for them, but he wasn't the star then we later came to appreciate, though he was in the national team.

In hindsight I kick myself that I was concentrating on Mortensen that much that I didn't really notice Schmeichel. But that is how scouting can go. If you're targeting a goalkeeper and they're playing in a good side, as Schmeichel was then, it is so much harder to notice them or be impressed by them.

I did have a good goalkeeper at the time in Bryan Gunn, so a keeper wasn't the top of my wish list, but any Premier

League manager or coach will tell you that they are always looking for the next star who can improve their team. I managed to sign most of my targets, though, because they were not all that expensive, most of the time.

GERRY SUMMERS

*Managed: Wolverhampton Wanderers (caretaker
1968); Oxford United (1969–1975); Gillingham
(1975–1981)*

MY BIG DEAL

Steve Bruce: Wallsend Boys Club to Gillingham on a
free transfer in 1978

Steve Bruce was my biggest and best signing by a country
mile. He had been rejected by all the north-east clubs and
probably many more. He had a great attitude that I admired,
he worked hard and went on to represent England at youth
level before moving on to Norwich City and then obviously
Manchester United where he became a prolific cup winner
and a great leader for Alex Ferguson.

He played 40-odd games for me in each of his first
two full seasons at Gillingham, which shows how well
he settled in. Steve was a great example of hard work and
determination. I wouldn't want to take much credit for
Steve's career as he did it all himself but I am pleased to
have been part of his journey at Gillingham.

THE ONE THAT GOT AWAY

Peter Beardsley: Wallsend Boys Club to Gillingham on
a free transfer in 1978

I was always keen on the development of young players, but
because of the size and financial status of my club, I had to
be careful how many youngsters I took on. I had several near
misses but my biggest regret is definitely Peter Beardsley. Not
because I couldn't get him but because I didn't take him on
at Gillingham when I had the chance, after he came down

for trials with Steve Bruce from Wallsend Boys Club in the north-east.

He was so keen he even offered to help the ground staff, but I just thought he wasn't good enough. I don't know why now all these years on but he must have been lacking something in my mind. But he clearly did have what it takes because he went on to have a great career, starting at Carlisle United.

In fact, he played against us in a league match and scored a hat-trick. I knew then I had made a huge mistake and that was even before he went on to have the decorated career he did!

BRIAN TALBOT

Managed: West Bromwich Albion (1988–1991); Aldershot (1991); Hibernians (Malta) (1993–1996); Rushden & Diamonds (1997–2004); Oldham Athletic (2004–2005); Oxford United (2005–2006); Marsaxlokk (2006–2008)

MY BIG DEAL

Ugo Ehiogu: Globe Town to West Bromwich Albion on a free transfer in 1988

My best signing was Ugo by a country mile. From the very first day I saw him I knew he would be a player. It was an amazing, almost freakish sequence of events as to how it came about. They [Globe Town] were a small club based in the East End of London and they made me an honorary member of their club, which I was pleased to accept. They asked me if they could send me any players of promise and I agreed of course but never honestly expected that relationship to bear any fruits for me as a manager.

But about a year later, someone from the club called me to say, 'There's a player we'd like you to take a look at.' Out of courtesy more than anything we invited him up to a trial. When Ugo came it was quickly obvious that it was a no-brainer for us to sign this lad as a YTS [Youth Training Scheme]. He was outstanding. I was gobsmacked at how he had slipped through the net.

He played at the back for me but at first in the youth team he played everywhere: in defence, midfield, even up front and wherever he played he was the standout player. He was confident, powerful, strong, commanding, he made good decisions, didn't waste the ball – the lad didn't realise how good he was.

The youth team coach told me how well he was doing and advised me that we needed to fast-track him into the first team, which we did. He learned quickly and you only needed to tell him something once and he had it, so it was never a problem to promote him so soon as he proved himself as someone who could be trusted to do the job you wanted from him.

Ugo was a gamble in a way because he was coming from a small club but once we got him up to the club it was clear we had got ourselves a gem of a footballer, so it quickly transpired that we had a bargain. We didn't have to pay a transfer fee, maybe just £1,500 in equipment for the club. West Brom later sold him to Villa and he went on to have a great career, even playing four times for England.

Paul Underwood would be another one of my best recruits from Enfield to Rushden & Diamonds.

THE ONE THAT GOT AWAY

Luther Blissett: Watford to West Bromwich Albion

I played with Luther at Watford so I knew what I would be getting. He was 30 at the time, which is a great age for a striker, especially for a club like we were then, in the old Second Division. There was to be a small fee involved and we were going to pay him £600 a week but Bournemouth, who had just been promoted into our league, somehow managed to find £1,200 a week wages for him and once he received that offer we had no chance of competing with it.

Luther was very honest and spoke to me on the phone and I couldn't blame him as they were paying him double to what West Brom could afford. It was a shame because he would have made a difference to us: he scored goals for fun, he stretched defences, was a good, positive influence in the dressing room,

I also tried to sign Terry Butcher, my old team-mate from Ipswich, and bring him to West Brom after he left Rangers. His experience and influence would have made him a terrific signing for us. But he chose to go to Coventry as player-manager instead as it gave him a start in management, which you can't blame him for.

STAN TERNENT

*Managed: Blackpool (1979–1980); Hull City
(1989–1991); Bury (1995–1998); Burnley (1998–
2004); Gillingham (2004–2005); Huddersfield
Town (2008)*

MY BIG DEAL

Ian Wright: Celtic to Burnley on a free transfer in 2000

It's really difficult to say who was your best signing and not wanting to be disrespectful to other players you signed. I also signed Paul Gascoigne of course. But Ian certainly had the desired effect when he came in, by helping us to promotion [into the First Division as was at the time]. He was coming to the end of his career but he still had a very positive impact around the club, on and off the pitch. I knew him from Crystal Palace when I worked at Selhurst Park for about a year with Steve Coppell so it wasn't like I didn't know him. I knew he had great faith in his own ability and was an out-and-out winner.

The move came about after I had a conversation with Mitchell Thomas, who was a senior player of mine and also a big pal of Ian's. I said, 'How's Satch getting on up at Celtic?' Satch was Wrighty's nickname and what we called him. Mitchell told me he wasn't too happy as he was getting into television at the time and it meant a lot of travelling between London and Glasgow. I said, 'Tell him if he ever fancies a few games here he'll be very welcome.' Mitchell came back to me a few days later and said, 'I spoke to Wrighty and he wants to know if you're serious.' Of course, I was deadly serious and told Mitchell to get Ian to call me.

Fortunately, we managed to get a deal done and it gave everyone associated with Burnley a massive lift, especially the players and the supporters. I never thought I would manage to persuade someone like Ian Wright to play for Burnley in the old Third Division [the second tier, prior to renaming as League One], but we did! I don't think the financial implications were of great consequence to Ian at that stage, he just wanted to play football and be happy doing it. I knew he had media commitments down in London, so I was prepared to be flexible with him.

I made a promise to his representatives that whether he wanted to come up to Burnley three days a week, two days, five days, three months, whatever it was, we would work things around him. Because I knew we had to make the move attractive to Ian Wright. He still knew how to score a goal and was great for us, so it worked well for both parties. His attitude was infectious, he was a terrific trainer and, ultimately, he is one of the greatest goalscoring strikers this country has ever produced, he's a legend, so we were very lucky to have him, even if it wasn't for a long period.

THE ONE THAT GOT AWAY

Peter Crouch: Queens Park Rangers to Burnley

I delayed a holiday in America to go down to London to meet him and his agent, Jonathan Barnett. I drove down to meet them at a motorway service station on the M40. I took my secretary with me and I was quietly hoping they would sign there and then but that didn't pan out. He ended up going to Portsmouth but I had a real go for him.

We bid £1.25m but Harry [Redknapp] went that bit further and they ended up getting him for £1.5m I think it was. Crouchy apparently said after signing for Pompey that the riots up here put him off. But he was a London boy anyway and I think that move just suited him more.

I signed Gareth Taylor afterwards instead and he was great for us. But Crouchy was my first choice and was a no-brainer. I liked him very much and his ability was pretty obvious. He had fantastic feet and people never gave him the credit that he deserved, because he's tall, thin and six-foot-whatever it was.

He was a very talented player and I thought it was clear that he would go on and have a very successful career, as it proved. You don't go playing for great clubs like Spurs and Liverpool for so long if you can't play. And he had some great years at Stoke City towards the back end of his career and Tony [Pulis] is no fool, he knew what he was doing bringing Crouchy in. He really is the one that got away for me.

COLIN TODD

Managed: Middlesbrough (1990–1991); Bolton Wanderers (1995–1999); Swindon Town (2000); Derby County (2001–2002); Bradford City (2004–2007); Randers (2007–2009); Darlington (2009); Randers (2012–2016); Esbjerg (2016)

MY BIG DEAL

Eidur Gudjohnsen: PSV Eindhoven to Bolton Wanderers on a free transfer in 1998

One thing in management that always used to annoy me was how managers come into a football club and get credit for someone who they didn't sign and who the previous manager brought in. I know a new manager can sometimes come in and extract better performances but let's not forget the manager who brought that player to the club in the first place.

In my case, it frustrated me that Sam Allardyce came in after me and got a lot of the credit for the players who I had signed before he arrived. I brought Jussi Jääskeläinen to Bolton for about £170,000 – he stayed there for over ten years and they could have cashed him in for £6m easy at one point. There was Per Frandsen, Ricardo Gardner, Mark Fish, Claus Jensen, Saša Ćurčić, Alan Thompson and many others. But the best one by a long way who I signed through my whole career was Eidur Gudjohnsen.

He was at PSV but had injured himself and he returned to Iceland to get himself fit. I then got a phone call from an agent asking if I would be interested to have a look at him and it was clear from his past record that he had something to offer. His time at PSV and a useful goalscoring record for Iceland under-21s meant his pedigree was good. There were not many too keen to take him because through the injury he had at PSV a story was going round saying he wouldn't play again. But I felt we had nothing to lose as we would only have given him a contract if a) he showed up well as a footballer and b) he proved his fitness. It was a good position for us to be in really because if he had not have had his injury we would never have been able to compete with the top clubs for his signature.

I was in Dublin at the time in a pre-season when he came over to join us so we could take a look at him. He was clearly overweight when he joined us but I could see that he had lots of potential to work with if we could get his weight right. I liked his ability to link up play, he could hold the ball up, retain possession, was dangerous around the box, wasn't the quickest but was strong and could turn and go at people. There was a lot to like.

The club obviously ended up making a lot of money from the signing of Eidur when he was sold to Chelsea for something like £4.5m. When you see what he achieved later on in his career with Chelsea and Barcelona, it puts it into perspective how well we did at Bolton to sign him for nothing.

There are quite a few I was pleased to sign. I already mentioned the lads at Bolton, and there were others like Robbie Mustoe for Middlesbrough and he stayed there for 12 years.

THE ONES THAT GOT AWAY
No one

There really wasn't a player I can remember badgering a chairman about and not getting. If there was a player we wanted to have a dart at and maybe money came into it and was a problem, it would usually be a reason to move on and not worry too much about.

JOHN TOSHACK

Managed: Swansea City (player-manager 1978–
1983 & manager 1983–1984); Sporting Lisbon
(1984–1985); Real Sociedad (1985–1989, 1991–
1994 & 2001–2002); Real Madrid (1989–1990
& 1999); Wales (1994 & 2004–2010); Deportivo
La Coruña (1995–1997); Beşiktaş (1997–
1999); Saint-Étienne (2000–2001); Catania
(2002–2003); Real Murcia (2004); Macedonia
(2011–2012); Khazar Lankaran (2013); Wydad
Casablanca (2014–2015); Tractor (2018)

MY BIG DEALS

Džemal Hadžiabdić: Velež Mostar to Swansea City for
£100,000 in 1980

Ante Rajković: FK Sarajevo to Swansea City for
£90,000 in 1981

To pick one signing for me is very difficult. I'll have to go
for two. Of all the players I've had, it's not the same signing
someone for Swansea City as it is to sign somebody for Real
Madrid. You could relate to someone signed for £2,000 and
sold for £20,000, or someone you signed who enabled others
to play better. Or someone on a free transfer.

Tommy Smith and Cally [Ian Callaghan] were terrific
signings for me at Swansea and helped me a lot. They
were free transfers when everyone had given up on them
and said they were finished. They came down to us on a
Thursday for a game on a Saturday and one time Smithy was
shouting and screaming at me because I'd said the weather
in Swansea was fine, he travelled down and then the game
was snowed off!

Cally was OK and understanding, but they had to stay down over the weekend and Smithy, well even on a good day you tried to keep out of his way, he was bubbling. But those two were so important to me with the good habits they brought with them. They helped me get started. I doubt there has been two better free transfers.

My favourites, though, are the two from my time at Swansea because of what they did and how popular they were. In those days there weren't many foreign players over here. Osvaldo Ardiles and Ricky Villa came about the same time from Argentina at Tottenham.

Pound for pound they were excellent. I have worked in 12 countries and won trophies in five or six of them, but those two from Yugoslavia were super signings both on and off the pitch. They were the first foreigners Swansea had and we really hit the jackpot with the two of them.

First there was Džemal Hadžiabdić, who they nicknamed 'Jimmy' in Swansea. It was a lot easier that way! There was a Yugoslav journalist who lived in London, a friend of mine, and he put me on to Hadžiabdić. The civil war in the old Yugoslavia, as it was then, was breaking out, so we nipped in and got him over on a trial. We played Tottenham in a friendly and he was so good the crowd went berserk. He came off after 60 minutes, did a few bows. We had to sign him.

We were fortunate because we got him out of Mostar. When the war was starting there, we got their families over here as well, away from that awful conflict that took so many lives. 'Jimmy' was a terrific lad. He was a left-back and his distribution was fantastic. He was shy, but a lovely lad. He ended up buying a house in Swansea and he goes back there even now.

So Hadžiabdić was the first one. Then, the other Yugoslav lad was Ante Rajković. He was another international and a central defender. He was so strong. When he shook your hand, you shuddered. You ask Graeme Souness. Souness went to toss a coin with Rajković because he was captain the day when we played Liverpool. He shook his hand and Souness had to have treatment because he'd damaged his hand. Rajković had a smile on his face.

I've been fortunate, I've managed top clubs and I've played against top players, and Rajković is up there. It is generally recognised that with a hamstring injury you can't play, right? But I saw Rajković play 30 minutes of a game against Cardiff, the local derby, with a hamstring injury. The doctors and the physios afterwards said how the hell he has played with that?

His reading of the game was excellent, and he was so strong. I think Rajković has a house in Swansea too where he spends some time on holiday.

These two Yugoslavs were outstanding. There's a little bit of sentiment with it for me because it was Swansea, but Hadžiabdić helped pushed us through the divisions from the old fourth division and into the Premier League, as it is now.

In our first season in the old First Division, we were top of the league at the end of March. With six games to go it looked like we were going to be champions, but we blew up and lost five of the last six and ended up coming sixth.

Another good signing that I should mention, when I was at Real Madrid, was Fernando Hierro, who many will have heard of. He was a 19-year-old playing for Valladolid when I first saw him, and I encouraged the president to have a look.

In those days at Real Madrid, they were kind enough to let me sign one player a year. The president signed five or six and would say, 'You can have one.' I said there's a lad at Valladolid, he was a little bit awkward, ungainly, tall, but he was from a family of footballers, a couple of brothers played, but they weren't as good as him.

When I look back now at what Hierro achieved at Real Madrid [five La Liga titles, three European Cups] and the Spanish national team [89 caps, played in four World Cups and two European Championships, later became manager] he was one of my best.

There was also Carlos Xavier and Oceano, who I had at Sporting Lisbon and took to Sociedad. Another I have to mention is Meho Kodro, who I signed for Sociedad. Hadžiabdić went back home, and he phoned me, said I had to have a look at this centre-forward, Kodro. We ended up paying about £50,000 for him and three years later Barcelona paid ridiculous money for him, something like £10m.

THE ONE THAT GOT AWAY
No one

I like to think that when I went for someone, I got him. There must have been someone somewhere along the line, but I can't think of one.

Signings were very much a personal thing in those days. These days half the managers don't know who the player is they've signed with all the people now involved at clubs.

I never signed anybody unless I'd seen them play. When I was playing for Liverpool, Bill Shankly taught me all I knew and that was one of the things he said, look at the players you are signing. That all seems to have gone out the window now.

The truth is, when managing in Europe and abroad, as I did after Swansea, you don't sign the players while you are in charge. You might sign players, but they might not actually be what you want.

Real Madrid is a good example of what it's like. They let the manager sign one out of every half a dozen, but the president, with the agents and God knows what, signed the rest of them. So, I couldn't really answer that question because by and large it wasn't me going for a player, it was other people and then the coach must integrate them into the team.

GRAHAM TURNER

Managed: Shrewsbury Town (1978–1984
& 2010–2014); Aston Villa (1984–1986);
Wolverhampton Wanderers (1986–1994); Hereford
United (1995–2009 & 2010)

MY BIG DEAL

Steve Bull: West Bromwich Albion to Wolverhampton
Wanderers for £30,000, including the part-exchange of
Andy Thompson, in 1986

It has to be Bully when I think about what we paid for him
and his contribution over the years [with a Wolves record
306 goals], especially in those early dark days in the old
Third and Fourth Divisions – he scored lots of goals in every
season he played at Molineux. He was very raw when he
came to us, he needed plenty of chances to convert them
into one or two goals, but he would make those chances.

I first saw him play against Chelsea in the Full Members'
Cup and I was very impressed with the way he looked after
himself as much as anything. He was the type of striker who
would try to convert six chances in a match and four or five
of them might end up out the ground or by the corner flag
but he was equally likely to have grabbed one or two goals
as well.

My first problem was getting some money out of Wolves
owner Tony Gallagher to fund the transfer as I didn't have
anything to spend in my early days. But then out of the blue
I was told I'd got a little bit of money to spend – so I bought
two rookies from West Brom, which didn't go down too well
with many people at Wolves given the fierce rivalry between
the clubs. If I remember rightly the fee was £40,000 with
a top-up of another £20,000. Bully would have been about

£30,000 of that, I guess, with Andy Thompson also part of the package.

It took some work to get this transfer over the line, though. The West Brom manager Ron Saunders was quite keen to get the deal done eventually but it still took about three phone calls. The first two occasions he told me Bully was not for sale, but I pursued it. The third time I called him I detected there was a shifting in his attitude towards selling – whether he didn't really fancy him or whether he just wanted to create some money to bring someone else in, I'm not sure. But he gave in.

The West Brom chairman Sid Lucas needed a lot more persuading – it nearly broke his heart. I remember driving over to The Hawthorns to meet Sid Lucas with the forms for him to sign, thinking, 'I'm not going to let this deal slip through my fingers.' Fortunately, we agreed the deal there and then and I just had to meet the players the following morning to agree personal terms.

Bully probably took about two minutes to agree his contract and Thommo maybe two and a half minutes. They were just so excited to be wanted by Wolves despite the poor state we were in then as a club. I'm not sure they realised what they were coming to but still they dropped two divisions to come and help us out and thankfully we started getting a few decent results and they began to enjoy it at the Molineux. Bully scored six goals in his first eight games so I was quite relieved that what little money I had managed to prise from the chairman was put to good use.

People have asked me over the years did I get lucky with the signing of Steve Bull or was it more good talent identification and the simple answer is it's a bit of both. If you watch enough football you become adept at spotting talent, especially good, young players, and if you look at what I did at Aston Villa, I signed a young Martin Keown before he had really made his name. But, equally, spending £40,000 was a significant amount of money to Wolves at that time and it was a gamble because you can never guarantee that a player will be successful. And I signed two kids with no record or real pedigree. But it worked out well as history will show.

The other player I would mention is Martin Keown, when I was Villa manager. I watched him play as a 19-year-old for Arsenal against Liverpool and he didn't give Ian Rush a kick. I watched him at Old Trafford. Again, he didn't give Mark Hughes a kick. A few months later I saw a clip in the newspaper that George Graham was going into Arsenal as their new manager and he had about five players who were out of contract that he needed to re-sign, perhaps. I then found out where Martin lived, on the outskirts of Oxford, I went down there and knocked on his door and persuaded him to sign for Villa.

It went to a tribunal and I believe Villa paid £125,000. So that was an outstanding signing given the career he went on to have. It's just a shame I only had him for six games before I was gone.

THE ONE THAT GOT AWAY

Neil Webb: Portsmouth to Aston Villa in 1985

I watched him play for England under-21s and I really fancied him coming to Villa. I got him and his wife up to Villa Park to talk about the move and what we expected from him. He seemed fairly happy but he mentioned that he wanted to speak with his dad and bring him up the following week to finalise the move. We agreed to do that. I was very confident at that stage that we would sign him.

But his dad rang me 24 hours later to say he was going to sign for Forest. Even then I refused to give it up and said, 'Hold on, where are you, let me know and I'll get across to meet up to sort this out.' But his dad said it was too late as he had already signed. That was a big disappointment and I don't know the reason why it never happened for us, but I suspect he was offered better personal terms at Forest.

It was shame as I liked Webby a lot. He could get forward and score goals from midfield. It didn't surprise me that he went on to win a lot of England caps [26] and play at the top level, especially with Manchester United. Ironically, Webb was my first choice to bring to Villa that summer [1985], but when I missed out on him to Brian Clough at Nottingham Forest, I instead took Steve Hodge from Forest a couple of months later. Hodge actually made the 1986 England World Cup squad, ahead of Webb.

MARK WARBURTON

Managed: Brentford (2013–2015); Rangers
(2015–2017); Nottingham Forest (2017); Queens
Park Rangers (2019–)

MY BIG DEAL

James Tarkowski: Oldham Athletic to Brentford for
£300,000 in 2014

I have gone for James Tarkowski because of his journey;
how we took him from Oldham and he then did well in
the Championship, he got his move to the Premier League
and did well there as well before being picked for England.
So, he is proof of how, if you deliver on your potential, you
can develop to succeed at the highest level if you take your
opportunities.

We played Oldham and our analyst told me beforehand
that the only threat from Oldham was their centre-half
who keeps driving into midfield with the ball and he
is really comfortable with it. And I thought to myself,
'I remember he caused us no end of problems when we
played them last.' David Weir was my assistant and Frank
McPartland was our recruitment guy, so they're two top
people who know football, and when we looked at the
footage of James, his range of passing, his physicality, it
made you think 'wow'. Frank then worked his magic and
did a great deal by making sure we were able to bring James
to Brentford.

I was not only pleased to sign the player but I was also
delighted because it showed a recruitment process working
very smoothly. There were other clubs interested and
sniffing around him but they hesitated and we didn't. It is
not unknown that if these processes are not in good order

moves can be slow or be delayed and sometimes can lead to you missing a player, so thankfully that wasn't the case with us here. We didn't hesitate; Oldham had a tough financial position at the time and we were able to capitalise on that in the right way so it was a good deal for everyone. He was a top player for us from the moment he joined us, on and off the field.

I'm not surprised he has gone on to a much higher level. I saw a player who could play out from the back effortlessly, didn't panic with the ball when he was put under pressure, he could carry the ball comfortably into midfield, was a threat aerially in both boxes, could play left or right side of central defence, had a great range of diagonal passing, he really ticked every box when he played for me. So, it's not a surprise he has developed his game further, especially at Burnley under Sean [Dyche], who has a great knowledge and knows how to develop players.

I still believe there are many more players like Tarkowski who are plying their trade in the lower leagues and good enough to eventually move up to Premier League level. It might not be the romantic route that we saw a few years ago like how Ian Rush moved from Chester City to Liverpool, but we might well see more talented young players move from Leagues One and Two to a Championship club, as a stepping stone before going on to the Premier League. There is no doubt the talent is there – it is just a matter of giving these players the time and opportunity to develop at such a high level.

James Tavernier is another player I would like to mention who we took to Rangers from Wigan after he'd been on loan at Rotherham. He became club captain at Rangers and is a great example of another player who can play at a very good standard if given the opportunity. We bought James [£240,000] and Martyn Waghorn [£600,000] for the same fee that I paid for Tarkowski. James really impressed with his physicality and Martyn nearly scored 30 goals in his first season in Scotland so they did great for me and Rangers.

The best technical player I have ever worked with was Nico Kranjčar. I went to New York to sign him, as he was out there playing for New York Cosmos and, although he was past his best and a stone and a half overweight, we brought him back and got him fit and what a technical player he was.

He was such a good technician with a football at his feet. We did training drills when the players sometimes couldn't get the ball off him! He had everything. The impact he had on the younger players was fantastic.

THE ONE THAT GOT AWAY

Aaron Mooy: Manchester City to Rangers on loan

Brian Marwood, the former Arsenal player who is now high up at Manchester City, called me up one afternoon on the same day I had signed a player for Rangers earlier that day, when money was very tight. Anyway, Brian – who is someone I have a huge amount of respect for – asked me if I would like to take Aaron Mooy on loan – when the ink was still wet after I had signed another midfield player that day.

I knew all about Aaron Mooy and I thought to myself, 'Oh no!' because the budget was so tight there was no way we could afford both players. I didn't even cheekily ask the chairman for one more deal because I was well aware of the financial position. So, I had to tell Brian that although Aaron would be great for us and would get Ibrox buzzing, we simply couldn't afford him. Instead, he went to Huddersfield, helped them reach the Premier League and earned a permanent move to the Premier League for himself from there.

That was a massive disappointment for me because I knew he would have absolutely run the midfield and the

Ibrox crowd would have loved him. Just to prove I am not making this up, the player I had signed that same day was Joey Barton. I was still delighted to have Joey because he had been voted in the Championship Team of the Year that season and was Burnley's Player of the Year. It was just disappointing I couldn't have signed Mooy as well as I always considered him a tough Australian midfielder. He's definitely be the one that got away for me.

NEIL WARNOCK

Managed: Gainsborough Trinity (1980–1981);
Burton Albion (1981–1986); Scarborough
(1986–1989); Notts County (1989–1993); Torquay
United (1993); Huddersfield Town (1993–1995);
Plymouth Argyle (1995–1997); Oldham Athletic
(1997–1998); Bury (1998–1999); Sheffield United
(1999–2007); Crystal Palace (2007–2010 &
2014); Queens Park Rangers (2010–2012 &
2015); Leeds United (2012–2013); Rotherham
United (2016); Cardiff City (2016–2019);
Middlesbrough (2020–2021)

MY BIG DEALS

Craig Short: Pickering Town to Scarborough on a free transfer in 1987

Michael Brown: Manchester City to Sheffield United loan followed by a free transfer in 2000

The best player – I don't know what to say about that really. I spent a weekend thinking over this. It's not easy. I've done so many transfers. To begin with I had to write down all my clubs to remind me where I've been and who I've signed. I probably had two, which I couldn't really split and that's Craig Short and Michael Brown.

Craig Short was a bank clerk in Scarborough. He was on 20 quid a week, I think. He played in the reserves for us. He was a right-winger; then we tried him in midfield as he was a big lad; then we tried him at right-back; we tried him up front – we tried him everywhere. He just never fitted in anywhere.

But we played Birmingham City away in a reserve game and Peter Withe was up front for Birmingham in this

345

reserve game and I said to him, 'Look, Shorty, we've tried everything; I want you to go and mark Peter Withe and, wherever he goes, stop with him all day.' After about ten minutes Peter Withe's running to the touchline: 'Can you get this effing idiot off my back?' He says, 'He's like a rash.' Shorty never gave him a look-in and that's how we found his position.

In fairness he couldn't pass water. He used to take a bag of balls out, him and his brother, Chris, who also played for us; 40, 50 balls every day he used to take out and knock it with his right foot, left foot. He couldn't pass very well at all. I remember years later sending him a text when he was taking free kicks for Everton and I said, 'Can you remember Scarborough when you used to take those balls because you couldn't pass water?' There he was playing in the Premier League, taking free kicks for Everton!

With Brownie, Man City couldn't get rid of him quick enough. I took him on at Sheffield United and he was like a lost lamb really. He did well for me. I don't think we paid for him, we just got him on loan, then made it permanent.

He'd been out to Hartlepool on loan, then Portsmouth and then us before we signed him on. Portsmouth didn't want him, so they kicked him out for disciplinary reasons, and I took him on board. He had two of the best years ever and he got a move to Tottenham for half a million quid. He was a likeable rogue was Brownie. He's doing well now, a lovely lad.

Contribution wise, Short and Brown were probably the best two I had, never cost anything. I look around and, yes, I've had people like Adel Taarabt at QPR, Victor Moses at Crystal Palace, but value for money, those two, Craig Short and Michael Brown, they helped me win things.

THE ONE THAT GOT AWAY

Didier Drogba: Le Mans to Sheffield United for £100,000

I definitely know the one that got away. It was at Sheffield United and I had a scout, an ex-player of mine at Bury called Laurent D'Jaffo. He's a French lad and he rang me at Sheffield United when I first went in there. This was in the late '90s and he said, 'I've seen a striker, second division, in France. He's one for you, Gaffer.'

He then told me the club wanted 100 grand. I said, 'One hundred grand for a second division striker in France?'

He said, 'Yes, but he's good, Gaffer.'

I said, 'I can't Jaffo' – that's what we called him. 'I can't be paying 100 grand for a second division striker in France.'

Jaffo said, 'Well I just thought I'd tell you as I know you'd like him.'

I said, 'What's his name, anyway?'

'Didier Drogba,' Jaffo said.

Drogba was just starting out as an 18-year-old with Le Mans. And I didn't sign him! That's easily the one that got away from me.

I just thought second division striker, in France. Nah. Sheffield were in the Championship [the First Division at the time]. It took rough and tumble to play in there.

So we just didn't go for it. I didn't mind too much until Drogba then signed for Chelsea for £24m from Marseille in 2004 and scored a million goals for them.

So Jaffo reminds me of this every year!

HOWARD WILKINSON

*Managed: Boston United (1975–1976); Mossley
(1976–1977); England C (1979–1982); Notts
County (1982–1983); Sheffield Wednesday
(1983–1988); Leeds United (1988–1996);
England (caretaker 1999 & 2000); England U21
(1999–2001); Sunderland (2002–2003); Shanghai
Shenhua (2004)*

MY BIG DEAL

Gordon Strachan: Manchester United to Leeds
United in 1989

By the time I arrived at Leeds in October 1988, I had a
very clear picture of the strategic goals and timescales that
the chairman Leslie Silver and I had agreed. The first was
to get back into the top division as quickly as was humanly
possible and this meant promotion in our first or, at the
latest, second full season. From there on, the targets were
Europe and the championship of the [old] First Division.
This could only be achieved through judicious recruitment
and very careful selection.

In this respect the acquisition of Gordon Strachan
was crucial. I needed a player who could lead and perform
whatever the test on the pitch, in the dressing room and in
public. This was a lot to ask, but from our first meeting I
knew Gordon was that man. One man does not make a club
or a team, obviously, but his transfer was significant to our
subsequent success.

I was well aware of him right from his Aberdeen days
and what he did to help upset the balance of power north
of the border. Then he went to Manchester United, which
was a surprise as he almost ended up in Germany. As soon

as he became available he was someone I knew I needed to speak to.

In those days managers relied on tip-offs by reporters before stories went into newspapers and as a result of that I heard he was going to Sheffield Wednesday. I rang him after he met with Wednesday and persuaded him to come over to Leeds for a chat. That was a challenge because at the time I went to Leeds they were second from bottom in the Second Division and Sheffield were about seventh in the First. But Gordon bought into my vision and was there at the beginning of our journey.

The more we spoke it became clear we could both offer each other something. For him Leeds was an opportunity to prove he could still perform at the highest level when there was a feeling his best days were behind him at Old Trafford. In my case it was about placing the keystone in the arch. He embodied my values, he bought into the vision, he walked the walk and was the role model to which I wanted my younger players to aspire to for as long as we could make it last. History shows us that he was invigorated by the move and he did get a new lease of life. He did receive a very good contract but I knew it was important he recognised it wasn't just talk on our part.

Gary McAllister was another signing I was proud of. When I called his agent about the possibility of signing him from Leicester, Gary was speaking to Nottingham Forest at the time. And not many people chose to turn their back on Brian Clough. I'm sure Cloughy would have given me some stick for stealing him from under his nose.

And Gary Speed was someone I was pleased to nurture. While I didn't bring him to the club, as he was already in the youth team when I came to Elland Road, I did promote him from the youth team to the first team and in doing so was able to demonstrate the academy structure I wanted to build at Leeds. Gary had the perfect role model in Strachan to learn from. The great career he ended up having was a testament to the football education he received at Leeds.

THE ONE THAT GOT AWAY

Paul Gascoigne: Newcastle United to Sheffield Wednesday; Lazio to Leeds United

I became aware of him when he was around the England under-21s and I can remember him scoring against my Sheffield Wednesday team for Newcastle in his first full season. He was just 17 but played like a man. Whenever people ask me who was the most talented player I have ever seen I always say him. He was Lionel Messi and more. He could have played midfield, centre-half, up front, he was strong, he was quick, he was two-footed, he had great balance, great vision. He had everything. I would undoubtedly put him up there with [George] Best and Messi.

I made enquiries about him when he was at Newcastle but got nowhere. In hindsight I was wasting my time because he was always destined for bigger things than we could have offered him at Sheffield Wednesday at that time. Once I knew the ballpark figure of what they were after [Gascoigne signed for Tottenham for £2.2m] I knew that was us out of it and it was actually one of the reasons I left Sheffield Wednesday. At that time they had just come through some financial difficulties and were happy to run a safe ship. But I was more ambitious.

I made more enquiries when he was in Italy because, for whatever reason, it never really happened for him at Tottenham or Lazio. I went out to Italy to try and sign him for Leeds and was there about three days, but I couldn't do it.

It was a shame because I remain convinced that if we had have brought him to Leeds we could have given him a lot of help in terms of his lifestyle. They used to say Vinny

Jones couldn't stay on the park but he came to Leeds and got booked twice in two seasons and became a different player. Who really knows what would have happened to Gazza, but it would have been fun finding out!

TERRY YORATH

Managed: Swansea City (1986–1989 &
1990–1991); Wales (1988–1993); Bradford City
(1989–1990); Cardiff City (1994–1995); Lebanon
(1995–1997); Sheffield Wednesday (2001–2002);
Margate (2008–2009)

MY BIG DEAL

Alan Davies: Newcastle United to Swansea City on a free
transfer in 1987

I picked him up from Newcastle for nothing. In fact, he was
part of a double deal with Joe Allon. I seem to recall Willie
McFaul was the Newcastle manager at the time. It was an
easy deal to do and I was very pleased to sign him as Alan
had been a Wales international for a few years by then. I
scouted him myself as I'd seen him play many times.

He'd been around and learned his trade. Alan never
really managed to break through for any length of time at
Manchester United, where he had spent all his youth and
early years, but he had enough ability to make it there. The
stature of the club and what they're looking for sometimes
means good players will not always get the opportunities
they deserve. But make no mistake, he was a very, very good
footballer with great feet; he was just a natural footballer
through and through. If you put him in a five-a-side, he
would be the best player.

Alan was known for playing wide, which was where
he played when he won his FA Cup winners' medal for
Manchester United [in 1983], but he could play anywhere
across the park as he had such good feet. He was a playmaker
for me in the centre of midfield and was instrumental when
we won promotion from the old Fourth Division into the

Third. Other managers probably played him on the wing because he was slight, but he could look after himself. Although he was very slight of build, he had a steely will to win.

It was so sad that he committed suicide, he was so young [aged 30]; he always liked a laugh and a joke. He was great to have around actually. I enjoyed managing him and I appreciated him as a footballer, so much so that I bought him again when I went to Bradford City as manager. Unfortunately, that never worked out quite as well as he broke his leg. He was never the same again afterwards.

THE ONE THAT GOT AWAY

No one

I don't really recall missing out on any one player in particular. I always worked to a budget and never had any problems finding players within that budget.

I also found, at Swansea, that it was difficult scouting players with any great frequency purely because of the geography. There was Cardiff City down the road, then your next nearest ground was Swindon. It meant a hell of a lot of travelling so maybe I didn't get to see as many games for scouting as I would have liked.

Appendix 1

How the clubs and home nations are represented by
our contributing managers:

Leicester City (13 managers)
Sunderland (12)
Aston Villa (11)
Wolverhampton Wanderers (11)
Coventry City (10)
Crystal Palace (10)
Manchester City (10)
West Bromwich Albion (10)
Cardiff City (9)
Nottingham Forest (9)
Sheffield Wednesday (9)
Southampton (9)
Bolton Wanderers (8)
Queens Park Rangers (8)
Blackburn Rovers (7)
Derby County (7)
Middlesbrough (7)
Newcastle United (7)
Norwich City (7)
Plymouth Argyle (7)
Stoke City (7)
Swansea City (7)
Birmingham City (6)
Celtic (6)
Fulham (6)
Huddersfield Town (6)
Leeds United (6)
Sheffield United (6)
Tottenham Hotspur (6)
Bradford City (5)
Brentford (5)

Brighton & Hove Albion (5)
Everton (5)
Gillingham (5)
Hull City (5)
Liverpool (5)
Motherwell (5)
Portsmouth (5)
Preston North End (5)
Shrewsbury Town (5)
Walsall (5)
Watford (5)
West Ham United (5)
Bristol City (4)
Chelsea (4)
Grimsby Town (4)
Ipswich Town (4)
Motherwell (4)
Notts County (4)
Oldham Athletic (4)
Oxford United (4)
Port Vale (4)
Rotherham United (4)
Swindon Town (4)
Barnet (3)
Blackpool (3)
Bristol Rovers (3)
Burton Albion (3)
Charlton Athletic (3)
Exeter City (3)
Hereford (3)
Hibernian (3)
Manchester United (3)
Mansfield Town (3)
Millwall (3)
Rangers (3)
Reading (3)
Scunthorpe United (3)
Stockport County (3)

Torquay United (3)
Tranmere Rovers (3)
Wigan Athletic (3)
Wrexham (3)
Aberdeen (2)
Barnsley (2)
Bournemouth (2)
Burnley (2)
Cambridge United (2)
Carlisle United (2)
Chester City (2)
Colchester United (2)
Darlington (2)
Doncaster Rovers (2)
Gainsborough Trinity (2)
Hartlepool United (2)
Heart of Midlothian (2)
Kettering Town (2)
Leyton Orient (2)
Livingstone (2)
Luton Town (2)
Macclesfield Town (2)
Newport County (2)
Northampton Town (2)
Peterborough United (2)
Sligo Rovers (2)
Southport (2)
Weymouth (2)
Wimbledon (2)
Wycombe Wanderers (2)
York City (2)
Accrington (1)
Aldershot (1)
Altrincham (1)
Arsenal (1)
Ashton United (1)
Ayr United (1)
Bedford Town (1)

Bishop Auckland (1)
Boston United (1)
Bury (1)
Cheltenham (1)
Chesterfield (1)
Chorley (1)
Crewe Alexandra (1)
Dundee (1)
Dunfermline (1)
Dunstable Town (1)
Eastbourne (1)
Fleetwood Town (1)
Grantham Town (1)
Hibernians (1)
Hillingdon Borough (1)
Ilkeston Town (1)
Inverness Caledonian Thistle (1)
Limerick (1)
Lincoln City (1)
Linfield (1)
Maidstone United (1)
Margate (1)
Morecambe (1)
Mossley (1)
Northwick Victoria (1)
Nuneaton Borough (1)
Rochdale (1)
Rushden & Diamonds (1)
Scarborough (1)
Shamrock Rovers (1)
Shepshed Charterhouse (1)
Southend United (1)
St Mirren (1)
Woking (1)
Workington (1)

England (6)
Northern Ireland (5)
Wales (5)
England U21 (3)
Republic of Ireland (3)
Scotland (3)
England C (1)
England U18 (1)
Wales U21 (1)

Appendix 2

The featured managers

Aberdeen (2) – Keith Burkinshaw (caretaker); Mark McGhee
Accrington (1) – John Coleman
Aldershot (1) – Brian Talbot
Altrincham (1) – Tommy Docherty
Arsenal (1) – Terry Neill
Ashton United (1) – John Coleman
Aston Villa (11) – Ron Atkinson; Steve Bruce; Tommy Docherty; Gérard Houllier; Paul Lambert; Brian Little; Alex McLeish; David O'Leary; Martin O'Neill; Dean Smith; Graham Turner
Ayr United (1) – George Burley
Barnet (3) – Barry Fry; Mark McGhee; Alan Mullery
Barnsley (2) – Dave Bassett; Allan Clarke
Bedford Town (1) – Barry Fry
Birmingham City (6) – Steve Bruce; Trevor Francis; Barry Fry; Lou Macari; Alex McLeish; Harry Redknapp
Bishop Auckland (1) – Lawrie McMenemy
Blackburn Rovers (7) – Sam Allardyce; Mark Hughes; Paul Lambert; Gordon Lee; Don Mackay; Bobby Saxton; Graeme Souness
Blackpool (3) – Sam Allardyce; Gary Megson; Stan Ternent
Bolton Wanderers (8) – Sam Allardyce; Jimmy Armfield; Neil Lennon; Roy McFarland; John McGovern; Gary Megson; Phil Neal; Colin Todd
Boston United (1) – Howard Wilkinson
Bournemouth (2) – Tony Pulis; Harry Redknapp
Bradford City (5) – Lennie Lawrence; Roy McFarland; Bryan Robson; Colin Todd; Terry Yorath
Brentford (5) – Micky Adams; Terry Butcher; Steve Coppell; Dean Smith; Mark Warburton

Brighton (5) – Micky Adams; Steve Coppell; Brian Horton; Mark McGhee; Alan Mullery

Bristol City (4) – Steve Coppell; Joe Jordan; Tony Pulis; Denis Smith

Bristol Rovers (3) – Gerry Francis; Bobby Gould; Mark McGhee

Burnley (2) – Sean Dyche; Stan Ternent

Burton Albion (3) – Nigel Clough; Roy McFarland; Neil Warnock

Bury (1) – Neil Warnock

Cambridge United (2) – Ron Atkinson; Roy McFarland

Cardiff City (9) – Len Ashurst; Alan Durban; Bobby Gould; Kenny Hibbitt; Dave Jones; Lennie Lawrence; Mick McCarthy; Phil Neal; Terry Yorath

Carlisle United (2) – Keith Curle; Harry Gregg

Celtic (6) – David Hay; Neil Lennon; Lou Macari; Martin O'Neill; Brendan Rodgers; Gordon Strachan

Charlton Athletic (3) – Alan Curbishley; Lennie Lawrence; Alan Mullery

Chelsea (4) – Tommy Docherty; Bobby Gould (caretaker); Glenn Hoddle; Claudio Ranieri

Cheltenham (1) – Bobby Gould

Chester City (2) – Keith Curle; Kevin Ratcliffe

Chesterfield (1) – Roy McFarland

Chorley (1) – John McGovern

Colchester United (2) – George Burley; Paul Lambert

Coventry City (10) – Micky Adams; Ron Atkinson; Terry Butcher; Bobby Gould; Don Mackay; Gordon Milne; Phil Neal; Peter Reid; John Sillett; Gordon Strachan

Crawley (1) – Steve Coppell (director of football)

Crewe Alexandra (1) – Harry Gregg

Crystal Palace (10) – Sam Allardyce; Dave Bassett; Steve Bruce; George Burley; Steve Coppell; Trevor Francis; Lennie Lawrence; Alan Mullery; Tony Pulis; Neil Warnock

Darlington (2) – Brian Little; Colin Todd

Derby County (7) – George Burley; Nigel Clough; Tommy Docherty; Steve McClaren; Roy McFarland; John Newman; Colin Todd

Doncaster Rovers (2) – Brian Flynn; Lawrie McMenemy

Dundee (1) – Don Mackay

Dunfermline Athletic (1) – David Hay

Dunstable Town (1) – Barry Fry

Eastbourne (1) – Mark McGhee

Everton (5) – Sam Allardyce; Billy Bingham; Gordon Lee; David Moyes; Joe Royle

Exeter City (3) – Gerry Francis; John Newman; Bobby Saxton

Fleetwood Town (1) – Graham Alexander

Fulham (6) – Micky Adams; Roy Evans; Kevin Keegan; Malcolm MacDonald; Don Mackay; Claudio Ranieri

Gainsborough Trinity (2) – Brian Little; Neil Warnock

Gillingham (5) – Len Ashurst; Keith Burkinshaw; Tony Pulis; Gerry Summers; Stan Ternent

Grantham Town (1) – Martin O'Neill

Grimsby Town (4) – Alan Buckley; Lennie Lawrence; Lawrie McMenemy; John Newman

Hartlepool United (2) – Len Ashurst; Dave Jones

Heart of Midlothian (2) – George Burley; Joe Jordan

Hereford United (3) – John Newman; John Sillett; Graham Turner

Hibernian (3) – Terry Butcher; Neil Lennon; Alex McLeish

Hibernians (1) – Brian Talbot

Hillingdon Borough (1) – Barry Fry

Huddersfield Town (6) – Steve Bruce; Brian Horton; Lou Macari; Malcolm MacDonald; Stan Ternent; Neil Warnock

Hull City (5) – Steve Bruce; Brian Horton; Brian Little; Terry Neill; Stan Ternent

Ilkeston Town (1) – John McGovern

Inverness Caledonian Thistle (1) – Terry Butcher

Ipswich Town (4) – George Burley; Paul Lambert; Mick McCarthy; Joe Royle

Kettering Town (2) – Ron Atkinson; Alan Buckley

Leeds United (6) – Jimmy Armfield; Allan Clarke; David O'Leary; Peter Reid; Neil Warnock; Howard Wilkinson

Leicester City (13) – Micky Adams; Dave Bassett; Sven Göran Eriksson; Bryan Hamilton; Gordon Lee (caretaker); Brian Little; Mark McGhee; Gary Megson; Gordon Milne; Martin O'Neill; David Pleat; Claudio Ranieri; Brendan Rodgers

Leyton Orient (2) – Frank Clark; Kenny Jackett

Limerick (1) – Sam Allardyce
Lincoln City (1) – Allan Clarke
Linfield (1) – Billy Bingham
Liverpool (5) – Roy Evans; Gérard Houllier; Jürgen Klopp; Brendan Rodgers; Graeme Souness
Livingstone (2) – David Hay; Paul Lambert
Luton Town (2) – Lennie Lawrence; David Pleat
Macclesfield Town (2) – Brian Horton; Sammy McIlroy
Maidstone United (1) – Barry Fry
Manchester City (10) – Tony Book; Frank Clark; Steve Coppell; Sven-Göran Eriksson; Brian Horton; Mark Hughes; Kevin Keegan; Phil Neal; Peter Reid; Joe Royle
Manchester United (3) – Ron Atkinson; Tommy Docherty; David Moyes
Mansfield Town (3) – Billy Bingham; Nigel Clough; Keith Curle
Margate (1) – Terry Yorath
Middlesbrough (7) – Lennie Lawrence; Steve McClaren; Tony Pulis; Bryan Robson; Gordon Strachan; Colin Todd; Neil Warnock
Millwall (3) – Kenny Jackett; Mick McCarthy; Mark McGhee
Morecambe (1) – Sammy McIlroy
Mossley (1) – Howard Wilkinson
Motherwell (5) – Graham Alexander; Terry Butcher; David Hay; Mark McGhee; Alex McLeish
Newcastle United (7) – Sam Allardyce; Steve Bruce; Kevin Keegan; Gordon Lee; Steve McClaren; Bobby Saxton (caretaker); Graeme Souness
Newport County (2) – Len Ashurst; Terry Butcher
Northampton Town (2) – John Barnwell; Keith Curle
Northwich Victoria (1) – Sammy McIlroy
Norwich City (7) – Ken Brown; Bryan Hamilton; Paul Lambert; Gary Megson; Martin O'Neill; Dean Smith; Dave Stringer
Notts County (4) – Sam Allardyce; John Barnwell; Keith Curle; Neil Warnock
Nottingham Forest (9) – Micky Adams (caretaker); Ron Atkinson; Dave Bassett; Frank Clark; Steve McClaren; Alex McLeish; Gary Megson; Martin O'Neill; Mark Warburton

Nuneaton Borough (1) – David Pleat

Oldham Athletic (4) – Keith Curle; Joe Royle; Brian Talbot; Neil Warnock

Oxford United (4) – Brian Horton; Denis Smith; Gerry Summers; Brian Talbot

Peterborough United (2) – John Barnwell; Barry Fry

Plymouth Argyle (7) – Billy Bingham; Ken Brown; Lennie Lawrence; Tony Pulis; Peter Reid; Bobby Saxton; Neil Warnock

Portsmouth (5) – Steve Coppell (director of football); Kenny Jackett; Joe Jordan (caretaker); Tony Pulis; Harry Redknapp

Port Vale (4) – Micky Adams; Brian Horton; Gordon Lee; John Rudge

Preston North End (5) – Graham Alexander (caretaker); Sam Allardyce; Tommy Docherty; Gordon Lee; David Moyes

Queens Park Rangers (8) – Tommy Docherty; Gerry Francis; Trevor Francis; Steve McClaren; Alan Mullery; Harry Redknapp; Mark Warburton; Neil Warnock

Rangers (3) – Alex McLeish; Graeme Souness; Mark Warburton

Reading (3) – Steve Coppell; Mark McGhee; Brendan Rodgers

Rochdale (1) – John Coleman

Rotherham United (4) – Tommy Docherty; Kenny Jackett; John McGovern; Neil Warnock

Rushden & Diamonds (1) – Brian Talbot

Salford (1) – Graham Alexander

Scarborough (1) – Neil Warnock

Scunthorpe United (3) – Graham Alexander; Keith Burkinshaw; Allan Clarke

Shamrock Rovers (1) – Johnny Giles

Sheffield United (6) – Micky Adams; Dave Bassett; Steve Bruce; Nigel Clough; Bryan Robson; Neil Warnock

Sheffield Wednesday (9) – Len Ashurst; Ron Atkinson; Steve Bruce; Trevor Francis; Dave Jones; Gary Megson; David Pleat; Howard Wilkinson; Terry Yorath

Shepshed Charterhouse (1) – Martin O'Neill

Shrewsbury Town (5) – Ken Brown; Alan Durban; Harry Gregg; Kevin Ratcliffe; Graham Turner

Sligo Rovers (2) – Micky Adams; John Coleman

Southampton (9) – Dave Bassett (caretaker); George Burley; Glenn Hoddle; Dave Jones; Lawrie McMenemy; Chris Nicholl; Harry Redknapp; Graeme Souness; Gordon Strachan

Southend United (1) – Barry Fry

Southport (2) – Billy Bingham; John Coleman

St Mirren (1) – David Hay

Stockport County (3) – Dave Jones; Gary Megson; Sammy McIlroy

Stoke City (7) – Alan Durban; Joe Jordan; Paul Lambert; Brian Little; Lou Macari; Gary Megson; Tony Pulis

Sunderland (12) – Sam Allardyce; Len Ashurst; Steve Bruce; Terry Butcher; Alan Durban; Mick McCarthy; Lawrie McMenemy; David Moyes; Martin O'Neill; Peter Reid; Denis Smith; Howard Wilkinson

Swansea City (7) – Micky Adams; Brian Flynn; Harry Gregg; Kenny Jackett; Brendan Rodgers; John Toshack; Terry Yorath

Swindon Town (4) – Roy Evans; Glenn Hoddle; Lou Macari; Colin Todd

Torquay United (3) – Keith Curle; Roy McFarland; Neil Warnock

Tottenham Hotspur (6) – Keith Burkinshaw; Gerry Francis; Glenn Hoddle; Terry Neill; David Pleat; Harry Redknapp

Tranmere Rovers (3) – Micky Adams; Bryan Hamilton; Brian Little

Walsall (5) – John Barnwell; Alan Buckley; Kenny Hibbitt; Chris Nicholl; Dean Smith

Watford (5) – Dave Bassett; Sean Dyche; Kenny Jackett; Claudio Ranieri; Brendan Rodgers

West Bromwich Albion (10) – Sam Allardyce; Ron Atkinson; Keith Burkinshaw; Johnny Giles; Bobby Gould; Brian Little; Tony Pulis; Bryan Robson; Denis Smith; Brian Talbot

West Ham United (5) – Sam Allardyce; Alan Curbishley; Lou Macari; David Moyes; Harry Redknapp

Weymouth (2) – Len Ashurst; Bobby Gould

Wigan Athletic (3) – Steve Bruce; Bryan Hamilton; Gordon Milne

Wimbledon (2) – Dave Bassett; Bobby Gould

Wolverhampton Wanderers (11) – John Barnwell; Tommy Docherty; Glenn Hoddle; Kenny Jackett; Dave Jones; Paul Lambert; Brian Little; Mick McCarthy; Mark McGhee; Gerry Summers (caretaker); Graham Turner
Woking (1) – John McGovern
Workington (1) – Keith Burkinshaw
Wrexham (3) – Brian Flynn; Brian Little; Denis Smith
Wycombe Wanderers (2) – Paul Lambert; Martin O'Neill
York City (2) – Bobby Saxton; Denis Smith

England U18 (1) – Gordon Milne
England U21 (3) – Lawrie McMenemy; Peter Reid; Howard Wilkinson
England C (1) – Howard Wilkinson
England (6) – Sam Allardyce; Sven-Göran Eriksson; Glenn Hoddle; Kevin Keegan; Steve McClaren; Howard Wilkinson (caretaker)
Northern Ireland (5) – Billy Bingham; Bryan Hamilton; Sammy McIlroy; Lawrie McMenemy; Terry Neill
Republic of Ireland (3) – Johnny Giles; Mick McCarthy; Martin O'Neill
Scotland (3) – George Burley; Alex McLeish; Gordon Strachan
Wales (5) – Brian Flynn; Bobby Gould; Mark Hughes; John Toshack; Terry Yorath
Wales U21 (1) – Brian Flynn